Theological Education in a CROSS-CULTURAL CONTEXT

Essays in Honor of
John and Bea Carter

A. Kay Fountain
Editor

John and Bea in...

1963

2014

WIPF & STOCK · Eugene, Oregon

Wipf and Stock Publishers
199 W 8th Ave, Suite 3
Eugene, OR 97401

Theological Education in a Cross-Cultural Context
Essays in Honor of John and Bea Carter
By Fountain, A. Kay
Copyright©2016 APTS Press
ISBN 13: 978-1-4982-9482-9
Publication date 3/18/2016
Previously published by APTS Press, 2016

This edition is published by Wipf and Stock Publishers
by arrangement with APTS Press.

CONTENT

v	A Tribute to John and Bea Carter Carl and Terri Gibbs
7	Introduction A. Kay Fountain
9	John and Bea Carter: A Biographical Sketch Dave Johnson
33	Liberal Arts, the Sciences, and Christian Higher Education: The ICI Experience Robert A. Love
59	Workers Together with God: An Approach to a Christian Educational Psychology George M. Flattery
79	Assessing Missional Ministries in the Pentecostal Church Robert W. Houlihan
103	The Training Pyramid Carl B. Gibbs
133	Knowledge with Zeal: Biblical Examples of Using a God-Anointed Intellect in His Service Dave Johnson
153	Pentecostal Witness in the Public Sphere: The Civic Engagement of Three Faith-Based Organizations Among the Most Vulnerable People in Vallejo, California Joel A. Tejedo
179	A History and Components of Pentecostal Theological Education Paul W. Lewis
199	Tongues as a Sign: Reconciling Luke and Paul Robert P. Menzies
225	Is Servant Leadership Effective in Motivating Volunteers? Stephen Fogarty
249	Profiles of Contributors

A Tribute to John and Bea Carter

John and Bea Carter have been consistent mentors and friends. As young missionaries we were often welcomed into their home and shared as co-laborers in their ministry. As veterans, they continued to partner in creating structures for training worldwide, including Africa.

In over three decades of friendship, our respect for them has grown. Few missionary educators have left a more lasting mark on their mission's philosophy of training or touched the lives of so many, including ours.

Carl and Terri Gibbs

INTRODUCTION
by A. Kay Fountain, Editor
Academic Dean
Asia Pacific Theological Seminary

It is both a pleasure and a privilege to introduce this volume of essays in honour of John and Bea Carter. I have known the Carters for about 30 years, and have appreciated their gracious and forthright approach to both ministry and the Christian life. Friends and colleagues have contributed to this volume, with the underlying theme of Christian Education specifically in an intercultural environment. The first two articles reflect the close association that the Carters had with the International Correspondence Institute (now Global University) in the earlier days of their missionary service. The remaining seven articles are indicative of the wider influence they have had since their appointment to Asia Pacific Theological Seminary. The authors of these articles come from different streams within Pentecostalism, and from differing ethnic backgrounds. This is a fitting testimony to the influence that John and Bea have had in their ministry. They are truly global citizens and have shown an ability to work not only cross-culturally, but also across the spectrum of Christian theological education. John's influence in the development of the Asia Pacific Theological Association and, in latter years, in the World Association of Pentecostal Theological Educators, has been both visionary and significant in encouraging high academic standards in Pentecostal Education around the world. Bea's constant support, encouragement and hospitality has facilitated this ministry. They have been a great team, and will be sadly missed in Asia and the Pacific, now that they are retiring from the constant travel that this work has involved. It is my hope that this festschrift, produced in their honour, will be a fitting reminder of the global influence they have had on Pentecostal Theological Education, and will inspire others to continue with the work that they have begun.

JOHN AND BEA CARTER:
A BIOGRAPHICAL SKETCH
By Dave Johnson

Introduction

John and Bea Carter[1] have made an indelible impact on the Asia Pacific Theological Seminary (APTS) and many Assemblies of God theological institutions throughout the region. In 1991 John became APTS's academic dean and continued on in the capacity of president and later chairman of the APTS board of directors until March, 2016. During these years John and Bea ministered to seminary students, faculty and families from all over Asia and beyond. This short biographical sketch tells part of their story. It includes their early years with families who were not living for Christ and the story of the effect of the gospel on their lives, including their decisions to become missionaries. Through that decision and God's guiding them to pursue a somewhat unusual doctoral degree, God set John and Bea on a special life course. The result was years of fruitful ministry equipping ministers, missionaries and Bible school faculty to proclaim the gospel and train others to proclaim it to numerous people groups and nations in Asia and beyond to the glory of God.

---

[1]Since this sketch involves telling both John's and Bea's stories, I will forgo the normal academic tradition of referring to a person by their last name and simply refer to them by their first names or simply as "The Carters."

Background and Testimonies

John's Story

John was adopted into the home of Sydney and Florence Carter in Washington D.C. in 1942. About 30 months later, however, his parents divorced and he and his mother moved west, eventually settling in California.[2] His mother, although a nominal Methodist, had little Christian influence in her life and, over the course of the years, married and divorced several times as well as having common law relationships with a number of men. Despite these difficulties, God had planted a seed of faith in young John's heart. John explained how he came to faith in Christ in his own words:

> I never attended church on a regular basis, but did go to the Methodist church Sunday school in Fairfield, CA from time to time. Unfortunately, I never really heard the Gospel in those meetings. But I did have some degree of faith in God and can remember very clearly two times when God intervened in my life to provide an answer to prayer.
>
> The first occurred on a Friday night when I was thirteen. It was my mom's habit to "go out" on Friday nights. I knew that this meant she would return home drunk in the middle of the night, often accompanied by some man who would spend the night. On this particular evening, she had already been drinking and announced that she was "going out." I can clearly remember going into my room and in a prayer of desperation praying, "Dear God, don't let her go!" Within a few minutes I heard her calling, "Fred,[3] come

---

[2]Email from John and Bea Carter to the author, September 9, 2008.
[3]During those years and until I went to graduate school, I was known by my middle name "Fred."

here and help me get undressed. I'm going to bed." I can still remember feeling overwhelmed by the idea that God had actually answered my prayer!

The second instance came about a year later after we had moved from Fairfield to Vallejo, California and I enrolled in a new junior high school at mid-year. The first day, as I was opening my locker in the hall, I bumped the boy next to me, resulting in an altercation with someone whom I later learned was known as the school bully. Later that day, I went to my first gym class and, when I located my gym locker, I discovered that it was next to his. I remember breathing a prayer, "Dear God, move my locker." Without saying anything about this or mentioning it to the gym teacher, the next day when I came to gym class, the teacher, said, "Carter, come here, we've moved your locker!" Amazing. . . .!

One morning a short time after we moved to Vallejo, and just a few months before I turned fourteen, my mother went to a small neighborhood grocery store and met a lady named Catherine there who struck up a conversation with her. Learning that we had just moved to the city, Catherine invited my mom and me to go to church with her the following Sunday. Mom agreed and that morning Catherine came by and picked us up to go to First Assembly of God in Vallejo. There, I joined a junior high Sunday school class taught by a man named Tommy Tucker. Tommy was a WWII veteran who peppered his Sunday school lessons with stories of the war, which kept all of us boys intrigued. Several times a month, he would also come by on Saturdays and pick-up the boys from his class to play ball or do other fun things. In many ways, I found in Tommy the father-figure I never had at home. Every Sunday, Catherine would faithfully come by to pick us up, although my mom did not always attend with me.

One Sunday morning the following summer, someone at the church approached me and asked if I would like to go to Junior High youth camp the next month, saying that the church would pay my way. I had never even heard of youth camp, let alone attended one, so I excitedly agreed. . . . The days were filled with sports and games, and the mornings and evenings with youth-oriented evangelistic services. After listening to the speaker for several nights, on Thursday, August 9, 1956 after hearing a sermon on Hell, and deciding that I didn't want to go there, I came forward and gave my life to Christ. The next night, the speaker talked about the Baptism in the Holy Spirit and that sounded pretty good too, so I responded again and was filled with the Spirit and spoke in tongues for the first time.[4]

Bea's Story

Bea also was born to parents who were not living for Christ in her early years. Her father's miraculous healing turned her family around. Bea told her story this way:

> I am the daughter of a Missouri share cropper named Elmer Burleson who moved his family to California to pursue better employment opportunities. Both my mom (Martha) and dad were backslidden Pentecostals. . . .
>
> However, as a child, I had a friend who invited me to Sunday school. Her mother would let her go with me to the movies on Saturday, if we would promise to attend Sunday school and church the next day. At one point, I responded to an altar call and gave my life to Christ, but lacking any Christian influence or nurturing at home, my Christian life did not flourish. I did not consider myself a Christian, but also did not get involved with the "vices" of so many of my friends.

---

[4]Email from John and Bea Carter to the author September 10, 2008.

In 1956, my dad had two gall bladder surgeries that went badly because of the extensive scar tissue that had developed over the years from passing gall stones. Being too weak for further surgery and running out of insurance coverage, he was sent home to "get better" so they could do another surgery. However, it was clear that he was wasting away in bed at home and that he had been sent home to die. He had tubes that came from his side to drain the bile from his liver. When he ate, he had to swallow a tube to pour the bile into his stomach to digest his food. The acid from the leaking bile had caused open sores on his side where the tubes exited and he was too weak to get out of bed without help. Clearly he was dying. . . .

One morning my friend's mother called to talk with my mother and found her distraught because of the deteriorating condition of my dad. She asked if she could have her pastor come by to pray for him. My mom agreed, and the pastor of Hollister Assembly of God dropped what he was doing to come over about 10:00 am that morning. He prayed for my dad and comforted my mom, but nothing dramatic happened.

At noon, I came home for lunch and while my mom and I were eating in the kitchen, my dad came running into the kitchen, pounding on his side, saying "I'm healed. I'm healed. Praise God, I'm healed." The tubes came out of his side that night, the open wound closed up and within a week, he was back at work. What we didn't know was that while in the hospital a Bethany Bible College student who worked as an orderly had witnessed to my dad and led him in the sinner's prayer.
As a result of seeing my dad's dramatic healing, both my mom and I began to go to church and within several months gave our lives to Christ. . . . A few months later,

in July 1956, my mom and I both received the Baptism of the Holy Spirit on the same night.

The doctors tried to determine how my dad was living since his internal 'plumbing' had been disconnected. He drank barium so they could trace it through to his stomach with a fluoroscope. But they could only follow it so far when it disappeared, only to appear again in his stomach! They never did determine how he could be alive. Even our atheistic doctor began to go to church because of my dad's miracle. I enrolled in Bethany the next year to study to be a missionary.[5]

Education, Marriage and Children

Bethany Bible College and San Jose State University

In early 1962, while John and Bea were both attending Bethany Bible College, John began serving as the youth pastor and choir director at the church Bea attended. Even though they had become casually acquainted at school, they did not begin to really get to know each other until John began serving at the church. At one point in their dating, they began to discuss a possible future together. John recalled:

> Bea was a missions major at Bethany, so she actually had a call to missions before I did. On one occasion while we were dating, I casually asked her if she had ever thought of being a pastor's wife? Having attended a small church that tended to be hard on its pastor and his wife, her response was 'No way!' A few minutes later, she asked, 'Have you ever thought of being a missionary's husband?' Obviously she prayed harder that I did.[6]

They were married about three months after they first started dating.

---

[5] Ibid.
[6] Email from John Carter to the author November 15, 2015.

As often happens, marriage and additions to the family interrupted their educational plans. John did not finish his degree in Pastoral Theology until 1967 and Bea finished her degree in missions in 1969.[7] During this time, Bea worked in a department store and John in several jobs as a salesman and for four years as a deputy sheriff. While John does not feel that this position helped in shaping his professional career, perhaps it taught him how to discipline those who err—a vital asset to an academic dean! During this time, their children, Kim and Steve, were also born, adding great joy and responsibility to their lives.

In researching this article, I asked John to reflect on how his past assignments had prepared him for the leadership roles that he would assume at APTS with the understanding that God prepares people at every level in life for future responsibilities. John related two noteworthy lessons he learned outside the classroom during his Bible school days. While in school, he worked as a salesman to support his family. Rather than focusing on the sales themselves, his manager taught him to focus on what he could control, such as making contacts with people, knowing that if he did that, he would make the level of sales expected of him. Later on, he would apply this to goal setting to his academic career knowing that if offered a quality program, something he could control, the students they wished to train would be drawn to the school.

The second lesson he learned in this time period was patience. When his church got a new pastor, he once explained to John that there were many things in the church that he wished to change, but that he needed to wait a year in order to learn why things were done the way they were. In applying this to APTS, John observed that this was a wise course of action. Another Bible college president once mentioned that making changes at a theological institution was like trying to bulldoze a cemetery; there were memorials to the past everywhere![8] Waiting also afforded him time to build the needed relationships with his co-workers in order to foster the trust, understanding and cooperation needed to make necessary changes.

---

[7]Ibid.
[8]M. Wayne Benson, personal conversation with the author, n.d.

John studied Pastoral Theology at Bethany under the assumption, which was quite common at the time, that he would join most of his classmates in pastoral ministry. He also became interested in psychology.[9] When doors to possible pastorates closed following graduation, John and Bea felt led by the Lord that he should enroll in a bachelor's degree program in psychology in nearby San Jose State University where he graduated in 1969.[10] It would be this degree, more than the pastoral degree from Bethany, that would define their future.

Graduate School at the University of Illinois

Only months after graduation, the Carters loaded up the kids and moved to the Champaign-Urbana, Illinois area, about halfway across the continent, for John to pursue doctoral studies at the University of Illinois (U of I). He had looked at several schools but concluded that Illinois was the best place for them because this university had one of the most highly rated programs in educational psychology at the time. They also offered him a full ride scholarship plus a small monthly stipend for living expenses.[11] There he pursued studies in the Psychology of Classroom Learning with a minor in Experimental Psychology of Human Learning, finishing a master's degree, with thesis, in 1970 and a Ph.D. in 1972.

While at the U of I, he had an opportunity to see behind the scenes at the inner workings of a department at a major university, another step in God's preparation for leadership at APTS:

> During my third year of graduate study at the University of Illinois, I was invited to participate as the graduate student representative on the administrative committee of the Educational Psychology Department. This committee was involved in every aspect of the department, from reviewing programs to determining

---

[9]Email from John Carter to the author, November 15, 2015.
[10]Ibid.
[11]Ibid.

the salaries of professors. Through this I learned a great deal about the administration processes of an academic institution.[12]

Meanwhile, Bea, whom John described as "The consummate partner and 'helpmeet,'" worked to support the family, well earning the commonly given unofficial but time honored degree of PHT (Put Hubby Through).[13] She also bore the brunt of raising Kim and Steve, providing the stability they needed, particularly as John was focused on the demands of his developing academic career. While he was at U of I, Bea also found time to complete the coursework for a master's degree in Educational Psychology, although she did not write the required thesis. Since her main goal was to understand what John was doing to give them something to connect on besides family matters, she achieved her goal without the degree.[14] She would have many opportunities to discuss this subject with her husband in the years that followed.

John's Academic Career

In The Secular Arena (1972-78)

Following his Ph.D. graduation in 1972, the family moved even further east to Syracuse, New York, for John to teach at Syracuse University. He had offers from three different schools but chose Syracuse because it offered a better salary and provided an atmosphere that was conducive to research and writing, which John relished.[15] Here, he also had an opportunity to see the inner workings of a university, this time from the prospective of a junior faculty member:

... I was asked to be one of the members of the Dean's Advisory Committee for the School of Education. This

---

[12]Email from John Carter to the author, September 7, 2015.
[13]Email from John Carter to the author, September 14, 2015.
[14]Ibid.
[15]Carter, November 15, 2015

committee involved representatives from all the departments of the School of Ed and included professors from all ranks, from Assistant Professor to Full Professor. Again, it provided many insights into the operation and administration of a major academic institution.[16]

Many lessons in administration at Syracuse would prove to be beneficial in his service at APTS. For example, his department chairman understood and valued teamwork in accomplishing goals, going to great lengths to include both faculty and graduate students in decision making.[17] John applied this lesson early in their tenure at APTS when seminary president Bill Menzies (1984-85, 1989-95) asked him and Bea to organize and host the annual faculty Christmas party in their home. At first, he planned to invite only the faculty members. Menzies asked him to consider inviting the other missionaries on campus and his initial reaction was to not do so because they weren't faculty. Then, thinking of the value of inclusivity and collegiality, he changed his mind and invited the others. This was a wise move considering the organic nature of APTS where all faculty and other missionaries serving the school in other capacities lived on campus and excluding the others could have easily led to hurt feelings.

In 1974, the Carters moved back to California for John to serve as a civilian research psychologist for the United States Navy. Here, he gained experience as a team leader in conducting academic research, which no doubt contributed to his outstanding ability to help students develop and execute behavioral sciences research, which included research design and statistical analysis. I myself benefited from John's expertise in these areas. The research design for both my master's thesis and doctoral dissertation were done under his excellent tutelage. Like others, I found studying under him to require discipline and be demanding, but he was also fair and helpful. The result was that I learned much in the process.

---

[16]Email from John Carter to the author, September 7, 2015.
[17]Carter, September 7, 2015.

One of John's doctoral degree students at Syracuse was from Iran. John received an invitation from this student, who had since been called home, to move to Tehran and lead a team in developing Educational Radio and TV for that country. Sensing that this would give them their first opportunity to live, work and teach cross-culturally, John and Bea accepted a two year assignment. Here, John served as the team leader for eight American consultants who were training Iranians in instructional development, course evaluation and career counseling. He also managed a project staff, conducted education research and oversaw the development of teaching materials for a continuing educational program. In addition, he supervised a program in educational development that allowed the students to gain credits from Syracuse University.

Life outside the job also offered numerous opportunities to experience other cultures. At the time, the Shah offered at least minimal religious freedom and the Assemblies of God had an international church that met in the capital, not far from Tehran University, that the Carters attended along with many Armenian and Assyrian believers. Kim and Steve attended the Tehran American School with several thousand other American children whose parents were living in Iran and working for American companies doing business there.[18]

Looking back on this time nearly forty years later, the Carters believe that God was preparing them for missions from the beginning.[19] Before they went to Iran, the Lord began to draw them into missions through an invitation from the International Correspondence Institute, (ICI), now known as Global University. At that time, ICI was located in Belgium and had thousands of students scattered all over the world. John explains:

> In late 1975, we received a letter from Dr. George Flattery [the founding president of ICI] about writing a course for ICI in Brussels. As we learned more about ICI, we became convinced that God was leading us

---
[18]Carter, November 15, 2015.
[19]Ibid.

toward missionary ministry with this new educational ministry. In fact, it was obvious that all of John's academic training and experience was ideally suited for the work of ICI in developing courses for distance education.[20]

Sensing that this might be the Lord's leading, they began inquiring about applying. The local Assemblies of God church leaders in Southern California encouraged them to apply and took the lead in contacting the national office of the Assemblies of God World Missions (AGWM) in Springfield, Missouri. When they did so, however, they identified John as a "practicing psychologist." The AGWM leadership politely responded that no such personnel were needed in missions![21] Then Flattery intervened, explaining to the leadership that John was an educational psychologist and that they did, in fact, need someone with John's qualifications in their innovative ministry. Due to the great respect the leaders had for Flattery, they reversed their opinion and encouraged the Carters to apply.

Ministry at ICI and Southern California College (1978-1991)

When they first arrived at ICI Brussels in 1978, John's first position was that of the Director of Course Development. This entailed managing a staff of about twenty career and short-term missionaries who developed education courses for various levels of ICI programs in several media formats such as print, audio and video, gaining experience that would be valuable in his role of the academic dean at APTS. While the core curriculum development team were all AG missionaries, the authors of the various courses came from all over the world, giving him valuable experience in cross-cultural ministry.[22]

When the Carters arrived, there were about sixty-five courses that were in various stages of development. Once an author finished writing the course materials, the process of

---

[20]Email from John and Bea Carter to the author, September 9, 2008.
[21]Ibid.
[22]Carter, November 15, 2015.

editing the course, writing and editing study guides, exams and other items took time. During their four years there, his team completed all of these courses and many others that were constantly being created.[23]

Beyond this, however, he also learned some key lessons that would influence his leadership style at APTS:

> I continued to gain experience in administration and team building. One of the things I learned from ICI President, Dr. George Flattery, was the importance of a compelling vision in motivating exceptional commitment to a purpose. Everyone who worked at ICI in those days had a sense that what they were doing was contributing significantly to a Kingdom purpose.[24]

He also learned a few lessons of what not to do. At that time, ICI did not allow missionaries assigned there to have significant ministry outside of ICI, such as teaching at the nearby Assemblies of God Continental Theological Seminary. By nature, most missionaries are capable of successfully juggling a number of responsibilities simultaneously and many have a bit of an independent streak when it comes to hearing the voice of God directing their lives and ministries. Therefore, many did not receive this restriction well and as a result, some left ICI to pursue other ministry.[25]

At APTS, John adopted the attitude that the faculty were welcome to pursue whatever outside ministries they wished to do as long as they also fulfilled their responsibilities at the seminary. He also believed that when faculty members exercised their gifts in outside ministries it actually expanded the influence of the seminary in sharing its resources with the local and national church ministries of the region.

John also noted that "competence is more important than agreeableness" and noted that some of the best workers there

---

[23]Ibid.
[24]Email from John Carter to the author, September 7, 2015.
[25]Ibid.

could be hard to get along with.²⁶ He came to the conclusion that giving such people some liberty to pursue their work as they saw fit led to high productivity. That does not mean, however, that relational tension should not be addressed. John noted that a number of missionaries left ICI because of relational breakdowns where leaders did not intervene.²⁷ He would have ample opportunity to apply this lesson at APTS, where the multi-cultural faculty and students all lived and worked right on campus.²⁸

While John was executing his responsibilities at ICI, Bea was busy on the home front raising the children, a daunting task for any parent that is even more challenging in a foreign context. The situation was made even more complex given that Kim and Steve attended a variety of schools during this time, the limits of a missionary budget being a primary consideration in school selection.²⁹ She also provided hospitality for their many guests, something she had also done in Iran, as well as assisting from time to time at the ICI office when they needed an extra hand.³⁰

By the time John and Bea completed their three year term and returned to the States, Kim was ready for college and Steve was going into high school. This is a difficult point in life for most missionary families, who love their families and also value their ministries. Many families opt to remain on the field, but some feel the need to look for a stateside assignment to help their children through the transition from adolescence to adulthood. This is the route the Carters felt led by the Lord to take, at least for a time.

John was offered a position as an associate professor of psychology at the Assemblies of God's Southern California College (now Vanguard University) in Costa Mesa, California and taught psychology. A year later he also became the

---

²⁶Ibid.
²⁷Ibid.
²⁸For a broader discussion on the challenging of living on a multi-cultural campus, please refer to my book, *Led By the Spirit: The History of the American Assemblies of God Missionaries in the Philippines*, (Mandaluyong City, Philippines: ICI Ministries, 2009), 336-40.
²⁹Carter, November 15, 2015.
³⁰Email from John Carter to the author, September 14, 2015.

chairman of the Psychology Department. In this capacity, he was responsible for the overall administration of the department, which consisted of four faculty members, curriculum and budget planning. While their time there was probably enjoyable, God wasn't finished with them in missions.

At the end of John's contract with Vanguard in 1985, God spoke to him and Bea to return to ICI in Brussels, which they did after a period of itineration. They arrived back in Brussels in 1987. This time, John became a professor of Education and Dean of the ICI College program. In this capacity, he was the chief administrator of a college of over 9,000 students enrolled through national offices in 120 countries all over the globe. The college offered bachelor's degrees in Bible, Theology and Church Ministries. In this capacity he planned curriculum, recruited faculty and planned, monitored and evaluated course development.[31]

In 1991, as they completed this term of missionary service, ICI moved its headquarters from Brussels to Fort Worth, Texas, mainly for financial reasons. The Carters, however, felt that their time overseas was not yet complete and accepted an invitation from Bob Houlihan, the regional director for AGWM in the Asia Pacific from 1987-1998, to fill an unexpected vacancy as the academic dean at APTS.

The APTS Years (1991-2016)

Academic Dean (1991-1996)

Because John's predecessor had vacated the position unexpectedly, the Carter's availability was a godsend to APTS. Despite the lack of opportunity for a smooth transition, John found the situation in the dean's office to be in good order, with one exception. The school was in the process of preparing for an upcoming official visit by ATESEA (Association of Theological Education in Southeast Asia), a major accrediting association. Though the visit was scheduled for soon after the Carters'

---

[31]John and Bea Carter, September 7, 2015.

arrival, nothing had been done to prepare the faculty for this event. That year, as one faculty member noted, the annual faculty retreat was dedicated to finalizing a self-study of the entire school in preparation for the visit.[32] The fact that APTS continues to be accredited with ATESEA suggests that the visit went well.

John brought a wealth of experience to his new position. In his own words:

> By the time I arrived at APTS, I had already had a 20-year career in various aspects of higher education including the U of Illinois, Syracuse, ICI and SCC/Vanguard . . . so my philosophy of Christian higher education was already well in place. I have always considered myself more of an implementer than a visionary. I've often seen "visions" fall by the wayside when the "visionary" lacked the skills to organize and implement the vision, so both at ICI and at APTS I took it upon myself to get the things done that were considered important to the school.[33]

During John's tenure as dean, APTS completed phasing out the bachelor's degree programs that had been part of the school since its founding in 1964. The phase out had been planned from the beginning, correctly anticipating that the Bible schools in the region would then be able to upgrade their programs to include a fourth year once their teachers had completed their master's degrees, which many did at APTS. This phase out, then, suggests that APTS was well on its way to achieving their goal of providing qualified Bible school instructors for the Bible schools in the Asia Pacific part of the world. Doing away with the bachelor's programs enabled APTS to focus on its master's degree programs, with several more disciplines being added during John's tenure.

---

[32]Email from John Carter to the author, September 14, 2015.
[33]Ibid.

President (1996-2004)

The Carters served under the leadership of Dr. Bill Menzies, who was president of APTS (1984-85, 1989-95). In August, 1995, the entire campus was saddened when Doris Menzies, Bill's wife, suffered a heart attack and they had to go to the States for treatment. Within months it became obvious that they would not be able to return, forcing Bill to resign as the APTS president. With no time to form a search committee and look for a successor, the board appointed John to fill the remainder of his term in March, 1996, and gave Menzies the honorary title of president emeritus as well as chancellor. John would prove to be a wise choice.

Since John's replacement as the academic dean, Wonsuk Ma, would not arrive until August, he was forced to handle both roles. When the business administrator left in June, John picked up that assignment as well, simply because there was no one else to take the job until January, 1997. Bea's unwavering support, along with that of the faculty, staff and students, who rallied to the occasion, helped lighten his load.[34]

Asia Pacific Center for the Advancement of Leadership and Missions (APCALM)

When John became president, the board had been discussing building a missions center on campus for several years, Being, by his own confession, an implementer more than an innovator, he asked the board to either move forward with the project or take it off the table.[35] By this time, the school was also developing a number of summer institute programs for various ministries such as youth and media. In 1997, APTS hosted a summer program for training Asian missionaries through the now defunct Assemblies of God Asian Missions Association (AGAMA). In 1998, they began the Institute for Islamic Studies in cooperation with the Center for Ministry to

---

[34]John Carter, *President's Report to the Board of Directors*, Asia Pacific Theological Seminary, March 19, 1997, 1.
[35]Carter, September 14, 2015.

Muslims (now Global Initiative), a program that has now expanded to more than twenty locations around the world. Also, the school was receiving numerous requests from outsiders to use the campus for retreats and seminars. John himself saw APTS's role in training missionaries not only as a fulfillment of the one of the mandates for the school's existence, but also in keeping with "the growing involvement of Asian churches in missions," which he saw as one of the most "significant trends of the late 20th and 21st centuries."[36] The board agreed and decided to move ahead with the project because they believed that bigger facilities would address the growing need for space.[37]

In March, 1999, ground was broken for a 5,200 square meter (55,000 sq. feet), seven story building on the lower part of the campus that involved as many as 250 construction workers.[38] This was a tremendous challenge for John, who had never built anything larger than a tool shed in his own backyard in California.[39] The building was dedicated at graduation in March, 2001, although the construction was not completed until later.

While this was going on, the Carters went through some personal trials. Bea became seriously ill and had to return to the States alone. For some time, the question remained if they would even be able to continue in missions. Despite this situation, however, both the board and the Carters were adamant that they were following God's leading and pressed ahead. In time, Bea recovered and rejoined her husband in the Philippines.[40]

Academics

In July, 2000, the school opened its first post-graduate program, a Master of Theology degree, under the leadership of Wonsuk Ma. In February, 2002, the school opened a doctorate in ministry program, the first doctoral level studies in the

---

[36] John Carter, *The APTS Missions Training/Conference Center Project*," n.d., 1.
[37] Carter, March 19, 1997, 2.
[38] John Carter, *President's Report to the Board of Directors*, March, 2001, 3.
[39] John Carter, "Fulfilling Your Vision," *The Courier*, Vol. 9. No. 3, December, 2000, 1.
[40] Ibid.

history of the school. The next month, John could report to the Board of Directors that the school now had a "Full range" of academic programs.[41]

Wonsuk Ma fully agreed with John's assessment, but concluded that additional academic programs also placed greater stress on the faculty, which was amplified by the unexpected loss of two Asian instructors in the same year that the D.Min program began.[42] Nevertheless, Ma emphasized APTS's bright future stating that the school was continuing its "'ascending thrust' impacting not only Asian Pentecostals and the international Pentecostal world, but also the Asian Evangelical World."[43]

Part of the reason that Ma felt that APTS was increasingly making an impact in Asia was due to the intentional moves the school had made to Asianize the faculty. In the mid-1980s, the school began a Faculty Development Program that provided financial resources for potential faculty members to get their post-graduate degrees, Ma himself being among the first to do so. Ma felt that the addition of the post-graduate programs, which would make it possible for more Asians to obtain post-graduate degrees, would also "improve the 'Asian' image of the seminary."[44]

No one summed up John's tenure as president better than Wonsuk Ma who, perhaps worked with John more closely than any other individual:

> The era of his presidency saw a significant leap in seminary life, reputation and influence. The construction of the massive conference building (now called the Global Missions Center) is only a small part of his accomplishment. The school reached its peak in faculty strength. Once I counted 12 full-time faculty members from 8 countries, approximately 10 had PhD degrees and 50% of them were Asian, maintaining an

---

[41]Carter, March, 2002, 1.
[42]Wonsuk Ma, *A Report to the APTS Board of Directors*, March, 2003, 1.
[43]Ma, *A Report*, 2.
[44]Wonsuk Ma, *A Report to the Board of Directors*, March, 2004, 1.

ideal balance. The seminary added post-graduate programs: a Master of Theology, a Doctor of Ministry and the Wales Ph.D. program hosted by the seminary. Academic activities increased in frequency and impact: through an increase in enrollment, extensive on-site programs, the publication of a journal and monographs, an annual lectureship and occasional lectures, the school became a premier institution in advancing Pentecostal studies in Asia. The seminary also led several regional networks: the Asia Pacific Theological Association (APTA) and the Assemblies of God Association of Mission in Asia (AGAMA). With its accreditations by the Asia Theological Association (ATA), Association of Theological Education in Southeast Asia (ATESEA) and APTA, the scope of engagement was broadened. Under John's leadership, APTS was an active member of Asia Graduate School of Theology-Philippines (AGST-Phil), often providing valuable contributions.[45]

Bea's Activities and Ministries

While John went about his duties in the office, Bea was busy at home and on campus. Throughout their APTS years, she became well known as a great hostess, performing her role as the dean's and, later, the president's wife, with excellence. She was particularly known and loved for her great cooking. She also taught in the English Language program and, over the years, edited hundreds of term papers for students struggling to express themselves in English. When their son, Steve, came to APTS to work on his master's degree, he lived with them and she enjoyed having him "home" again.

Early in their tenure, Bea hired a maid named Juliet Pascual, a local Filipina who was a new Christian. Pascual worked in their home for several years and described both Carters as kind people who treated her well, making sure that she was paid fairly and on time. The relationship reached such a depth that

---

[45]Email from Wonsuk Ma to the author, November 17, 2015.

she came to see them as her adopted parents, which was especially meaningful to her since she did not grow up in a Christian home.[46] Later, Bea encouraged her to apply for a job on campus, which she got and has been a valuable part of the APTS team ever since.

Kay Fountain had fond memories of both Carters. Speaking of Bea she related:

> Bea is the perfect partner to John. She is a people-person, and she is intuitive in her awareness of the feelings of others. She is hospitable and caring, and also very intelligent. She also makes a great cup of tea. In their years at APTS she was the perfect entertainer, and she cared for all faculty, their spouses, and very specially, their children.
>
> I was personally really helped by them both when I had a series of incidents with heart palpitations as a student. They had me stay in their home until I could get down to Manila for a check-up, and then Bea accompanied me to Manila and back again on the bus!!! One very funny thing happened on the bus on the way back - we were sitting in the very back seat - high up over the back wheels, and higher than the seats in front of us. The bus stopped very suddenly and we fell forward collapsing the backs of the seats in front of us, so that those sitting in them were kind of squashed under us![47]

Tham Wan Yee,[48] current APTS president, and Alex Fuentes[49] also agreed that Bea was the perfect partner, stating that she kept him grounded, providing balance in his relationships with others.

---

[46] Email from Juliet Pascual to the author, November 10, 2015.
[47] Email from Kay Fountain to the author, November 18, 2015.
[48] Yee, November 16, 2015.
[49] Email from Alex Fuentes to the author, November 24, 2015.

A number of students and colleagues saw Bea as a second mother. Former faculty member Bob Menzies, a former faculty, remembered that Bea "adopted" younger faculty members and their children into her own extended family.[50] Joel Tejedo mentioned that Bea's spirituality was noted in her faithful chapel attendance.[51] Steve Fogarty remembered Bea as both "intelligent and articulate."[52] Perhaps no one summarized Bea's role better than long time faculty member and former dean, Wonsuk Ma: "Bea was a catalyst of the community life, especially supporting ladies (including spouses of students) and children. In spite of the physical challenges she endured, she gave herself freely to the community. In fact, how she and John dealt with life's challenges, including her illness, became an important inspiration to many on campus."[53]

Continuing Service to APTS (2006-)

After vacating the presidency, the Carters went to the US for a year of itineration and then returned to campus for two years while John continued to teach. He purposely moved into a new, smaller office in the APCALM building (now GMC) and when someone would come to him with a problem that the president would normally handle, he simply sent them to see the new president, Dr. Wayne Cagle. There was never any question of his support for the new president or for Rev. Tham Wan Yee, who succeeded Cagle in 2009.

In 2006, the Carters decided to return to the US so Bea could have needed back surgery. However, upon learning of their intention to leave APTS, they were invited to go to Australia to work with Southern Cross College, the Assemblies of God National School, to assist in their development towards becoming a Christian university. After determining that Bea could obtain back surgery in Australia from a highly regarded neurosurgeon, they agreed to move there in early 2007. They

---

[50]Email from Bob Menzies to the author, November 17, 2015.
[51]Email from Joel Tejedo to the author, November 16, 2015.
[52]Email from Steve Fogarty to the author, November 17, 2015.
[53]Email from Wonsuk Ma to the author, November 17, 2015.

subsequently moved to the US in late 2008 in preparation for their eventual retirement, although John continued to serve as APEO Director until 2010 and continued to return to campus to teach block courses. In 2012, he accepted a two year appointment as chairman of the board and, in 2015, accepted the board's request to extend his term until March, 2016. At the time of this writing, it appears that his departure from the board in March, 2016, will likely end their formal involvement with APTS. We will be sorry to see them go.

Other Opportunities and Responsibilities

Throughout their tenure at APTS and beyond, John has served the broader movement of the Assemblies of God education in several significant ways. For many years, he served in various capacities for the Asia Pacific Theological Association (APTA), the Assemblies of God accrediting agency for theological institutions in the Asia Pacific Region. This critical organization provides for a school accrediting process, teacher certification and an annual theological symposium that has brought greater stability to the schools it serves. John headed the Accreditation Commission for fifteen years and served two terms as the chairman of the board. He also lent his considerable administrative skills to many APTA committees to help ensure that things ran smoothly. In addition, John served from 2005 to 2010 as the head of the Asia Pacific Education Office, another AGWM ministry to Bible schools, as a consultant for the Bible schools in the region.[54]

Beyond this, John has served as a consultant to the AGWM's Bible school efforts in other regions of the world, specifically in Europe and Africa, in launching organizations similar to APTA. He was also the founding chairman of the World Alliance of Pentecostal Theological Education (WAPTE) from 2009-13. WAPTE, according to its website, is a "A global cooperative fellowship of Pentecostal and Charismatic theological

---

[54]Dave Johnson, *Led by the Spirit: The History of the American Assemblies of God Missionaries in the Philippines*, (Mandaluyong City, Philippines: ICI Ministries, Inc., 2009), 327.

associations, denominational offices, and missions agencies that provide educational services to theological and/or ministry training schools."[55]

Conclusion

God's hand has obviously been on both John and Bea over more than fifty years of marriage, education and ministry. Both of their children are also serving the Lord faithfully in their chosen lifestyles and locations, Kim with her family in Southern California and Steve with his family in his wife's native Sweden. While their family is their greatest legacy, they have also left behind a legacy of integrity, compassion, kindness, and excellence in education. Through this legacy they have provided precious tools for spreading the gospel and maturing the church to thousands of students and many colleagues from numerous nations throughout the years. To God be the glory for the lives and labors of John and Bea Carter!

---

[55] The World Alliance for Pentecostal Theological Education, www.wapte.org accessed 24 November 2015.

Liberal Arts, the Sciences, and Christian Higher Education: The ICI Experience
by Robert A. Love

Introduction

In the spring of 1981, my wife Helen and I flew to Brussels, Belgium, for an official visit to the headquarters of the International Correspondence Institute (ICI; now Global University). At that time, this degree-granting, distance-learning educational institution had emerged as one of the premier missions entities of the Assemblies of God. We looked forward to potentially joining the staff of its Academic Division, headed by Dr. John F. Carter, who was serving as dean.

For some years, I had been the Dean for Science and Mathematics at Prince George's Community College in Largo, Maryland (USA). Those and other credentials plus my general "track record" had been examined prior to our visit; and once there, I was also asked to speak in chapel and to conduct a seminar. While these evaluation measures in themselves may have been considered adequate, ICI administration was looking at us primarily to determine if and where we would "fit in." I emphasize the term "fit in" because, as we soon learned, fitting in was critically important. It involved a great deal more than meeting the criteria for a position. If we were to serve with ICI, we would find ourselves working with a multitude of highly diverse people, developing distance education curricula for a worldwide student body, traveling to places we had never been, answering questions about the institution, preaching and teaching without prior notice, counseling, advising, eating whatever was set before us. Not being able to meet that definition of "fitting in" could severely harm ICI and its ministry.

Our relationship with John Carter and his wife Bea was launched at a picturesque restaurant, where we were treated not only to European cuisine, but also to an evening of wonderful conversation and discussion. That evening marked the beginning of a lifelong friendship for which we will be forever grateful. It was also the beginning of a professional association that involved working together and consulting off and on for over 30 years. John Carter was an able administrator, a wise and considerate mentor, a creative solver of problems, an eloquent speaker, a gracious host, and a consummate team player. These qualities were exactly what ICI needed in those days. I recall Dr. Carter reminding me that I should learn to tolerate ambiguity. That was good advice, as there was plenty of it to go around.

In this paper we will consider the development of the ICI college degree programs. Special emphasis will be given to the liberal arts and general education offerings. Most importantly, we will describe the significant contributions made by Dr. John Carter during our association in the decade of the 1980s. Dr. Carter's leadership and influence on Assemblies of God higher education was outstanding. The continuing outcomes of his efforts during those early days include the national and regional accreditation of the Global University and the expansion of the degree programs to include the Master of Arts, the Master of Divinity and the Doctor of Ministry. Moreover, the university is now offering academic programs in the Middle East, India, China, Viet Nam, and, quite literally around the world.

One problem that ICI encountered early on had to do with the inclusion of "general education"—which included science and mathematics— in a Bible-Theology curriculum. At the time, most Bible college educators in America regarded distance education as being substandard. Perhaps distance methods might be acceptable (even necessary) in Africa, Asia, and India; but to offer an accredited undergraduate degree program that included a general education component by distance education methods in Europe was almost unthinkable. Moreover, there was a concern that such a program might make its way back across the Atlantic to provide competition for the American Bible colleges, which were then teetering on the financial brink. The leaders of the Assemblies of God, which is based in Springfield, Missouri (USA),[1] saw this coming and were quick to limit ICI's influence to those lands beyond "the shining seas."

The issues facing ICI were complex and multi-faceted. For example, a plan of study must be developed that would provide ministerial training for the multitudes of students who did not have access to traditional education. The curriculum must include the courses—and their distribution—that are required for a Bachelor of Arts degree, and these courses must be developed in such a way that students could study by themselves in any part of the world. Also, the curriculum must include the liberal arts, albeit in their modern forms and extensions. An instructional design would, of necessity, govern the way all ICI courses were developed. Evaluation systems for both the courses and the programs must be established early on. Moreover, it was of prime importance that the curriculum and all its components be of high quality and worthy of the degree to be earned.

There are, of course, some principles that can be applied in course content development and the delivery of instruction, whether in the classroom or by distance methods. It was recognized, however, that both content and instruction would be significantly influenced by the way in which the course developer "saw" the teaching-learning experience. As the years go by and the cost of higher education keeps increasing, the question constantly arises as to the necessity of an education that declares itself specifically as *Christian* education. This is the problem facing students—and their parents—who are considering a Christian college or university. A Christian university can be significantly more expensive than a secular school that provides similar instruction and certifications. Let

---

[1]Springfield has been regarded as the quintessential Midwest American city. At the time of ICI's founding, 85 percent of its residents had been was born in or near the city, which is geographically land-locked and relatively isolated. Springfield was an ideal location for establishment of the pre-WWII Assemblies of God; but in the following decades, a more international focus would be needed. Although founded there in 1968, ICI was soon "hustled off" to Brussels, which remained its home until 1990.

us consider at this point, lest it slip from our thinking, the reasons why Christian higher education is of such high value.

- Justification for the Christian higher education experience tends to stress the general ethos of a Christian school and the Christian worldview of its staff, especially the faculty. If we are going to think about Christian education, we need to discuss the notion of worldview, what it is, and why it's so important.
- Also of concern for Christian education is the "general education" component, which is required by all accrediting commissions for curricula leading to a bachelor's degree. In this regard, we need to think about how the Christian worldview intersects with that part of the curriculum which relates to the world and its wisdom. Are Bible and Theology really all-sufficient, or is it also necessary and worthwhile to study some secular subjects?
- Finally, we need to consider the way in which Christian education treats studies—especially those within the liberal arts and the sciences—that seem to be in conflict with Christian doctrine. For instance, what positions and attitudes do we take with regard to the sciences and the pronouncements of the scientific community? Why should the ministerial student study science at all? And what should be the goals of science courses for those seeking to become pastors, teachers, and evangelists?

A Christian Worldview and Christian Higher Education

The question arises as to whether the worldview of the curriculum planner and or teacher has a place in the delivery of content that does not fit the first and obvious definition of Christian education. When we think of secular education in the 21st century, we can see how the instructor's worldview can affect his or her teaching of the social sciences, literature, art, music, drama, and even medicine and the healing arts. But how, if at all, might the teacher's worldview affect his or her understanding and teaching of mathematics or of science?

First, let us consider the following questions. What is a worldview and how do we "get" one? Did Jesus have a worldview? Just what is a Christian worldview? And how does our worldview affect the way we learn and the way we approach various areas of study? The answers to such questions may lead us to begin recognizing the differences in education obtained at a Christian college or from a Christian teacher versus a secular college or a non-Christian teacher. Those answers may also help us make a determination as to whether sending our children to Christian schools and colleges is worth the extra cost. Secondly, let us consider how the sciences might be taught legitimately and honestly while maintaining, within that teaching-learning experience, the essence of Christian education.

What Is a Worldview and How Do We "Get" One?

A "worldview" has been described variously as a systematic way of looking at the world, as a comprehensive framework of one's basic beliefs about things, or as a set of presuppositions. In their book, *How Shall We Now Live?* Chuck Colson and Nancy Pearcy[2] suggest that a worldview is a system that allows us to answer, to our satisfaction, such questions as "Why am I here?" and "Where am I going?" Regent University philosophy professor Michael Palmer defines a worldview this way:

> [It] is a set of beliefs and practices that shape a person's approach to the most important issues of life. Through our worldview, we determine priorities, explain our relationship to God and fellow human beings, assess the meaning of events, and justify our actions. Our worldview even speaks to the most ordinary practices in everyday life, including the types of things we read and

---

[2]Chuck Colson and Nancy Pearcy, *How Shall We Now Live?* (Wheaton, Illinois: 1998), xi.

view, the types of entertainment and leisure activities we seek, our approach to work, and much more.[3]

It is interesting to note that millennia before the term "worldview" was coined and adopted, the Bible identified the essence of ourselves using the term "heart." *"Watch over your heart with all diligence,"* warns King Solomon, *"for from it flow the springs of life"* (Proverbs 4:23). Dallas Baptist University philosophy professor David Naugle points out that everybody has a worldview, which seems to be an inescapable characteristic of being human, and that it is likely the most important thing about us.[4]

How Might Jesus' Worldview Have Been Described?

Let us accept the assumption that (1) we all have, whether by design or default, some kind of worldview, and (2) our worldview affects not only our learning processes, but also what we enjoy learning, what we choose to learn, how we interpret that which is taught to us, and our apprehension of intellectual content. Applying those assumptions to Jesus, what might we recognize as the elements within his worldview?

Studying the four gospels, we get a good picture of the worldview of Jesus at work in his life. Those who experienced and or saw his miracles wondered greatly, remarking, *"Behold, what manner of man is this?"* (Matthew 8:27). Even at age 12 (and likely before that), he had questions—*"All who heard him were amazed at his understanding and his answers"* (Luke 2:47). Jesus exercised his intellect.

We recognize that Jesus lived in a day that has been called "pre-scientific." The notion of the Earth as one planet in a system of planets, the laws of motion, the concept of gravity, the nature of matter, and the precise measurement of time were to

---

[3]Michael Palmer, "Elements of a Christian Worldview," in *Elements of a Christian Worldview*, compiled and edited by Michael Palmer (Springfield, MO: Logion Press, 1998), 24.

[4]Richard Weaver, *Ideas Have Consequences* (Chicago: University of Chicago Press, Phoenix Books, 1948), 3.

be "discovered" centuries later. The concepts of space, time, energy, and mass were not matters of concern in those days. Rather, the great issue was the nature of God as revealed in the Law and the Prophets, the Psalms, and the Writings. What could be known of God and of doing His will were the overwhelming concerns.

It may sound strange to suggest that Jesus could have been a scientist, but the notion is not unreasonable. He used logic, and he reasoned from evidence. The Law and the Testimony were accepted as fact. Jesus could read and interpret what he read. He selectively challenged entrenched opinions and was successful in debate, even with hostile opponents. What we observe in operation throughout His life and public ministry is a finely tuned intellectual honesty.

What Is a Christian Worldview?

As already noted, a worldview is primarily a set of beliefs that shapes a person's approach to what he or she perceives as the most important issues in life. It can include practices and things we *do* in response to our set of beliefs, but what we *think* about things comes first. Thus, formation of a Christian worldview requires selection of a set of beliefs that a 21st-century Christian should regard as important. Let us consider those beliefs which are of sufficient importance for Christians to order their lives by them.

Such a worldview begins with a belief in the existence of God, the Creator of the universe, the Earth, and all living things, including human beings who were made in His image. The Bible, which a Christian reveres as the written word of God, reveals that man has fallen from an original perfect relationship with God, that he is sinful and requires redemption, and that God has provided for that redemption through Jesus' life, atoning death, and resurrection. A Christian also holds that humans, created in God's image, are rational beings able to observe an order of things in the created universe.

Given this expectation of order, we humans have been able to formulate verbally and mathematically the statements (or laws) that describe this order. A Christian believes that each one of us bears the image of God and thus is worthy of respect. A Christian recognizes that God provides mankind a suitable habitat for life and entrusts to mankind appropriate allocation of resources. A Christian also understands that God will ultimately bring the deeds of men into judgment and will execute that judgment righteously.

The notion of a Christian worldview is not new. Consider, for example, the Apostles' Creed, which was set down by the twelve apostles and appeared in written form by the late 2nd century:

> I believe in God the Father almighty, creator of heaven and earth. I believe in Jesus Christ, his only Son, our Lord. He was conceived by the power of the Holy Spirit and born of the Virgin Mary. He suffered under Pontius Pilate. He was crucified, died, and was buried. He descended to the dead. On the third day again, He ascended into heaven and is seated at the Father. He will come again to judge the living and the dead. I believe in the Holy Spirit. I believe in the holy Catholic Church, the communion of saints, the forgiveness of sins, the resurrection of the body, and the life everlasting.[5]

The apostles certainly would not have thought of the Creed as a description of a worldview. But we can readily see it as a set of beliefs that are included in a Christian worldview. What we do *not* see in the Creed are specific statements with regard to knowledge not revealed in Scripture or to social relationships, including respect for other humans or to economics or to stewardship of the environment. And most importantly, we do not find in that Creed an indication of what to do with our scientific knowledge and technology. Thus, we must surmise that the difference in worldview between then and now is due to the information which has been gained from general

---

[5] *Apostles' Creed*, in *Oxford Dictionary of the Christian Church* (Oxford: University Press, 2005), 90.

education. What to do about "modern problems" is part of a modern worldview and should, therefore, be included in a modern curriculum.⁶

A Christian Worldview and Educational Curriculum Development

It may be tempting to conclude that the Apostles Creed or similar ones of the church are adequate to describe a Christian worldview, even today. Certainly, the creeds contain timeless theological truths. We place them very close to the Scriptures in terms of their expression of Christian doctrine. But they simply do not deal with the issues that a believer today must face.

Secularists often argue that Christianity is just fine as long as it is kept within the walls of the church. This view was popularized by paleontologist Stephen Jay Gould, who advocated "non-overlapping *magisteria*," which means, simply, that science and religion are to be regarded as separate and distinct domains, each with the exclusive authority to teach within its domain. The sheer pomposity of this concept sends up a red flag at the outset. The assertion that science and religion do not overlap at all is a naïve notion that was advanced apparently to silence religious objections while appearing to be conciliatory.

Non-overlapping *magisteria* politely enjoins theologians to refrain from commenting on scientific conclusions, about which, it is presumed, they know nothing. Likewise, the scientific community is graciously offering to refrain from commenting on religious topics that they regard as unworthy of discussion. While there continues to be debate over where the boundaries should be, Australian philosopher Russell Blackford weighs in as follows: "The idea that science and religion have authority in entirely separate domains and do not come into

---

⁶Arthur McGiffert, *The Apostles' Creed: Its Origin, Its Purpose, and Its Historical Interpretation*. https:// archive.org/details/apostlescreedits00mcgi. (Accessed 3/1/15).

conflict is, in a word, rubbish. However, it's remarkably persistent rubbish."[7]

Of course, in the day-to-day work and practice of theology vis-à-vis the secular professions, separation has been practiced for a long time. The problems occur at the interface where, for example, a scientific pronouncement is offered that is clearly at odds with the beliefs held in a Christian worldview. This often happens when pronouncements related to the development of living things are expanded to include the requirement that the creation of living things must be explainable by natural law. The whole process is incorrectly referred to as "evolution," to which science demands exclusive rights. Woe be to the practicing scientist today who would dare whisper anything that even appears to agree with the Christian position.

Conversely, a scientific finding may fly in the face of a theological position, such as occurred when Galileo (1564-1642) observed the moons of Jupiter and the phases of Venus. These phenomena were impossible to explain using the geocentric assumptions required at the time. Theologians held that the earth must be at the center of the universe and that orbits must be perfect circles. Admittedly, Galileo was undiplomatic in presenting his observations and conclusions. He publicly ridiculed the Pope and put limits on his authority.[8] Galileo was forced to recant, and the church reigned supreme for a time on these essentially scientific issues.

As we consider the ways in which educational systems must respond to such "turf battles," we may well ask ourselves what our curricula might include to prepare Christians for life in the 21st century. This is even more important when we consider the curricular content of ministerial training programs. Is it adequate to systematically teach the Bible and the theological

---

[7]Russell Blackford, "A Very Short Introduction to Non-Overlapping Magisteria," under "Content and Discussion." http://old.richarddawkins.net/articles/575220-a-very-short-introduction-to-non-overlapping-magisteria (accessed September 15, 2014).

[8]In a letter to Grand Duchess Cristina of Tuscany, Galileo writes: "With regard to [opinions] which are not directly matters of faith, certainly no one doubts that the Supreme Pontiff has always an absolute power to approve or condemn; but it is not in the power of any created being to make things true or false, for this belongs to their own nature and to the fact. Therefore, in my judgment one should first be assured of the necessary and immutable truth of the fact, over which no man has power."

positions that are derived from it? Can we simply just include some instruction in the practice of ministry and perhaps some church history?

Even before doing any research on the matter, we can rightly conclude that a minister needs to know about a wide range of subjects, many of which are outside the realm of theological studies. Here are just a few examples. Music is important in the church. A minister needs some preparation in the handling of legal problems that may arise. Also, a minister must have some understanding of the arts and sciences that affect our lives in so many ways. In fact, he may well be preaching to people in his congregation who have trained for and make their living in those areas. And if a minister wishes to earn an accredited degree, the curriculum must include the liberal arts. So let us consider here the liberal arts, why they are intrinsically important, and why they have endured the test of time.

The Liberal Arts and Christian Higher Education

When we think of Christian education, we may initially recall our experiences in Sunday school—the stories, activities, and teaching materials provided. Or the thought of Christian education may evoke memories of the antics in the junior boys' class and the youth group we enjoyed as we got older. We may also think of the materials made available for new converts or for church membership classes. Such are typically doctrinaire approaches to living the Christian life and being a member of the church.

Most church-related colleges have a degree or a certificate program in Christian education. College-level Christian education is not to be confused with the professional education programs offered to pre-service teachers, nor does it prepare one for the pastoral or evangelistic ministry. Christian education as a *major* area of study is often undersubscribed; it is simply not a primary item of focus when it comes to career preparation. And as a *minor*, it fares only a little better. The peripheral nature of Christian education in the professional ministry is usually in the background when a school attempts to recruit Christian Education students.

Christian Education is, of course, a great deal more than Sunday school and simplified age-graded doctrinal instruction. Education itself can legitimately be regarded as Christian when designed and delivered in the light of the Christian worldview. For instance, what implications might mathematics have for Christian education? We could ask the same question about the relationship of Christianity to the study of grammar, the sciences, the technical aspects of public speaking, etc.

From ancient times it has been recognized that educated people should be exposed to certain arenas of knowledge. The Greeks identified seven important things to learn and know about—music, astronomy, arithmetic, geometry, grammar, logic, and rhetoric. In the Middle Ages, a diligent Bible student discovered Proverbs 9:1, which read, "*Wisdom has builded her house. She has hewn out her seven pillars.*" Well that was it! The Greeks' early curriculum development was sanctified as the "Liberal Arts," which continue in their modern forms to this day. We could argue the hermeneutical merits of allegorical interpretations, which were often done in those days. Whether right or wrong, it nevertheless caught on; and the seven liberal arts became the basis of the curriculum for years to come.

Much later, while elitism was stubbornly hanging on in Europe, things were a lot more "democratic" in colonial America. The concept of education for all may have started in 1799, when George Washington left a special bequest in his last will and testament to establish a national university (although there's no record of where the money actually went).[9] Sadly, education stagnated when we had to take "time out" for the War of 1812, the Civil War, and World Wars I and II. Following the Second World War, however, the GI Bill was established to educate our war veterans. The liberal arts, at that time, were considered too narrow for the highly diverse American population. Everybody needed to be educated, while

---

[9]John S. Brubacher and Willis Rudy, *Higher Education in Transition* (New York: Harper and Rowe, 1958), 217.

maintaining the notion of a core of studies. Thus, the liberal arts became "general education."

If they were called in today as accreditation reviewers, the Greeks and the Scholastics would recognize at least a fourth of most undergraduate curricula. A block of thirty-two or more credits has been set aside for general education, which, in words of the Higher Learning Commission, is:

> Understanding and appreciating diverse cultures, mastering multiple modes of inquiry, effectively analyzing and communicating information, and recognizing the importance of creativity and values to the human spirit not only allow people to live richer lives but also are a foundation for most careers and for the informed exercise of local, national, and international citizenship.[10]

The liberal arts have endured for centuries, maintaining their place since the time Christianity began in Jerusalem and Judea then moving westward. With their modern expressions and extensions, the liberal arts are rightly required in college curricula. Even a cursory review of their history reveals that they have an intimate relationship to Christ and the church. The Bible, theological studies at all levels and the Christian experience have inspired the very best of art, music, and scholarship. Christian education is a confluence of all that's good in the striving of our human race to learn and develop.

The Sciences and ICI's Curriculum Development

In development of the ICI Bachelor of Arts degree program, ICI's leadership recognized that a general education block of courses needed to be included. However, at the time (1968), many within the Assemblies of God viewed with suspicion the general education courses that were required and had to be

---

[10]North Central Association: Statement on General Education. https://www.umkc.edu/provost/ committees/general-education-advisory-task-force/higher-learning-commission-statement-on-general-education.pdf. (Accessed 2/27/15).

reviewed by secular authorities. Why, they reckoned, should one spend time learning secular subjects when we had no more than one generation in which to prepare for the end-time events (a view often, broadly, and convincingly proclaimed)? Was not the preaching of the gospel always of prime importance?

In the early days of the denomination, the study of subjects not related to the ministry of the Word was regarded at best as a diversion and at worst a threat. Jonathan Thigpen, of the Evangelical Training Association (ETA), cites David R. Breed, a professor at Western Theological Seminary, who wrote the following in the July 1927 *Biblical Review Quarterly*:

> The [Bible] institute was developed to meet a demand for Christian training for many who could not have a college education but were worthy candidates for Christian service. . . . In the vast majority of cases the institutes have remained orthodox in their teachings, which cannot be said of all the seminaries. I think this one thing more than anything else has drawn men away from the seminary to the institute.

Thigpen then goes on to say:

> In 42 years (1927 to 1969) the emphasis of the Bible institute movement turned from training those who "could not have a college education" into a full-fledged program of undergraduate studies leading to a degree. Even as the American Association of Bible Colleges (AABC) was experiencing growth and receiving long sought for academic recognition, the Evangelical Teacher Training Institute (ETTA) continued to work with Bible colleges, Christian liberal arts colleges, seminaries and traditional Bible institutes. From 1947 to 1969, the ETTA membership roll grew from 50 schools to over

100, with much of the growth coming in the Bible institute area.[11]

This is precisely where the Assemblies of God schools (including ICI) were in 1968. By the mid-1970s, ICI was in full pursuit of accreditation. At that time, the only accrediting commission willing to review correspondence programs was the National Home Study Council (NHSC), which has since become the prestigious national accrediting association known as the Distance Education Accrediting Commission (DEAC). And the NHSC required a general education component in any degree program.

If ICI's education program must include the liberal arts, we could understand the need for music and rhetoric, which translated directly into Christian vocational programs as instrumental music, vocal music, public speaking, and grammar. Even arithmetic and geometry (categorized as mathematics) were seen as practical, useful—and non-threatening. Logic, however, deemed by many as being "human reasoning," presented a serious problem. For from it would flow the natural sciences, felt to be just a short step to the social sciences, including psychology, which had long been regarded with suspicion. Perhaps the natural sciences could be approached a lot like mathematics, considered as having a safe, internal logic of its own. A satisfying approach to the natural sciences was reached by formulating a physical science course that both met the accreditation requirements and was "safe" theologically.

In the mid-1980s, the new ICI science course was developed. It was primarily a survey of the physical sciences—physics, chemistry, astronomy, and geology. One section addressed the impacts of science on human life, with attention given to those science-related issues that were sensitive in the Christian community. The course also included a discussion of astronomy versus astrology.

---

[11]Jonathan Thigpen, "A Brief History of the Bible Institute Movement in America," Evangelical Training Association. www.etaworld.org/?bibleinstitute (accessed September 19, 2014).

The theory of evolution was touched on but not extensively treated. Instead of arguing against evolution, the course placed strong emphasis on God as Creator of all things. While the text recognized the natural development of living things and their adaptation to the environment, the term "evolution" was limited to changes in response to both the environment and genetic influences, which are not always onward and upward. Living species can change for the worse and can become extinct. Hence, the course's discussion of evolution in the scientific sense could not be construed as agreement with the atheistic perspective in which God did not exist or was not considered necessary.

After considerable thought and discussion, it was decided that ICI's physical science course would recognize the assumption that the universe (including our Earth) is of finite age. The scientific community has been in general agreement that the universe had a beginning. Strong evidence indicates it to be 14 billion years old and the Earth about 4.5 billion years old. Our decision placed us in the category of "old earth creationists." Some felt that we should have adopted the "young earth" position, which was regarded as more biblical. We did not argue the point, but rather placed a strong emphasis on the truths conveyed in the Bible, while recognizing that scientific findings are probably correct within reasonable limits. This allowed us to teach and champion the biblical revelation of God as Creator, while treating science as science. Both of these concepts are highly important and can legitimately be held in a state of moderate tension.

In 2010, an interactive distance education laboratory course was developed to accompany the Physical Science course. The science experiences took the form of experiments, observations, and descriptions. The experiments involve measurements and the reporting of such with appropriate precision. They also involve application, with the student carrying out procedures, generating data, and converting those data into meaningful forms. Comprehension is evidenced by the requirement to observe phenomena then describe them. There are also opportunities, in the study of principles and concepts, to analyze, synthesize, and evaluate. The course was written with a student's entire cognitive domain in focus.

A key outcome of the ICI science laboratory course is the understanding that a theoretical value can be verified by experiment. In fact, that's how the theoretical value got there in the first place. Newton formulated the law of gravity in both written and mathematical forms. His equation required the placement of a gravitational constant. He didn't know what the value of that constant was but knew it had to be there. Later, Cavendish determined, by measurement, the gravitational constant's value in the laboratory. Then the formula could be used to predict the actual force of gravity. One way of studying gravity is to determine its action on a free-falling body. In our laboratory course, the students are able to use the formula by which the action of a falling body may be estimated. The experiment carried out demonstrates the truth of the formula in a real-world situation.

Consider another example. Experimental data are provided to measure the loss of oxygen in the decomposition of potassium chlorate. The students are required to make sense of the data and draw a conclusion. While most of them recognize that the oxygen lost and the potassium chloride remaining is predictable and demonstrable by experiment, some have observed that the experiments and their outcomes, although interesting, are not enough in themselves to prove the truth of the theory. When they make such an observation, we know the students are on their way to an internalized understanding of the scientific method.

Importance and Implication of Science Education for the Christian Education Student

Let's suppose that there is no external pressure at all to include science or mathematics or logic in our Christian education programs. Would their study still be beneficial, even necessary? We would argue that the sciences have significant importance for the theologian, the minister, and, in fact, every believer for at least two reasons.

Firstly, science is the study of a finely tuned creation, and we are all well served by learning about the Earth on which we live and the universe surrounding it. It also provides insight into the mind of the Creator, for there are characteristics of God that can be deduced from the findings of science.

Secondly, science provides us with an increasing number of practical advantages and conveniences that improve our quality of life—advantages and conveniences that we benefit from every day and even have come to expect. Scientific research has had its influence on us from birth forward, resulting in a life span that has almost doubled over the last 100 years. It has also increased or otherwise impacted for the better our safety and security, our modes of transportation, our methods of communication, the medicine and the healing arts, our forms of entertainment, the means of warfare. The list goes on.

Now, let us consider what science does for us relative to our thought life. We have already discussed "worldview" and noted how important it is that we have a right way of thinking. A great deal has been said in the response to the question, "What would Jesus do?" We may also well ask, "What would Jesus think?" followed by "What then should we think?"

In Jesus' day, concerns were primarily political, relational, and religious. People back then no doubt marveled at the wonders of nature; and Jesus pointed out that one could make a fair estimate of what the weather would be (Matthew 16:3). These might be regarded as rudimentary scientific observations; but remember, "back then" was not an era that produced scientists. Rather, it produced sages, poets, mystics, and activists. Observations of the heavenly bodies were given phenomenological rather than scientific interpretations. The Psalmist described the apparent movement of the sun across the sky but made no attempt to explain it. The sun rises in the east and hastens to the west, *"rejoicing as a strong man to run a race"* (Psalm 19:5).

We continue to use this same phenomenological language today, although we now understand that it is the Earth that is moving, turning on its axis from west to east. This seems counterintuitive because we do not feel the motion of the Earth, and we perceive that the sun is moving around the Earth. We refer to the sun's daily appearance and departure as "sunrise" and "sunset." Even astronomers use these terms. Thus, the study of science is of value in helping us understand what we observe.

Next, let us consider why or how our Earth smoothly and ceaselessly rotates on its axis while it revolves around the sun. Enter Isaac Newton, who explained that an object at rest will remain at rest and an object in motion will remain in uniform motion unless acted upon by an outside force. This is Newton's first law of motion—the law of inertia; and it is in the study of physical science that we learn this.

We may further ask how the Earth or any other planet can remain in orbit around the sun. Again, Newton demonstrated mathematically that there exists between massive bodies a force called gravity. Left to itself, gravity would pull our Earth into the blazing center of the sun, for the Earth wants to continue in a straight line—but an exact balance is maintained. And while we may not know how the universe began, we can describe with precision the movements of major bodies in the universe.

Isaac Newton provided these explanations, and they have stood the test of time. In fact, it would be accurate to say that we think of the visible universe in Newtonian terms. A force is that which is necessary to accelerate a mass, which means that something has to move. If there is no movement, we do not have force. This is the way we think, which is why the question has been raised—Since God is a Spirit, is it even possible for God to move a quantity of matter in the physical universe?

But what of the non-visible universe? When we look into the atoms and molecules that make up the universe, we find tiny universes of sub-atomic particles in motion. Do Newton's laws still work? Yes . . . but the mass contained in each of these particles is so small that its effects on gravity approach zero and a whole new set of mechanical rules take over, which is referred to as "quantum mechanics." Within the sphere of quantum mechanics, many things can occur without any external evidence that motion has taken place at all.

To illustrate, let us consider the compact disc (the CD). It's a plastic disc coated with materials that allow information to be imprinted. This information can later be retrieved. The imprinting process involves the reorientation of molecules on the disc's surface, and vast amounts of information can be stored in this way. Yet there is no visible motion of the Newtonian variety to indicate that the disc is now a different entity. A blank CD costs anywhere from a dime to a dollar. A CD that contains a two-hour Hollywood film costs upwards of ten dollars. One on which is written a major computer program (e.g., Microsoft Office) would cost several hundred dollars. And one containing classified government defense information could have astronomical value; in fact, it may even be worth your life if it were known that you possessed this information. But what's so important to realize is that none of these CDs differ in appearance. We are not aware of any difference by just looking.

For a serious reader of the Bible, it is not hard to see a parallel between the nature of God and the works of God. Highly visible events, such as creation of the physical universe, are attributed to him. Human observers want to see dramatic, observable miracles; and God is able to do them. So why doesn't He do them more often? We tend to feel that, if He did more great miracles, the whole world would believe. This, Jesus pointed out, is not the case. Miracles there may be, but men do not believe because of them. In fact, they do not believe or trust even if one should rise from the dead (e.g., see Luke 16:19-31).

Oddly (at least we consider it so), there are a myriad of works of God that no one can see. From the dawn of history, it is recorded that men and women pray to God. And we are given to understand that God hears and answers in His time and manner and that He speaks to us directly. When God speaks, in some instances, the mountains may move and lightning may flash; but in others, there may be no visible sign at all. Rather, His speaking may be the very still and very small voice that is imprinted on our minds and hearts. Indeed, the parallel is unmistakable when God says, *"I will write my laws upon their hearts"* (Jeremiah 31:33; Hebrews 8:10). It is interesting to consider that the process of praying is not unlike the imprinting of information on a CD. Our study of science suggests that possibility, and such can enable us to endure the imprinting which we believe is changing us for the better.

So science is important for those who are studying for the ministry. For they will, after all, likely be preaching to, teaching, and interacting with those who are scientifically trained and think like scientists. But the study of science and mathematics involves a great deal more than that. God is the Creator; and in the sciences, we learn about creation. He made all things beautiful in their time—and there is likewise a beauty in the sciences and mathematics. Although this beauty is not far from the surface, nonetheless, one has to dig for it. God has provided His sons and daughters with a beautiful blue planet containing all things freely to be enjoyed, albeit with wisdom. And the study of science can help us be good stewards of this planet He created. Science also gives us hints about the glories of a world to come, for, according to scientific laws, nothing disappears without a trace.

A Recap of "The ICI Experience:" The Issues, Their Resolution and John Carter

The International Correspondence Institute was established almost fifty years ago as a multi-level school within the context of the Assemblies of God foreign missions organization. Every effort was made to create the image that it was (aside from its distance education mode of delivery) a traditional school. Its officers held the academic titles that would be found at a university; and its faculty members were assigned the traditional ranks of professor, associate professor, etc. The perception was fostered that ICI was an academic community and that the contributions of its staff would stand on their merits. This approach was expected by the growing cadre of faculty members who had been trained in American universities.

In point of fact, the ICI international office in Brussels tended to be operated as a proprietorship. Under this organizational structure, it was bewildering to its top leaders that alternative suggestions were offered. The president/proprietor may well have wondered why staff members thought it necessary to contribute ideas and comments. Does not the proprietor own the business and thus control its operation? Indeed, the influence of the ICI proprietor extended to the smallest of details.

There were two factors in the ICI equation that probably saved the institution and permitted it to become what it is today. (1) The founding president was a man of vision, unfeigned spirituality, and goodwill. The penchant for micromanagement and favoritism for family members was so ingrained in his thinking that he is hardly to be blamed for not shaking loose from it. Any other management approach would not have occurred to him nor would it have been negotiable had it been suggested. (2) The institution needed the academically-trained, doctorate-holding members of its leadership. An uneasy truce was established. If the act of voicing an idea was considered subversive, the academics could endure the compromise position that open discussion was tolerated. The academics were patronized, but they were heard.

As ICI rocked along through the 1980s and into the 1990s, development of its programs—and indeed the reputation of the institution—required sensitivity to the views of the largely clerical senior leadership and to the requirements curriculum development. Dr. Carter understood this and was willing to walk that fine line. His influence was significant through the ongoing curriculum development and implementation processes, the result of which was continued national accreditation and, ultimately, regional accreditation by the Higher Learning Commission of the North Central Association.

The day came when planning started for a new ICI science course. Were we going to write the course in such a way as to avoid all controversy, sidestepping key issues and avoiding the rightful claims of science? No, we were not; nor were we going to deny the clear inference that the creation points to and describes a wise and loving Creator. We would provide for ministerial students (and now many others) a course that is both true to the tenets of science and honoring to God.

For example, within the pages of the ICI course in physical science, we consider the phenomenon of solar eclipses, where the moon moves directly in front of the sun, thus eclipsing the sun's light. For a few minutes, those who are fortunate enough to be in the path of an eclipse can see the edge of the sun and the corona of light that surrounds it. It is a truly awesome sight. Then as the moon continues to move relative to the sun, the light from the sun gradually reappears. If one should continue to gaze at the sun with unprotected eyes, he could suffer serious injury to the eyes or blindness. Herein lies the question—"If the glory of creation is unendurable, how will we face the uncreated Light?"[12]

In a secret meeting, conducted at night and away from the political and religious leaders and the multitudes, Jesus engaged a prestigious ruler who had questions. In contrast to most of Jesus' inquirers, Nicodemus was an honest seeker. We can guess what those questions might have been, but the response Jesus gave him was simply, *"You must be born again"* (John 3:7); that is, something has to happen to recreate you, to make you new again—something like a resurrection.

There are, to be sure, a number of miracles reported in the Bible that present problems for the scientifically trained mind, but the treatment of the resurrection is as close to a scientific report as one is likely to find in Scripture. Jesus was executed by crucifixion on the order of the Roman governor. He was certified dead by a Roman officer, and was buried by Jewish officials in a guarded tomb. He rose again the third day and appeared alive to a significant number of honest and qualified witnesses. In discussing the resurrection, the Apostle Paul did not resort to theological arguments, but rather treated it as a fact to be reported. And if an event of that importance can be thus reported, can we not hold in tension the reports of events about which we still may have questions? American novelist and poet John Updike writes:

> *Make no mistake: if He rose at all*
> *it was as His body;*

---

[12]Robert Love and Franklin Niles, *Studies in Physical Science* (Springfield, Missouri: Global University, 2008), 203.

if the cells' dissolution did not reverse, the molecules
reknit, the amino acids rekindle,
the Church will fall.

It was not as the flowers,
each soft Spring recurrent;
it was not as His Spirit in the mouths and fuddled
eyes of the eleven apostles;
it was as His flesh: ours.

The same hinged thumbs and toes,
the same valved heart
that—pierced—died, withered, paused, and then
regathered out of enduring Might
new strength to enclose.

Let us not mock God with metaphor,
analogy, sidestepping, transcendence;
making of the event a parable, a sign painted in the
faded credulity of earlier ages:
let us walk through the door.

The stone is rolled back, not papier-mache,
Not a stone in a story,
But the vast rock of materiality that in the slow
grinding of
Time will eclipse for each of us
The wide light of day.

And if we have an angel at the tomb,
Make it a real angel,
Weighty with Max Planck's quanta, vivid with hair,
opaque in
The dawn light, robed in real linen
Spun on a definite loom.

Let us not seek to make it less monstrous,
For our own convenience, our own sense of beauty,

Lest, awakened in one unthinkable hour,
we are embarrassed
By the miracle, and crushed by remonstrance.[13]

A Tribute to John F. Carter

A college dean is seldom universally beloved. Typically, this "academic middle manager" is seen by the top administrators as a keeper of the peace, the one who get the work done while holding the faculty at bay. The faculty, on the other hand, view the dean as their first-among-equals protector, the one who obtains from the recalcitrant administrators the privileges and honors they so richly deserve. If the dean can serve as the president's man in the trenches and, at the same time, serve as a tribune of the faculty, he may be seen as having considerable talent. John F. Carter accomplished that with skill and grace and was, in so many ways, our beloved dean.

Thank you, John Carter, on behalf of myself and the many others you have led, for your faithfulness, for your determination, for your unfailing kindness and encouragement, for your example, and for your friendship.

---

[13] John Updike, *"Seven Stanzas on Easter"* http://thegospelcoalition.org/blogs/justintaylor/2012/04/07/ seven-stanzas-at-easter-john-updike/. (Accessed 3/1/15).

Bibliography

Blackford, Russell. "A Very Short Introduction to Non-Overlapping Magisteria," under "Content and Discussion," http://old.richarddawkins.net/ articles/575220-a-very-short-introduction-to-non-overlapping-magisteria. (Accessed 9/15/14).

Brubacher, John and Willis Rudy. *Higher Education in Transition.* New York: Harper and Rowe, 1958.

Colson, Charles, and Nancy Pearcy, *How Now Shall We Live?* Wheaton, Illinois: Tyndale, 1998.

Love, Robert and Franklin Niles. *Studies in Physical Science.* Springfield, Missouri: Global University, 2008.

McGiffert, Arthur Cushman. *The Apostles' Creed: Its Origin, Its Purpose, and Its Historical Interpretation (2008).* https://archive.org/details/apostlescreeds00mcgi. (Accessed 3/1/15).

North Central Association: Statement on General Education. https://www.umkc.edu/provost/ committees/general-education-advisory-task-force/higher-learning-commission-statement-on-general-education.pdf. (Accessed 2/27/15).

Oxford Dictionary of the Christian Church. *The Apostles' Creed.* Oxford: University Press, 2005.

Palmer, Michael. "Elements of a Christian Worldview." *Pneuma.* Springfield, Missouri: Logion Press, 1998.

Thigpen, Jonathan. "A Brief History of the Bible Institute Movement in America," Evangelical Training Association, https://www.etaworld.org/?bibleinstitute. (Accessed 9/19/14).

Updike, John. "*Seven Stanzas on Easter.*" http://thegospel coalition.org /blogs/justintaylor/ 2012/04/07/seven-stanzas-at-easter-john-updike/. (Accessed 3/1/15).

WORKERS TOGETHER WITH GOD:
An Approach to a Christian Educational Psychology
By George M. Flattery

Introduction

Christian education is both a divine and a human task. Because it is a divine task, theology and the work of the Spirit are essential considerations. Because the task is also human, educational psychology should be studied and applied. Educational psychology can contribute a great deal to our understanding of how to teach divine truth and apply that truth to life.

Drawing from these sources, my focus will be on how we work together with God to have an impact on the learner's development. I will begin with comments on a Christian framework for educational psychology since our educational psychology must harmonize with our theological foundations. Then I will comment briefly on the discipline of educational psychology. After that, I will discuss several specific aspects of the learner's development, including perception, emotions, and motives.[1]

A Christian Framework

As workers together with God (2 Cor. 6:1), we have a definite framework for a Christian psychology of education. As suggested above, the central truth of this framework is that Christian education is both a divine and a human endeavor. All

---

[1] In my book entitled *Teaching for Christian Maturity*, I treated eight aspects of the learner's development: percepts, concepts, emotions, attitudes, motives, the will, social development, and service. My presentation here draws from the discussions in this book.

aspects of the framework relate to this central truth. With this in mind, let us take a look at some of the key points.

Goals

The Biblical goals of Christian education are: (1) to lead men to believe in Christ as Savior, (2) to help believers grow in the image of Christ, (3) to relate well to other people, and (4) to train people for service in the kingdom of God. All four of these goals involve behavioral change. However, we are not just teaching for behavioral change; we are teaching for change in a given direction. In a word, Christ-likeness is our goal. This direction is firmly rooted in our theological understandings of God, man, sin, and salvation.

Nature of Man

The Biblical view of man is that he was made in the image of God. However, Adam, the first man, fell. Without delving into the subjects of original sin and depravity, we all agree that all men are sinners and are in need of salvation. The intellectual and emotional condition of the ungodly is described by Paul in Ephesians 4:17-19:

> This I say therefore, and affirm together with the Lord, that you walk no longer just as the Gentiles also walk, in the futility of their mind, being darkened in their understanding, excluded from the life of God, because of the ignorance that is in them, because of the hardness of their heart; and they, having become callous, have given themselves over to sensuality, for the practice of every kind of impurity with greediness.[2]

---

[2] Unless otherwise indicated, all quotations of Scripture are from the NASB, 1995.

Conversion

Through Christian education, we can introduce a person to Christ, but we cannot educate him or her into the kingdom of God. As Jesus said (John 3:3) to Nicodemus, "unless one is born again, he cannot see the kingdom of God." Ultimately, every person must choose to come to Christ in repentance and faith. When they do, then their spiritual life as a child of God begins.

It is important to think about the impact of this theology on children. Obviously, children need not be radically separated from God before accepting Christ. Many children grow up in Christian homes and naturally make their own faith commitment to him. Leading children to make this commitment is an important part of Christian education.

Growth and Development

As all educators do, Christian educators recognize that children grow and develop. Children grow physically. Their development is intellectual, emotional, and volitional, but also social. All of these aspects are interrelated with spiritual development. Spiritual development takes place through an ongoing relationship with God. Although Jesus was a unique person, he grew in normal ways. As Luke (2:52) puts it, "Jesus kept increasing in wisdom and stature, and in favor with God and men."

Except for physical growth, all aspects of development continue in adulthood. Spiritual development, for example, is a lifelong process. Even the apostle Paul, late in his ministry, said (Phil. 3:13-14): "Brethren, I do not regard myself as having laid hold of it [perfection] yet; but one thing I *do*: forgetting what *lies* behind and reaching forward to what *lies* ahead, I press on toward the goal for the prize of the upward call of God in Christ Jesus."

Educational Psychology

Educational psychology is essential to the field of education. Much educational practice is derived from its concepts and theories. Both theologians and Christian educators benefit from the research and writings of this discipline. The Christian educator can draw from various theories of educational psychology in constructing teaching and learning sequences.

Definition and Scope

We may think of educational psychology as a behavioral science dealing with human behavior and education. As a science, educational psychology studies those factors that help us understand, predict, and control behavior in educational settings. The scope of this discipline includes the nature of the learner, theories of the development of the learner, studies of motivation, learning theories, and teaching strategies. All these theories are applied to the instructional process. Consequently, various aspects of instructional design, such as writing instructional objectives, developing instructional sequences, and testing are included.

Approaches

The subject of educational psychology is presented in various ways. It is not my purpose to review all of these ways, but rather to focus on the aspects of intellect, emotion, and will. Many educational psychologists, even though they may use different terms, cover these aspects of the learner's development.

One educator, Herman H. Horne, dealt extensively with the learner's development. He was the leading idealist philosopher of education of the first part of the twentieth century. Much that he wrote, such as his book *Jesus--The Master Teacher*, was from a Christian perspective. We need not agree with his philosophical idealism to benefit from his thinking about educational psychology.

In one of his books, Horne develops his views on the *psychological* principles of education. As he states, his work is organized around "the threefold nature of the mind, viz. the intellectual, the emotional, and the moral [the will], and by the relationship of mind as a unit to divinity, the spiritual" (1915, 79). Horne maintains that the spirit of man is his whole consciousness in relation to deity (1915, 333). Because many theologians think of mankind in terms of intellect, emotion, and will, they can relate well to his approach.

Additionally, William Yount has written about educational psychology from a Christian perspective. In his revised book, published in 2010, he writes about thinking, feeling and valuing, doing, relating to other people, and other topics. Woven into these discussions is his treatment of spiritual development. Likewise, he relates each of these domains to learning theories, both past and present (2010, Unit 3).

Perception

We turn now to our discussion of the process of perception. Perception is one of the processes in intellectual development. Near the end of his life, Moses reminded the children of Israel of all that God had done for them. Then, Moses (Deut. 29:4, KJV) said: "Yet the Lord hath not given you a heart to perceive ("know," NASB, 1995, "a mind that understands," NIV), and eyes to see, and ears to hear, unto this day."

Helping people properly perceive, know, or understand the Word of God remains a challenge for the teacher today. Focusing on perception will help us meet this challenge. We shall consider, therefore, the nature of perception, factors that influence its development, how the teacher can help the student improve perception. Finally we will comment on the work of God in perception.

The Nature of Perception

Herman Horne identified two kinds of perception: (1) sense perception, or the knowledge of individual, sensible, present things, and (2) inner perception, or the knowledge of the self and meanings. In his view, through inner perception, the mind looks inward at itself and becomes aware of itself, its thoughts, feelings, or intuitions; or, the mind becomes aware of the meaning of any theory, thing, or truth. Horne agrees, though, that the unqualified term perception usually refers to sense perception (1915, 97-98).

As the term perception is normally used, two major steps are involved. The *first* step is that, through our senses, we become aware of the presence of things around us. Both the presence of things and the awareness of them are essential. We do not say that we have perceived anything until we have become aware of it. The *second* step is to assign meaning to the objects upon which we have focused our attention. Different people perceive the same objects in different ways. Moreover, the meanings we assign often change with the passing of time. The fact that our perceptions can change makes education possible.

Influences on Perception

Several factors influence our perception. One is the acuity, or sharpness, of our senses. If we lack this sharpness, we are unable to make clear distinctions between tones, colors, tastes, and the like. Another factor is the organization of the stimuli around us. For example, we all have taken note of optical illusions. In such cases we are deceived by the organization of what we see. Our perception of the many stimuli around us, however, is not always a passive process. We often actively examine the stimuli, select those to which we want to pay attention, and organize them into patterns that are meaningful to us.

A third factor is physical growth. At first a child perceives indistinct masses; then, because of physical growth, he begins to perceive distinct specifics. An infant's sensory experience is usually very vague and lacking in detail. As he reacts to the large masses which he first senses, he begins to distinguish some objects from the rest. He may, for example, begin to notice his blanket is different from other items in the room.

Improving Perception

The teacher can improve the student's perception of the Bible by providing sensory experiences for him that relate to the truths being taught. Jesus frequently taught truths by using things that the people could see, touch, taste, and otherwise experience. On one such occasion, he used a coin to teach some conniving Pharisees a lesson about meeting their obligations to the government as well as to God. With the denarius in sight, He said (Mt. 22:21): "Then render to Caesar the things that are Caesar's; and to God the things that are God's." His point was very clearly made.

Another way to improve perception is to teach abstract truth through the use of concrete language. Words that refer to things that appeal to the senses are concrete; words that refer to things that do not appeal to the senses are abstract. Both of these words, "concrete" and "abstract," are more abstract than concrete.

A teacher can help his students perceive what he is teaching by organizing the lesson so that his points will be clearer to them. It is usually wise to give a preview of the lesson first so that the students will have a general idea of what is going to be covered. Having glimpsed the whole, they will be able to relate the parts better to the whole. Then, the teacher should present each of the parts of the lesson. Students will more easily grasp the meaning of the lesson if the parts are taught in some logical order. Finally, the teacher should quickly review and summarize the lesson for the students. This will sharpen their perception of what was said.

A Miracle of God

In drawing us to Him so that we might perceive Him, God makes use of our natural senses. There is no greater evidence of this than the fact that He gave His Son to be incarnated in the form of human flesh. Because God made it possible for Jesus to be physically seen, John could say (I Jn. 3:16, KJV): "Hereby perceive [know, NASB, 1995] we the love of God, because he laid down his life for us: and we ought to lay down our lives for the brethren."

Besides showing us some things about himself through our natural senses, God desires to reveal himself inwardly to us through our spiritual senses. God has given us a soul that, as Tozer affirms, "has eyes with which to see and ears with which to hear" (1948, 58). However, God will not use these spiritual senses until he has miraculously cleansed them from sin and made them alive unto him. When he restores our spiritual senses, he sends his Spirit into our hearts to communicate with us. Concerning our ability to understand spiritual matters, Paul (I Cor. 2:11-12) writes:

> [11] For who among men knows the *thoughts* of a man except the spirit of the man, which is in him? Even so the *thoughts* of God no one knows except the Spirit of God. [12] Now we have received, not the spirit of the world, but the Spirit who is from God, that we might know the things freely given to us by God.

Emotions

Another aspect of the learner's development is emotion. Life would be reduced to a very sterile existence without emotion. What such a life would be like is described by three doctors, Strecker, Appel, and Appel, as follows:

> Emotions and feelings supply the energy which makes the mind work. Without emotion (emotional energy)

man, although he could live, would be inert, existing in a vegetative state, not necessarily asleep or unconscious but immobile, almost as in a stupor. Without emotion he would lie prone in bed. . . . In short, it is emotional energy which enables man to get out of bed in the morning, to dress himself, to eat breakfast, to go to work, to play, to make love, to care for his children, to fight, to build bridges, or to paint pictures. Without emotions he would do none of these things, but repose, a breathing lump of clay. (1958, 103)

The emotions, that are so vital to every other area of our lives, are equally essential to the expression of our faith. People who feel there ought to be no emotion in connection with their faith are really saying they do not want their faith to have anything to do with their lives, worship, or service. Such an attitude stands in direct contrast to Paul who urges us (Rom. 12:11) to be "fervent in spirit [or Spirit], serving the Lord." The work of God, like all other endeavors, benefits from emotions.

The Nature of Emotions

Emotions involve the whole of one's existence and life. In describing these states, Mouly writes:

Emotions are composite affairs, involving at least three interrelated aspects: (a) varying degrees of feeling covering the whole range of such continua as annoyance-satisfaction and pleasure-displeasure; (b) rather extensive visceral changes such as increased heartbeat and increased circulation of the blood; and (c) certain impulses involving the skeletal muscles such as an urge to fight when angry or to flee when afraid. The feeling aspect of an emotion is, in a sense, the most important phase of the emotion: it may even be considered *the* emotion. (1960, 74)

Our feelings, as well as the visceral changes that accompany them, are usually involuntary responses to our environment. However, we can exercise a measure of control over our emotions. For example, just because we may feel like striking at others, physically or verbally, does not mean that we are compelled to do so. Just as thoughts and actions are affected by feelings, so feelings can be brought under control by regulating our thoughts and actions.

The Development of Emotions

As a child grows physically and learns about his environment, he develops emotionally. Two different approaches to emotional development are described, as follows, by Bridges and Horne.

According to Bridges, emotional development occurs in three ways (1932, 324-341). One, as a child gets older, a gradual differentiation of emotions takes place. For example, at birth an infant displays a general state of excitement. During his first three months the infant's excitement begins to be expressed as distress and delight. Two, children develop emotionally through the modification of the way they act in response to each specific feeling. Early in a child's life, he displays his anger in the form of temper tantrums; at about the age of three this type of behavior is altered into the more subtle forms of sulking, obstinacy, and contrariness. Three, as the meaning of situations changes for an individual, the emotions aroused by them are different. A friend's pet dog is more likely to arouse fear in a five-year old than in an adult.

Besides the usual analyses, such as the one above, Horne recognizes three states of growth with regard to the objects to which our feelings attach themselves (1915, 204-206). First, the child's feelings are *egoistic*; that is, they center on himself or herself. The child loves himself/herself, pleasure, wants to possess things, has pride and vanity, and expresses fear, anger, joy, and grief. Next, in early adolescence, feelings are attached to others. These are the *altruistic* feelings and include love and hate, friendship, respect, sympathy, and emulation. Finally, the growing person, in late adolescence and maturity, attaches his or her feelings to certain ideals. Among the objects of these *ideal* feelings are truth, beauty and goodness. The pursuit of these ideals is satisfying. The three stages stand in relationship to each other like a series of concentric circles, each one larger than the last.

Training Emotions

To a degree, wholesome emotional life can be taught. Thus, teachers ought to commit themselves, not only to intellectual matters, but to training feelings as well. Here are some ways to do this:

Since our thoughts affect our feelings, the teacher can direct emotional life by the ideas and principles they present. Ideas and principles should be taught that will lead people to feel appropriately about their duties to themselves and their families. It is important, also, to teach people ideas that will cause them to have compassion for others. Our feelings, for ourselves and others, must be enlarged to include Biblical ideals such as truth, love, justice, and goodness.

Besides teaching stimulating ideas, it is essential that praxis be provided. Unless people become involved in God's work, it is not likely that they will develop adequate feelings for spiritual matters. Much learning takes place through doing.

If teachers desire to develop the emotional lives of others, they must set a good example themselves. The emotions of Jesus, our perfect pattern, stand out in scripture. For example, the Bible (Mark 6:34) tells us: "He saw a great multitude, and He felt compassion for them because they were like sheep without a shepherd; and He began to teach them many things."

A Divine Impartation

Mankind is unable to control and express emotions ideally. Undesirable emotional reactions are without doubt the most pervasive sickness of the human race. Anger and fear abound, expressed in many different forms. Because mankind reacts to life holistically, emotional maladjustment often leads to physical illness. Even worse than this is the fact that many emotional expressions are sinful and cause people to be separated from God. Concerning this state, Paul (Rom. 2:5) writes: "But because of your stubbornness and unrepentant heart you are storing up wrath for yourself in the day of wrath and revelation of the righteous judgment of God."

Bound by emotional habits that weaken them morally and dissipate energies, human beings, left alone, can only cry out, as Paul (Rom. 7:24) did, "Wretched man that I am! Who will set me free from the body of this death?" Fortunately, help is available. With the mighty apostle (Rom. 7:25) mankind can say, "Thanks be to God through Jesus Christ our Lord!" By turning to God man can crucify (Gal. 5:24) "the flesh with its passions and desires." A new capacity to love God and others will be born in them.

Because God loves us, he has provided the Holy Spirit to help us live a mature, Christ-like emotional life. The Holy Spirit imparts the fruit of the Spirit to us. All of these fruit—"love, joy, peace, patience, kindness, goodness, faithfulness, gentleness, self-control" (Gal. 5:22-23)—involve our emotions to some degree. The mind and will are also involved, but the role of emotions must be recognized. The man who is filled with the Spirit will display a completely new life of feeling.

Motives

A major concern in educational psychology is motivation. The local church teacher is faced with several challenging motivational problems. To start with, he has to attract people to class on a voluntary basis. Then, the teacher has to inspire the students to learn what he or she is teaching. Finally, there is the problem of getting people to live according to Biblical principles and to assume their role in the Body of Christ.

The Nature of Motives

When we consider motives, two main issues are involved. First, what incites, or causes us to act? Second, what are the things that give direction to our actions? What causes us to direct our behavior toward one goal instead of toward another? In short, motives have to do with what "arouses" and "directs" behavior.

Students of these issues have pointed to many things that have a part in determining why we behave as we do. However, most of these things can be grouped under the following categories: (1) inner conditions such as needs, drives, wants, and interests, (2) external factors such as food, water, money, praise or blame and the attention of others, (3) purposes or goals, and (4) the human will.

Our goals may include the satisfaction of an inner condition, such as hunger, or obtaining some external factor, such as food. Sometimes we include both our need and the external factor in stating our goal. A hungry man might say that his goal is to satisfy his hunger by eating food.

Our will affects what we do in at least two ways. One, we select the needs, such as thirst, to which we will pay attention. Two, with our will we select from the available external factors, such as water or milk, the ones we will seek to satisfy our needs.

To which of these four factors does the term "motives" refer? In a broad sense this term, which literally means, "to move," can refer to all of them. Each of them is in some way connected with "moving" us to do what we do. However, psychologists often use the word in a more restricted sense to refer to our needs (inner conditions) and our goals. In everyday conversation the word is usually employed in an even narrower sense, referring to our goals. In other words, by "motives" most people mean our purposes.

Theories of Motivation

Theories of motivation and learning are interrelated. As Yount says: "*Learning Theory* focuses on the establishment and strengthening of new behaviors, attitudes and concepts. *Motivation* focuses on the energy, vitality, and intensity of learning, on the learner's own intention to learn" (2010, Chapter 13). He emphasizes three major groups of learning theories: behavioral, cognitive, and humanistic (2010, Units 3 and 4). Then, he discusses the motivational theories associated with these groups as well as other theories of learning and motivation. He makes the following statement:

> Learning is complex—and *motivating* students to learn is complex as well, requiring a variety of motivational approaches. We will present motivation as a matter of reinforcing desired behavior (traditional behaviorism), providing appropriate models for behavior (social learning theory), creating a sense of curiosity (cognitive learning theory), making material meaningful (information processing theory), meeting personal needs (humanism), and encouraging achievement through successful experiences (aspiration and achievement theories). (2010, Chapter 13)

Abraham Maslow highlights personal needs in his theory of human motivation. He proposed a hierarchy of needs (1943, 370-396). According to him, the basic needs of man are as follows: (1) physiological needs, (2) safety needs, (3) love and belonging needs, (4) esteem needs, (5) self-actualization, or self-fulfillment needs, (6) cognitive needs, or the needs to know and understand and (7) aesthetic needs. In 1968, he added transcendence as an eighth category.

In Maslow's view an individual's needs at the lower level tend to be met before he attempts to satisfy his needs at a higher level. He admits, however, that this is not a hard and fast rule. Actually, it is doubtful that a person's needs at any level are ever completely met. Thus, we cannot apply Maslow's general rule in an absolute way.

Relating the Gospel to Man's Needs

As teachers, we should seek to relate the gospel to the needs of men. This will have a positive impact on the students' desire to learn. Even a cursory study of the Gospels will reveal that Jesus made strong appeals to the needs of his hearers. In relating the Gospel to needs, the teacher should know and communicate the following important truths.

The first truth is that God wants to meet all of our needs. The apostle Paul (Phil. 4:19) said, "And my God shall supply all your needs according to His riches in glory in Christ Jesus." Although he probably refers here to material needs, the statement applies aphoristically, or in principle, to all other needs as well.

We must not allow the abuse of this principle to keep us from teaching it. Many people distort the truth by confusing "needs" with excessive "desires." Almost any truth can be taught or grasped in distorted ways. We can be too cautious and not really share the good news of God's providence for his children. When properly taught, the children of God can take great comfort in knowing He takes great joy in meeting their needs.

Second is Christ's paradoxical teaching (Luke 9:24) that "whoever wishes to save his life shall lose it, but whoever loses his life for My sake, he is the one who will save it." Applied to our needs, this means that if we seek to satisfy them without Christ, we will be unsatisfied in the end. On the other hand, if we put him and his work first, he will ultimately satisfy our every need. By losing our lives, we gain them.

The third truth is that as our hearts respond to the needs of others, God enables us to meet their needs and in the process supplies our own needs. As Paul (2 Cor. 9:8, Phillips) says, "After all, God can give you everything that you need, so that you may always have sufficient both for yourselves and for giving away to other people."

A New Center

When a man or woman is saved, and as they grow in Christ, God transforms the entire motivational structure of their life. Before a person is transformed by the Holy Spirit, they make themselves the center of their life. Afterwards, they place Christ at the center. As they grow in Christ, they are increasingly able to say with Paul (Phil. 1:21), "For to me, to live is Christ, and to die is gain." By this Paul meant that Christ was the person who motivated the whole of his existence. It was Christ who aroused him to act and directed his behavior.

After we have put Christ at the center of our lives, we decide what we will do on the basis of whether or not it will benefit the kingdom of God. The interests of all other people are best served when the kingdom of God is advanced. Furthermore, it is marvelously true that what is best for the kingdom is ultimately best for us. Paradoxical, but true! In my opinion, this is why the psalmist said (Ps. 37:4), "Delight yourself in the Lord; And He will give you the desires of your heart."

Conclusion

In Christian education we are workers together with God in a task that is both divine and human. The fact that Christian education is a work of God does not lighten our responsibility to teach. Neither does the fact that we are responsible make the work of God unnecessary. A part of our responsibility is to pray that God will do his work in the lives of our students. We should pray for our students as Paul (Eph. 1:16-19, Phillips) did for the Ephesians:

> I thank God continually for you and I never give up praying for you; and this is my prayer. That God, the Father, will give you spiritual wisdom and the insight to know more of him: that you may receive that inner illumination of the spirit which will make you realize how great is the hope to which he is calling you–the

magnificence and splendor of the inheritance promised to Christians—and how tremendous is the power available to us who believe in God.

As we have seen, both theology and educational psychology deal with many aspects of a learner's development. With intellect, emotions, and will in mind, we have specifically discussed perception, emotions, and motivation.

It is the divine part of the task that distinguishes Christian education from education in general. A Christian approach to educational psychology, therefore, must take this distinction into account and build on it.

Let us work together with God! Because of the human aspects of teaching, we will benefit from a study of educational psychology, learning theory and instructional design. Then, because we must rely fully on the Holy Spirit, let us commune with God until we (Luke 24:49) "are clothed with power from on high." The Holy Spirit will enable us to accomplish our educational task.

Bibliography

Articles

Bridges, Katherine, "Emotional Development in Early Infancy," *Child Development*, III (1932), 324-341.

Maslow, A. H., "A Theory of Human Motivation," Psychological Review, L. No. 4 (1943), 370-396.

Books

Ausubel, David P., Novak, Joseph D., Hanesian, Helen. *Educational Psychology: A Cognitive View*. New York: Holt, Rinehart and Winston, 1968.

Biehler, Robert F., and Snowman, Jack. *Psychology Applied to Teaching*. Boston: Houghton Mifflin Company, 1982.

Boehlke, Robert R. *Theories of Learning in Christian Education*. Philadelphia: The Westminster Press, 1962.

Bruner, Jerome S. *The Process of Education*. New York: Vintage Books, 1963.

Carter, John F. *Educational Psychology: A Study Guide*. Brussels: International Correspondence Institute, 1985.

Flattery, George M. *Teaching for Christian Maturity*. Springfield: Gospel Publishing House, 1968.

Horne, Herman H. *Jesus--the Master Teacher*. Grand Rapids: Kregel Publications, 1964.

_____. *The Philosophy of Christian Education*. New York: Association Press, 1919.

_____. *The Philosophy of Education*. New York: Macmillan Co., 1930.

_____. *The Psychological Principles of Education*. New York: Macmillan Co., 1915.

Kingsley, Howard L., rev. Garry, Ralph. *The Nature and Conditions of Learning*. Englewood Cliffs: Prentice-Hall, Inc., 1957.

Klausmeier, Herbert J. and Goodwin, William. *Learning and Human Abilities: Educational Psychology*. New York: Harper and Row, Publishers, 1966.

Marsh, Leon. *Educational Psychology for Christian Education*. Fort Worth: Southwestern Baptist Theological Seminary, 1982.

McDonald, Frederick J. *Educational Psychology*. San Francisco: Wadsworth Publishing Co., Inc., 1959.

Meier, Paul D., Minirth, Frank B., and Wichern, Frank. *Introduction to Psychology and Counseling: Christian Perspectives and Applications*. Grand Rapids: Baker Book House, 1982.

Mouly, George J. *Psychology for Effective Teaching*. New York: Holt, Rinehart and Winston, 1962.

Strecker, Edward A., Appel, Kenneth E., and Appel. John W. *Discovering Ourselves*. New York: Macmillan Co., 1958.

Tozer, A. W. *The Pursuit of God*. Harrisburg: Christian Publications, 1948.

Yount, William. *Created to Learn: A Christian Teacher's Introduction to Educational Psychology*, Second Edition. Nashville: B&H Publishing Group, 2010.

Zuck, Roy B. *The Holy Spirit in Your Teaching*. Wheaton: Scripture Press Publications, Inc., 1963.

Assessing Missional Ministries in the Pentecostal Church
by Robert W. Houlihan
College of Christian Ministries and Religion
Southeastern University, Lakeland, Florida, USA

The growth of the Church in the 21st century is due in part to the distinctives of Pentecostal missions theology. It has been stated by many that the 20th century was a "Pentecostal century."[1] One of the reasons for this is the critical link between Pentecostal theology and Pentecostal missions. The advance of missions is in part based upon the understanding of one of the key verses of Pentecostal theology, ". . . but you shall receive power when the Holy Spirit has come upon you; and you shall be My witnesses both in Jerusalem, and in all Judea and Samaria, and even to the remotest part of the earth" (Acts 1:8 NAS). The words of Jesus clearly link the necessity of the power of the Holy Spirit with the declaration of God's truth in the nations of the earth. One without the other is inadequate to take the gospel to the world. For this reason, the early Pentecostal leaders talked much of the Word and the Spirit. One must have the Word of God, the *kerygma*, the message of Jesus' life, death, and resurrection but also the dynamics of the Spirit-signs and wonders to get the gospel to the remote parts of the earth.[2]

---

[1] Allan Anderson, "Towards a Pentecostal Missiology for the Majority World," *Asian Journal of Pentecostal Studies* 8:1 (2005): 29-47. "Pentecostal have been around for only a hundred years, but today are the main role players in the world missions, representing perhaps a quarter of the world's Christians and perhaps three quarters of them are in the Majority World. . . Most of the dramatic church growth in the twentieth century has taken place in Pentecostal and independent Pentecostal-like churches."

[2] Gary B. McGee, *Miracles, Missions, and American Pentecostalism* (New York: Orbis Books, 2010), 5.

Historic Pentecostal Foundations that Impact World Evangelism

The foundations laid by these early Pentecostals have proven to be biblical and effective. When one considers the fact that there are 584 million Pentecostals/charismatics in the world, growing by 20 million a year, then it is not difficult to see the impact of Pentecostal missions.[3] Also of great importance is the fact that the Pentecostal/charismatic segment of the Church is growing fastest in the non-Western world: Africa, Asia, and Latin America. Peter Jenkins made the interesting observation that of the three great ideological people movements of the last century, National Socialism, Communism and the Pentecostal Church, it is the last movement that had the most enduring impact on the world, because the former two, for all intents and purposes, have ceased to exist.[4] The following foundations have characterized Pentecostal missions: The relationship between the Spirit and the Word and the need to attack Satan's kingdom through the miraculous, the critical link between eschatology and missions and the mandate to reach all nations/people groups.

Closely linked to Pentecostals' equal emphasis of the Spirit and the Word is the truth that Jesus came to destroy the works of the Devil (I John 3:8). The attack against Satan's kingdom was initiated at the opening of the ministry of Jesus, but it is also being fulfilled as the gospel goes to the nations of the earth. In Mark's gospel, Jesus began to preach about the kingdom of God (Mark 1:15). This was critical because another kingdom, Satan's, was in control of planet earth.

After opening his ministry concerning the kingdom of God, Jesus immediately went to Capernaum and began the counterattack by casting out demons.[5] He came to bring in the kingdom of God by doing violence against the kingdom of Satan. The early Pentecostals understood this truth and brought back

---

[3] R. C. Crosby, *A Pentecostal Growth Explosion – Over a Fourth of Christendom.* http://www.patheos.com/blogs. 2012/05. (Accessed: June 15, 2015).
[4] Philip Jenkins, *The Next Christendom* (New York: Oxford University Press, 2007).
[5] Ibid., 9.

into the life of the Church the "signs and wonders" of Jesus. The emphasis upon this neglected area brought much criticism from other evangelicals or "Word only" people. But up to the time of Pentecostal missions, the growth of the Church was stagnated. It was only with the renewed emphasis upon not only the "preaching" of the gospel but also the dynamics of the Spirit that the Church began the advance to the remote areas of the earth. Pentecostal missions move forward by the miraculous.

Another area of Pentecostal theology and spirituality that has greatly impacted world evangelism is the link between missions and eschatology. Early Pentecostal preachers talked much of the second coming of the Lord. Whether they fully understood this from a missiological point is not known. However, when ministers were baptized with the Spirit, they began to reemphasize the coming of Christ for the Church.

The preaching of the coming of Christ brought with it several important emphases. The first was the call to holiness. If the Lord can come at any moment, then Christians need to be prepared. The parables of the Lord were often used to substantiate the truth of the imminent return of the Lord.

This led to the second eschatological emphasis: missions must be done quickly. To wait until later was viewed as a temptation from Satan to cheat Christians from receiving their rewards in heaven. With this theological framework, Pentecostal churches began to send out missionaries almost from the time they were founded. Full-Gospel churches seemed in a "hurry" because a night was coming when no man could work. Long range plans were not really considered.

A last eschatological emphasis has to do with the closure to the "age of the Gentiles." Early Pentecostals believed that the gospel must go to all nations before the end of the world could come. Matthew 24:14 was the theological basis for the advance of the Church in the entire world before the end of time. Then in order to "hasten" or "speed up" (2 Peter 3:12) the coming of the Lord, missionaries must be sent out to all nations. Without a doubt, there was confusion on this point in some quarters of Pentecostal theology, but as the Church matured, the meaning of nations (*ta ethne*) began to be understood. God is concerned with every people group. The importance of a biblical "worldview" was not an option; it was obligatory for Pentecostals. Every nation, every people group, must have the opportunity to hear before Christ comes again.

Issues Facing Missions Today

Based upon this brief historical sketch of the foundation of Pentecostal missions, this article will look at three overarching issues: the Traditions, the Trials, and the Trends of Pentecostal missions in order to assess strengths and weaknesses and suggest possible directions for the first quarter of the 21st century.

The Traditions of Pentecostal Missions

Tradition 1: New Territories

One of the main traditions that has made the Pentecostal mission strong in the 21st century is the emphasis upon going into new territories. As stated above, from the beginnings of the Azusa Street Mission, missionaries were sent out to the world. The more unreached and exotic the place, the more it was emphasized in local churches. For this reason, Africa, "the black continent," was the natural place for missionaries to go and do evangelism.

Pentecostals feel the need to go where no other missionaries have gone. Today Pentecostal Majority World missionaries can be found in Tibet, Inner Mongolia, the Islamic areas of Asia, remote areas of East Africa and a host of other countries. The clarion call of the early Pentecostals was sung for decades and knitted its truth to the fabric of the souls of its youth. . . . "To the regions beyond, I must go . . . I must go."[6]

Despite this, agencies have some concern about the numbers of missionaries needed to complete the task ahead. With the decrease of missionaries sent from the churches in

---

[6]A. B. Simpson and Margaret M. Simpson, *"The Regions Beyond,"* in *Hymns of the Christian Life.* (Harrisburg, PA: Christian Publications, 1936), #454.

Europe and the static number of cross-cultural missionaries being sent from North America, how will the growing world populations hear the message of redeeming love? One of the answers may lie in the growing number of young people in China who are called to cross-cultural missions. Whether one accepts the concept of the China youth's vision for "back to Jerusalem" or not, there are probably 100,000 young people with the hope of doing cross-cultural evangelism in the 10-40 window between China and Israel. It is a known fact that a majority of the unofficial churches in China are Pentecostal in theology.

Tradition 2: Planting Indigenous Churches and Empowering National Workers

Inspired by the works of Roland Allen[7] and then by the writing of Melvin Hodges,[8] Pentecostal missionaries were challenged to plant churches in a different way than their historical church brothers.[9] The emphasis was to be upon the "soil,"–the culture out of which the church was to be established. Many fellowships of missionaries had long and heated discussions on how to accomplish this, but in the end this became one of the traditions of Pentecostal Missions.

The indigenous model sharply contrasted with the model of church planting that for decades had centered around a western model of church building that became the symbol of the Christian community in the target culture. The motto of the latter model was, "Build it (the church building) and they will come." This artificial model was one of the reasons the church planting movement failed in China, Japan, and Korea for hundreds of years.

Possibly because of the lack of funds, Pentecostal missions were forced to use a different model that was indigenous that

---

[7]Roland Allan, *Missionary Methods: St. Paul's or Ours?* (Grand Rapids, MI: Eerdmans, 1962).

[8]Melvin L. Hodges, *The Indigenous Church* (Springfield, MO: Gospel Publishing House, 1976).

[9]Gary McGee, *Assemblies of God Missions Facing the 21st Century: Strategizing on the Run* (Springfield, MO: Gospel Publishing House, 2008), 6.

led to church planting not being dependent upon foreign funds. Gary McGee stated, "Four factors continue to shape the course of Assemblies of God missions: evangelical doctrine, Pentecostal doctrine and spirituality, the implementation of indigenous church principles concomitant with training leaders, and pragmatism in choosing delivery systems." He further stated:

> Assemblies of God missions have been committed to following "New Testament methods" in planting churches on the missions field. Regardless of this high-sounding goal, few missionaries knew how to put them into practice. . . . Notwithstanding, the vision of Alice E. Luce, Ralph D. Williams and Melvin Hodges, all of them skilled practitioners who adapted Pentecostal spirituality of Roland Allen's missiological perspectives, led to the seismic shift in mission policy from paternalism to partnership in the post war period. From the 1950's onward, the number of ministerial training institutions overseas skyrocketed. As missionaries turned the reins of leadership over to national leaders, church growth boomed in many countries.[10]

Empowering the national workers through training institutions and Bible Colleges became the hallmark of Pentecostal mission. This was done in many places "on the run," but when the missionaries understood their role as apostolic and not pastoral, church growth began to increase.

When the early historical church missionaries came to Japan, however, there had been a tendency to send their brightest converts to Germany for theological education. In his book, *Protestant Beginnings in Japan*, Wilburn T. Thomas states that one of the major reasons for failure of the church movement was the rise of biblical higher criticism by the Japanese scholars who were trained in Germany and other foreign countries.[11] This led to a dearth of church growth when

---

[10]Ibid., 9.
[11]Winburn T. Thomas, *Protestant Beginnings in Japan* (Tokyo: Charles Tuttle Co., 1959), 193-195.

there should have been a mighty movement in this very progressive country.

It is interesting to note that the Assemblies of God internationally has more Bible Schools and training institutions than any other world Christian fellowship. This was accomplished at a time when there was an aversion to theological training in the American Assemblies of God.

Tradition 3: Dependency on the Holy Spirit

The basic and most enduring tradition of the Pentecostal movement is the dependency upon the Holy Spirit for the advancement of the church in the world. If the work of missions is done through human strategies and plans, we get human results. It is only when we are led by the Spirit that we have a chance to destroy the works of the god of this world. Pentecostal mission that is done in the power of the Spirit has a Satan-ward view . . . realizing that we are fighting a formidable foe and the only way to overcome his control of the world's systems and people is in the same way our Lord accomplished it . . . by spiritual war. J. Philip Hogan, the Executive Director of the Division of Foreign Missions for more than two decades, said:

> I am overwhelmed and humbled before the moving of the Spirit's own sovereign presence in the world. Make no mistake, the missionary venture of the church, no matter how well planned, how finely administered and finely supported, would fail like every other vast human enterprise were it not that where human instrumentality leaves off, a blessed ally takes over. It is the Holy Spirit that calls, it is the Holy Spirit that inspires, it is the Holy Spirit that reveals, and it is the Holy Spirit that administers.[12]

---

[12] J. Philip Hogan, address given to the Evangelical Foreign Missions Association in 1970. Quoted by Gary McGee in *Assemblies of God Missions Facing the 21st Century: Strategizing on the Run*, 2-3.

The Trials of Pentecostal Missions

Together with a number of traditions, the incredible growth of Pentecostal missions has been cited above. This is nothing short of the blessings of God upon a revival movement that broke down some of the walls of class, race and poverty. However, today Pentecostal missions is facing several critical trials.

The Trial of a Misunderstanding of People Groups

As mentioned earlier, because of the political boundaries that separate countries, these demarcations were taken as the spiritual target areas to send missionaries. Missionaries were sent to Kenya, China, Malaysia, or a host of 200 other nations as the "uttermost parts of the earth." When several units were sent to a certain country, then the fellowship sensed it was fulfilling the Great Commission. While the home offices had to deal with political entities in order to obtain visas, it seemed that the focus was upon the countries rather than people groups in those countries.

Scriptures are very clear that "the field is the world" in God's view of the mission field. What was passed over by many was the meaning of the concept of "nations" in several passages (Matt. 24:14; Matt. 28:18-19). The *"ethne"* of these passages undoubtedly refers to culturally and linguistically similar groups of people who may live in a political country or may live in a land mass that covers several countries. Usually, there are many unreached people groups (UPGs) in a given country. For example, Myanmar, formerly known as Burma, has 135 distinct people groups. Any strategy to reach this "nation" would have to be sensitive to all these different cultural groups of people.

According to the Joshua Project, there are currently 16,598 ethne in the world and 7,165 are unreached constituting 41.5% of all people![13] It has only been in recent years that Pentecostal

---

[13] The Joshua Project website (accessed: May 12, 2013).

missions (at least in the American Assemblies of God) have followed the lead of other evangelical missions and begun to assign missionaries to people groups instead of countries. In a letter sent to the U.S. world missionaries in January, 2013 Executive Director Greg Mundis said:

> First, in cooperation with the Holy Spirit, we can strategically identify and focus on the neglected regions and send out workers to evangelize, plant churches, train believers to do the ministry, and minister to the poor and suffering. This pioneer work will not be easy–it never is–but it is necessary. Literally, hundreds of millions of people will not hear the message otherwise. Of course, we as AGWM don't bear the whole responsibility for every unreached people group, but we do bear a large responsibility because of God's favor on our mission. . . . Second, we can search our hearts to see if the Lord is whispering and directing us to be part of His plan and renewed strategic focus in AGWM to go to a neglected region and pioneer a work among unreached peoples. . . .[14]

This is a refreshing direction taken by the new Executive Director of world missions. One of the younger missions scholars, Alan Johnson, has had a great impact on this change by illuminating the biblical interpretation of the word "nations." He cites several biblical scholars to emphasize this point:

> In his work on the term *ethne* in Matthew 28:19, usually translated as nations, John Piper is concerned to show that the term is not limited to just geographic or political groups. He points out that even in English the term nations can refer to a people with a unifying ethnic identity as when we speak of the Cherokee Nation. Piper shows that the singular *ethnos* in the New Testament never refers to an individual but rather to a

---

[14] Greg Mundis, Letter mailed to Assemblies of God missionaries, January, 2013.

people group or nation. . . . The 18 references to *panta ta ethne* (all the nations) in the New Testament favor a people group view.[15]

The Trial of Confusion over the Biblical Concept of Ecclesia

Another difficulty that Pentecostal missions has faced in the last 100 years is the confusion of the meaning of the biblical concept of *ecclesia*. We in the West tend to associate the term with a certain place or building. This may come from the cultural heritage of the incredible cathedrals of Europe as the holy places of worship. Without a doubt, some of this thinking comes from our roots in the Roman Catholic tradition which places much emphasis upon places of worship. This is right within our western cultural context, but when this is transferred into another very different culture, misunderstanding may occur. For example, when early Protestant missionaries built church buildings in Japan, the buildings tended to look like western church buildings and not like the Asian buildings common in Japan. This at once made the Japanese view these structures as foreign and not part of their culture. It is difficult for the Japanese to enter into a religious building that looks "foreign."

In the New Testament, the followers of Christ did not have the luxury of "church" buildings. *Ecclesia* did not mean a special building for worship, but rather the gathering of believers wherever they might be–homes, caves, or fields. In my work with the Japanese Assemblies of God, they tended to be molded by this Western concept since it was taught to them by the early missionaries. The advance of the church was gauged by the number of church buildings the fellowship could count as part of their denomination. This was so engrained in their thinking that they could not think of believers meeting "wherever" in the name of the Lord as a "real" church. The growth of the church

---

[15] Alan Johnson, *Frontier Missions and Beyond: An Emerging Paradigm for Missions in the 21st Century*. Paper presented by the World-wide Mission into the 21st Century, 10-11.

was in some ways controlled by the philosophy of the pioneer missionaries . . . even though dead, they were still speaking.

The Trial of an Overemphasis on Evangelism

Another area that has caused some concern for Pentecostals in recent years is the realization that the early Pentecostals over emphasized evangelism and neglected cultural sensitivity and the social and justice issues of the poor. Pentecostals have always been aggressive in evangelism. Missions meant the proclamation of the gospel and the building of churches. McGee describes the first twenty years of Pentecostal missions as mostly "chaotic in operation." Reports filtering back from the fields tended to be newsletters of optimistic and triumphalistic reports of how many people were saved, healed and baptized. There were few reports of the cultural blunders or misunderstandings. If the people of a culture rejected the message, then the missionaries just "dusted the dirt off their sandals" and moved on to the next village or city. They gave little thought to trying to understand the culture of the target people group or ministering in a way to win their confidence. The motivation of missions was the imminent return of Christ and the need to get the gospel to the world. Evangelism was always viewed as more important than cultural understanding, education, social justice, or reaching children at risk.[16]

From a western worldview, many see holistic ministries and evangelism as completely separate enterprises. Obviously, compassion ministries may not be overly evangelistic; yet thinking that evangelism addresses the spiritual needs while holistic ministries address the physical needs is a false dichotomy. The separation of evangelism and social ministries creates a gap in Christian missions that has caused friction and disagreement among mission leaders, missionaries and national leadership.

More recently, Pentecostal scholars such as Murray Dempster have created a framework to help missionaries reflect

---

[16]Alan Johnson, *Apostolic Function* (Pasadena, CA: William Carey Library, 2009), 36.

on the biblical text and provide them with a social ethic to undergird their social practices.[17] With contemporary missionaries who are empowered by the Spirit, they recognize and practice a commitment to both evangelism and social concerns and see this ministry as holistic . . . both the "Word and Deed" are necessary for the gospel to be fully presented.

The Trial of the Unfinished Task

One of the main trials of Pentecostal mission agencies is the reality of the unfinished task of reaching the lost. Even with the growth of Pentecostal missions in the last 100 years, the percentage of Christians worldwide has not changed perceptibly with the increase in world population. In order to renew the challenge of reaching the lost, the U.S. Assemblies of God World Missions department launched the "Decade of Harvest" in the last ten years of the 20th century. Then the U.S. Home Missions department started a similar program with a goal to start 5,000 new churches in the United States. In some nations this program would be considered a success, but in the U.S. and many other nations it failed miserably. Pentecostals, as well as many evangelical groups, have launched world evangelism plans, but they have been unsuccessful in completing the task. The idea of "completing the task in our generation" has taken many forms, but no global evangelism plan has reached its goals.

Possibly, one of the reasons for this failure is the lack of the use of imagination and creativity in the church. We do things in the same way over and over again yet expect different results. If Pentecost brings anything to the issue of global evangelization, it is the concept of being led by the Spirit. The creative Spirit of God is the answer to help us break out of the cycle of failures in world evangelism. Churchill stated that "the empires of the future will be empires of the imagination." Maybe the Church should release the Spirit of God within itself to dream God's

---

[17]Murray Dempster, "The Structure of Christian Ethic Informed by Pentecostal Experience: Soundings in the Moral Significance of Glossolalia, in The Spirit and Spirituality," Eds. Wonsuk Ma and Robert Menzies (New York: T & T International, 2004), 108-140.

plan and not continue to do things in the ways we have in the past. David Bosch said it well: "The mission of the church needs constantly to be renewed and reconceived."[18]

The Trial of the Indigenous Principle

Another trial of Pentecostal missions has been the indigenous principle, the very principle that has been so fruitful. There are two obvious errors that missionaries can make with respect to the indigenous principle. One is to turn the responsibility of the church over to the nationals of a country before they are mature enough to lead the church. This tends to stagnate the growth of the church at its current level. The standardization of church processes tends to place an undue emphasis upon structure, leading to institutionalization and a decrease in growth. Even missionaries who may have helped launch the national church find it difficult to bring many new converts to the church because the balance of power in the church may shift. This is exactly the issue I faced when I endeavored to launch the Japan Evangelistic Association. The Japan Assemblies of God saw this new aggressive organization as a threat to their structure and would not accept new young leaders into their organization unless they were "saved" under one of their pastors or trained in their Bible College.

The other error that is being made today is the "over contextualization" of the approaches to reach the lost in a given culture. Contextualization assumes that every theology is shaped by the given context and the gospel must be present in a manner that will be understood by the people in the context of their culture. Jesus constantly "contextualized" his message depending upon the audience to which He was speaking. Contextualization is one of the most important and necessary skills that missionaries must employ. But there is a danger if missionaries go too far on the scale of contextualization. Some, in order to be relevant, have "over-contextualized" the gospel

---

[18]David Bosch, *Transforming Mission: Paradigm Shifts in Theology of Mission* (Maryknoll, NY: Orbis Books, 1991), 519.

message to the point that it is difficult for lost people to see the difference between what they currently believe and the message of the Bible. There is a current linguistic debate going on in missions circles on how to translate the name of God in Muslim cultures. Some would hold that it is acceptable to use the term "Allah" for "Jehovah" in the translation of the Scriptures into Arabic. Others would contend that whenever a Muslim reads the name Allah, the semantic meaning of that word in his context would not give him a picture of the God of the Bible. Those who are working in Islamic cultures will have to determine whether this is over contextualizing the word.

A recent article written by the scholars who work in Muslim contexts stated: "The issue at hand is much more than a translation strategy with missiological implications. The practice of removing from the text and/or redefining the divine familial terms of Father, Son, and Son of God with substitution of alternative terms in specialized Scripture translation for Muslims (or for non-Muslims) changes the very substructure of the gospel itself."[19]

I have had the concern for many of my missionary friends who, in their desire to reach Muslims, have adapted their whole life-style (contextualized). They dress like Muslims and grow beards; their wives wear *berkas,* they worship on Friday rather than Sunday, and attend the mosque for certain occasions to be part of the culture. In their desire to be part of the culture, have they lost the distinctiveness of the gospel? Would an Islamic friend understand the unique claims of Christ or would he just identify with the "Isa" of the Quran. In our quest to be contextual, we must not lose the distinctiveness and the unique claims of the gospel.

---

[19] Assemblies of God Missions Department internal paper, *The Necessity for Retaining Father and Son Terminology in Scripture Translations for Muslims* (April, 2012), 7.

The Trial of the Colonial Leadership Model

One of the main tenants of the colonial period was the role of leadership in the Majority World. Western missionaries were viewed as being more advanced educationally, so the role of leadership in the younger churches fell to them. Prior to the Pentecostals, most missionaries led the national churches in a Western leadership model. Since the church took much of its leadership model from the Catholic and Historical Churches, a hierarchical structure was developed. The missionary was the "head" of the local church and younger nationals became his assistants. While the Pentecostal emphasis upon the priesthood of all believers brought a new leadership model in the 21st century, nationals that tended to fill the positions vacated by the early missionaries saw themselves as "heads" of the church and continued the hierarchical model of the past.

The churches of the Majority World are having a difficult time changing to the new team leadership model. So also in the West, everything is in flux and wise leaders read the times to understand how best to lead people. Hirsch and Catchim in their book, *The Permanent Revolution*, state:

> ... the current decline of Christianity cannot be blamed on external factors alone. That is just a dodge, and a dangerous and irresponsible one at that. As significant as external factors are, much of the infertility arises from within the community of faith: in the dynamics of our human sin and unfaithfulness, our lack of audacious faith, and a historical, all-too-human penchant for doing things according to our preferences when it comes to running the church.[20]

Hirsch believes the church has neglected the biblical model for ecclesial leadership outlined in Ephesians 4:1-16. The historical church, including the Pentecostal church, has overemphasized the role of the pastor and teacher to the neglect

---

[20] Alan Hirsch and Tim Catchim, *The Permanent Revolution, Apostolic Imagination and Practice for the 21st Century* (Josey-Bass: San Francisco, 2012), xxxix.

of the apostles, prophets and evangelists. The leadership of the future in the Majority World as well as the West is team leadership based upon the Pauline model.

Trends and Suggestions on Future Directions

If organizations are not willing to change, they will be nonexistent within a few years.[21] The following trends and suggestions for change regarding those trends may help Pentecostal mission leaders chart a course to make trends and changes a part of our strategy.

The Internet and Technology: The Global Village

One current trend is the "global village" effect. Technology, advances of communications and travel have reduced the "size" of the world. Borders between countries are less significant today. Countries that blocked the introduction of the gospel in the past are now are part of the global village and cannot totally prevent their people from hearing the message of Christ.

This is especially true in "restricted access" countries. For example, the "China Net" has already put great amounts of information at the fingertips of millions of young inquisitive Chinese. The Chinese government may be able to monitor some of the information, but it will be impossible to keep ahead of all that invades the nation through satellites and cellular phones.

This technology impacts missions in that it allows for more decentralization than ever existed before. The early days of Pentecostal missions were powerful because the individual missionary felt a personal responsibility in taking the gospel to the lost. While many present day missionaries still feel the "burden" of missions, the slow, gradual growth of the centralization of missions programs has caused many missionaries to view themselves as being part of a corporate organization. This has greatly decreased the effectiveness of the

---

[21] See John Kotter, *Leading Change* (Boston: Harvard Business School Press, 1996); Jon R. Katzenbach, *Real Change Leaders: How You Can Create Growth and High Performance in Your Company* (New York: Times Books, 1995).

mission. But with the coming of technological advances, the power of decision-making can be placed where it should be, at the field level.

Alliances and Partnerships

Another trend today is the importance of alliances and partnerships. In the business world with a global economy, very few corporations can go it alone. For example, when Boeing builds one of its newest aircraft, there are 35,000 subcontractors in 25 countries producing all the parts that it takes to make an airplane.

Partnership is a dynamic strategy. The day when missions can fulfill their goals without other mission sending agencies is coming to a close. When the world was much "larger" and communications difficult, it was more acceptable for missions or missionaries to do their own thing. In many cases, they were alone in a given area with no other missions to relate to. But the day of isolation has come to a close. Nothing done in missions is accomplished in a "corner" or out of sight of others.

Since the worldwide Church has grown significantly—126 percent since 1970 when the world population has only increased by 60 percent—there are many two-thirds world mission agencies that are sending missionaries to the same target countries. In some Asia Pacific nations, there are five or six sending churches endeavoring to do missions work in the same receiving country from the same denomination. For example, in Thailand, the most Buddhist nation on earth, there are missionaries working from the following Assemblies of God fellowships: United States, Canada, Australia, Malaysia, New Zealand, and South Korea. When all of these churches work independently from each other in the same country, there can be much confusion in the local national church. When these missions are not in full cooperation, some areas of the ministry may have much attention, while others go completely untouched. The growing need for strategic alliances and planned cooperation is very evident. Integrated partnerships and global alliances will become necessary for missions to be effective in the 21st century.

In the past, some of the alliances in missions failed for a variety of reasons:
- Cultural differences among partners.
- Ineffective communication.
- Financial issues.
- Personality conflicts.
- Lack of clear goals.

The challenge is to develop "biblical partnerships" that have lasting relationships and agreed-upon objectives, while sharing their strengths and resources to obtain mutual goals. To have these kinds of alliances, it is important for the Christian community to be interdependent. Missionaries by nature are independent and sometime "loners." It is difficult for veteran missionaries to "turn over" responsibilities or share strategies with younger or immature workers, but this is a necessary component of the future.

For too long, the resources of the Western mission agencies have been disbursed at the will of the Western mission boards. The current need is for Western and non-Western agencies to work together sharing strategies, human resources, information, financial resources, and mission objectives in order to reveal to the non-Christian world the uniqueness of the universal Church of Jesus Christ. This strategic cooperation can greatly enhance the missionary task.

Information and Field Based Research Centers

There is a current need for field-based research centers. For many years, missions research has been conducted in the sterile offices of missions headquarters, thousands of miles away from missionaries. The need is for strategically placed research centers that are networked together electronically to assist leaders in developing strategies for the mission. Research greatly assists in the development of literature, radio programs, national church structures, national church demographics, and presents opportunities for church work. It can inform mission leaders about the critical current and future issues.

Missions Agencies as Learning Organizations

With the dynamic changes that impact our world, organizations need to adapt quickly in order to remain effective. Worldwide, bureaucratic structures are failing. Decades-old organizations are finding that the policies and programs that have led to success are no longer working. Status quo today quite often spells failure. To continue to be effective, organizations are learning to reinvent themselves.

In order to continue to "reinvent" the missions organization, it is important to focus on goals and objectives. The goals are the anchors that hold the mission steady during times of change. If every part of the mission (programs, committee resources, beliefs, and the decision-making processes) are in line with the goals and objectives of the mission, then the changes that come are more easily adapted to because all parts of the mission are in alignment.

To keep an organization in a learning mode, the leadership must believe in the concept of "lifetime learning." There are many resources and tools that are available in order to keep team members up to date. In this Age of Information, the means and methods for reaching the lost change constantly. Therefore, in order to be successful in the 21st century, the leadership of the mission must not be afraid to change programs, evaluate successes and failures, study all possible options, and allow the youth of the mission to be creative and try things that may be different from anything done in the past.

One of the strengths of a learning organization is the ability to translate individual vision into a shared-team vision. Because of today's complexity, it is important for team learning to occur which will heighten individual learning and speed up the accomplishment of a given task. The day of the individual "star" in missions is probably closed. The need of the hour is for apostolic teams that not only minister together but also do research, strategize, and plan together.

Embracing Change

The environment of the 21st century is one of ubiquitous change. It is possible in the next few years that the majority of missionaries will be from the Majority World and not the West. Missions, to fulfill the goal of taking the gospel to the whole world, must be prepared and embrace these changes and use them for the benefit of the church. Change may be the catalyst for the greatest open doors for missions in the 21st century. Rather than reject the new challenges that are brought about by change, the future of our work may depend to some extent on how we manage such changes and make them part of our strategy.

The changing world environment demands innovative ways for reaching the lost with the gospel. In order to accomplish this successfully, it demands the involvement of leadership at all levels–management, employees, missionaries, volunteers, and boards. The CEO cannot do this alone. If the CEO does make these kinds of decisions alone, compliance may be achieved, nonetheless, without fostering commitment and bringing about the deep change of those involved in the organization.[22] For this reason, the personnel of the mission need to see themselves at the center of things rather than at the periphery. The entire infrastructure–people at all leadership levels–must share the vision and understand the objectives of the mission. They must also completely understand and willingly move toward implementing the practical applications that will bring that vision into reality and accomplish the work. Individual leadership models will not be able to be flexible or adaptive enough to embrace change.

Leaders of missions must aggressively empower those under their supervision. In reality, real power is released when we

---

[22]Robert E. Quinn, *Deep Change* (San Francisco, CA: Josey-Bass Publishers, 1996), 148-150.

empower. Empowerment and networking are two of the "hot" words for our 21st century world. Empowerment implies decision-making responsibility before decisions are arbitrarily handed down. Networking implies not only technological links, but also personal contacts within the overall structure. Leaders must empower leaders under them and the entire missions family must be willing to be part of the network–linking arms and working together to achieve the mission of God.

Emphasis on Children's Ministries

The last trend in this paper is the importance of having a strategy to reach the children of the nations. For too long, Pentecostal missions was focused upon the conversion of adults in the target cultures. This is as it should be, but the largest unreached people group in the world is the children. If we are going to change the worldview of the target cultures, we must start with the younger minds in the culture and begin to raise up a people who identify themselves as Christians first and then nationals second.

First, children model the essence of saving faith and discipleship. In order to enter the kingdom of God, one must become like a child. Also, when we welcome a child, Jesus said that it is the same as welcoming Himself. The teachings of Jesus make it very clear that children are in a special place in the mind of God. For example, if anyone hinders, abuses, or neglects a child, the judgment of God will be upon him. The 4-14 Movement gives a clear missiological challenge to the church at large:

> *The texts [scriptures] make it clear that the role of the child is not one the church or families should ignore when it comes to pointing them towards God. Yet life often does that for children. Whether they are the victims of poverty, neglect, broken homes, or suffer as orphans, many children never have the chance to contemplate God or appreciate where they fit into His creation . . . . The task is large and grows more complex as families break up and as more*

people live in a secularized or unchurched environments. These realities, biblical, theological and missiological, call for us to think more deeply and concretely about how to reach those who are forming lifelong impressions of God.[23] *(italics in the original)*

Conclusion

This is a dynamic time with unparalleled opportunities for the church. Yet, these are difficult times where it is hard to discern what is really happening in some areas. Ambiguity and uncertainty go with the opportunities. Change is everywhere, which requires one to hold conclusions lightly, for what was right yesterday may be wrong and inadequate today.

First, we must realize the chaotic nature of the future. Things are never going to be like they were in the past. To be unprepared for all the crises coming in the future would be like the ostrich that puts its head in the sand. Not only must we recognize the changes that will come, we must thrive on these changes.

Second, we must be aware of future economic, societal, and governmental changes. To be caught unprepared for these events is to miss some of the "open doors" the Lord will give His church. It is important to evaluate all programs and forget the successes of the past. What made us successful could be the downfall of the mission tomorrow. Innovation and creativity must be the goals of future planning.

Third, we must ever strive to live incarnationally in the unreached cultures of the world. The ramifications of the incarnational model are obvious for missions. God has called us to become His communication in the "flesh," to live out kingdom life in the midst of alien cultures which are estranged from His Truth, Life, and Way. The words of Jesus ever ring in our ears, "As the Father has sent Me, so send I you" (John 20:21). When we live in this manner, we can move the lost

---

[23] 4/14 Movement Covenant: http://4to14window.com/covenant. April 30, 2010, 5. (Accessed: February 2, 2013).

from: darkness to light; illusion to truth; fantasy to reality; deception to knowledge; sin to righteousness; rebellion to belief; hatred to love; anxiety to peace; loneliness to fellowship; separation to unity; isolation to community; chaos to cosmos.

Bibliography

4/14 Movement. *Covenant*. http://4to14window.com. April 30, 2010. (Accessed February 2, 2013).

Allen, Roland. *Missionary Methods: St. Paul's or Ours?* Grand Rapids. MI: Eerdmans, 1962.

Anderson, Allan. "Towards a Pentecostal Missiology for the Majority World." *AJPS* 8:1 (2005): 29-47.

Assemblies of God Missions Department internal paper. *The Necessity for Retaining Father and Son Terminology in Scripture Translations for Muslims*. April, 2012.

Bosch, David J. *Transforming Mission: Paradigm Shifts in Theology of Mission*. Maryknoll, NY: Orbis Books, 1991.

Bradshaw, Bruce. *Bridging the Gap: Evangelism, Development and Shalom*. Monrovia, CA: MARC, 1993.

"Brussels Statement on Evangelization and Social Concern." *Transformation* 16, no. 2 (April 1999).

Crosby, R.C. *A Pentecostal Growth Explosion- Over a Fourth of Christendom*. http://Pathos.com/blogs. May 24, 2012. (Accessed: June 15, 2013)

Hirsch, Allan and Tim Catchim. *The Permanent Revolution. Apostolic Imagination and Practice for the 21st Century Church*. San Francisco: Josey-Bass, 2012.

Hodges, Melvin L. *The Indigenous Church*. Springfield, MO: Gospel Publishing House, 1976.

Jenkins, Philip. *The Next Christendom*. New York: Oxford University Press, 2007.

_____. *The New Faces of Christianity*. New York: Oxford University Press, 2006.

Johnson, Allan. *Frontier Missions and Beyond: An Emerging Paradigm for Missions in The 21st Century*. Paper presented to the Committee on World-Wide Mission Into the 21st Century.

_____. *Apostolic Function*. Pasadena, CA: William Carey Library, 2009.

Kallas, James. *Jesus and the Power of Satan*. Philadelphia, PA: Westminster Press. 1968.

Katzenbach, Jon R. *Real Change Leaders: How You Can Create Growth and High Performance at Your Company*. New York: Times Business, 1995.

Kotter, John. *Leading Change*. Boston: Harvard Business School Press, 1996.

Ma, Wonsuk, and Julie Ma. *Mission in the Spirit: Towards a Pentecostal/Charismatic Missiology*. Eugene, OR: Wipf and Stock Publishers, 2010.

Ma, Wonsuk and Robert Menzies, eds. *Pentecostalism in Context*. Sheffield, England: Sheffield Academic Press, 1997.

McGee, Gary. *Miracles, Missions, and American Pentecostalism*. New York: Orbis Books, 2010.

_____, *Assemblies of God Missions Facing the 21st Century: Strategy on the Run*. Springfield, MO: Gospel Publishing House. 2008.

Mundis, Greg. *RPTT, So all can Hear*. AGMD Letter. January, 2013.

Parks, Stan. *Missions Frontiers: Changing the Percentages*. Pasadena, CA: U.S. World Missions Center, Issue 35:3.

Quinn, Robert E. *Deep Change: Discovering the Leader Within*. San Francisco: Josey-Bass Publishers, 1996.

Robeck, Cecil M. JR. *The Azusa Street: Mission and Revival*. Nashville, TN: Thomas Nelson, 2006.

The Training Pyramid
By Carl B. Gibbs

I remember the exact moment I was exposed to the training pyramid. It was a significant "aha" moment when I realized that I had found something I would use for the rest of my life. I am grateful to Lois McKinney and a class she taught at Wheaton Graduate School for exposing me to the training pyramid (McKinney 1989, 64). I have in turn shared it with every institution where I have served and with leadership in a dozen countries. For some, this may be a review. In this case, this paper is designed to refresh one's memory and reinforce their zeal to train on all five levels. For those who have not seen it, I am confident that this will become an "aha" moment.

My perspective in this paper is colored by thirty-seven years as a missionary educator in the world's Southern Hemisphere. For almost four decades, I have focused on empowering local leadership through training and assisting revival movements to establish meaningful and structured training programs. The holistic approach represented by the training pyramid has significantly undergirded my philosophy of training.

What is the Leadership Training Pyramid?

The basic concept behind the training pyramid is that there are five essential levels of training that the church should *intentionally* and *simultaneously* implement. Without aggressive training on the lower half of the pyramid, the growth of a movement will be limited. Without training on the upper half, a movement will lack stability and continuity of doctrine from generation to generation.

Figure 1: The Training Pyramid

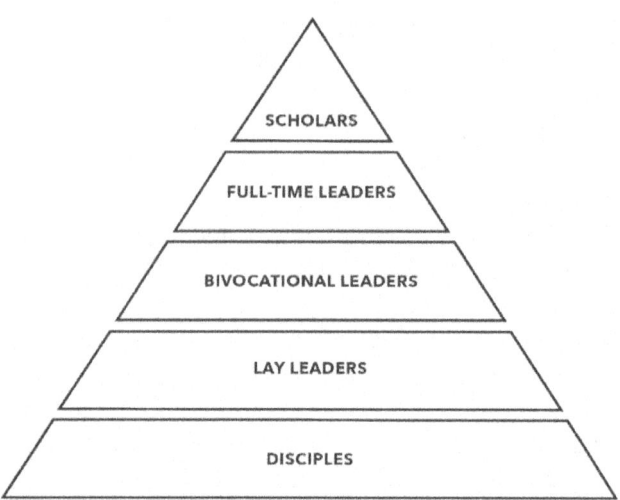

The numbers of people needing to be trained at each level diminishes at the higher levels of the training pyramid. The ratios may vary by the context, but here are broad suggested numbers:

1. Discipleship (1 to 1)
2. Lay leader volunteers (1 to 12)
3. Bivocational leaders of small and emerging congregations (1 to 30 or 40)
4. Full-time leaders such as pastors to larger congregations and missionaries (1 to 60)
5. Scholars (1 to 1000)

This paper will not include upper-level administrators. The purpose is not to describe a hierarchy of leadership. The concern is only on the type and extent of training needed for each level to effectively perform its ministry. A person who spends more time in ministry and has a more involved role is enabled to succeed in that ministry with adequate training. In general, the lower levels of the pyramid stress informal and non-formal methodologies while the higher levels stress formal methods and degrees.

Figure 2: Non-formal to Formal Training

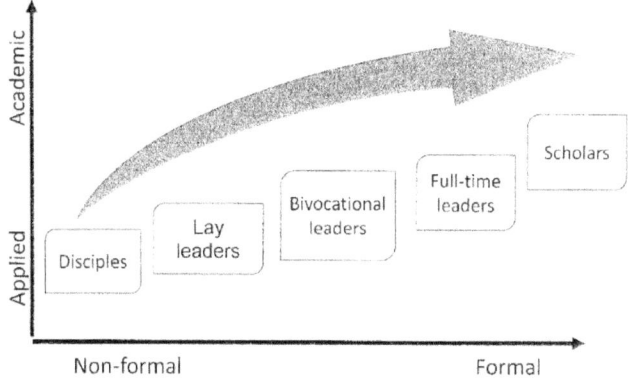

The bottom two levels are done at the local church. The middle level is best done through local church apprenticeship and practical formal training that allows for the minister to maintain a job and church ministry while learning. The upper two levels require more formal training that is beyond the resources of a local church. Thus they are normally supported by a group of congregations or a movement.

This middle level is the key to church planting. Finances in new church plants and smaller congregations often do not provide for full-time salaried pastors. Often leaders at this level volunteer as associates to a lead pastor but do not receive full salary. For this reason this level of leader is almost exclusively bivocational. However, they have a vital role. Without them a church movement will struggle to grow.

Most people will never be called to full-time ministry, but for those who are, the experiences and training at this level serve as a strong foundation for future training and ministry.

The training-pyramid model teaches that the church should *intentionally* and *simultaneously* implement training at these five levels. *Intentionally* implies that the training must be purposely planned and implemented. A West African proverb says that a village cow starves, that is, everyone in the village assumes someone else is feeding the cow when, in reality, nobody is. In the same way, someone has to assume responsibility and ownership at all levels of training. Otherwise, everyone will assume that someone else is going to "feed the cow."

Enson Lwesya (2003) describes planning as "an art and skill that makes you fully aware of what you are supposed to achieve (purpose) and how you are going to achieve it (strategy)." (73) That planning, along with the motivation to implement the plan, is what this paper defines as intentional.

Simultaneously implies that training should continually happen at all five levels. A church does not outgrow the need for lower levels of training nor can it neglect the higher levels of training. If any level is neglected, the church's power to grow spiritually and numerically is short-circuited. On the other hand, if a church movement actively engages in training at all of these levels, growth and stability will follow that training. Each level of training serves a unique purpose in the church:

1. **Discipled believers.** The purpose of this level of training is to keep new converts and encourage them to be faithful believers and motivated evangelists. Training at this level most directly affects the growth of a local congregation. The ratio of those needing to be discipled to members of the church is one to one (1:1). Every believer needs to be discipled.
2. **Lay leaders of small groups.** This level reflects the Sunday school teachers, Bible study leaders, altar workers, and other volunteer lay members. The ratio of this type of leader to church members is about 1 to 12.

For a local church, the mobilization of this group is the number one factor that promotes growth.
3. **Bivocational leaders of larger groups.** A local church will need one leader at this level for every 30 to 40 members in the congregation. A movement will depend on "tent-making" ministers to plant new congregations. Their training tends to be on-the-job apprenticeship learning. However, they are often involved in serious ministry and need some basic formal training in the Scriptures. They are the primary source of growth for a church movement. Without this group, new churches will rarely be planted and senior pastors will lack "Timothys."
4. **Full-time trained leaders.** Without trained pastors a revival will lack stability, and without full-time leaders new emerging churches will lack transitional leaders to take the movement from the planting stage to the harvest stage. Full-time leaders nurture converts through preaching and creative systems of discipleship. They train small-group leaders and mobilize church members to express their individual gifts. They tend to have more extensive and formal training. The ratio of this level of leader to members is one for every 60 to 80 congregants.
5. **Scholars.** Without biblically based scholarship a revival is not sustainable, and a movement will lack defense against false teachings and unbiblical practices. This level is trained to write the books, create the curriculum, and train the trainers. An important note of caution, however, is that higher-level training does not necessarily qualify one for higher levels of leadership. Although this is the highest level of training, it is not designed to limit leadership to the formally trained.

The Role of Training at the Lower and Higher Levels

In general, the three lowest groups are the primary sources for church growth. Without this training, the church will not experience dynamic growth. The training on these lower levels happens primarily on the local church level. Level three leaders may benefit from both apprenticeship learning in the church and limited semi-formal learning that allows them as bivocational leaders to remain in ministry (and in their jobs) while training.

The two highest levels contribute stability to the church. Training at this level requires more resources and specialization. Ironically, as the pyramid of training narrows, the cost of training increases. The cost and labor of maintaining faculty, academic resources, facilities, programs of study, record keeping, and so on, require that this level be done through a combined effort of multiple congregations or at a regional or national level.

Unfortunately, there is a tendency for higher-level training to operate completely independently from the local church or for the local church to reject graduates. Local churches without formally trained ministers tend to be more prone to doctrinal splits and lack stability in biblical training. On the other hand, Bible schools and seminaries without the support of national churches lack students at best. At worst, they tend to produce scholarship in churches that is formal, dogmatic, and stagnant.

Training Disciples

Some years ago I had preached in three of the Sunday services in a large church in East Africa. After I finished, someone else continued to minister in the remaining four Sunday services. That day, 127 responded to Christ in seven

altar calls. This was not due to the preaching that day. The number responding was not unusual. This church has gone from 11 members to 12,000 congregants in a little over a decade.

Many countries in the Southern Hemisphere are experiencing unparalleled revival. Often the growth has come suddenly, and the church is scarcely prepared to disciple the flood of seekers. Africa has gone from a handful of Christians in 1900 to 360 million today. The growth is similar in Asia where some claim there are 313 million who profess Christ (Jenkins 2002, 3). In Latin America there were 14,500 Protestants in 1938. Around that time the famous Peruvian author Carlos Mariategue commented that the Protestant church could only grow from social services and their possibilities for normal expansion were exhausted (Bonino 1995, 53). He was wrong. By 1950 there were already one million Protestants in Latin America; by 1980 there were 27 million, and by the turn of century, 65 million (Bonino 1995, 55).

Pentecostals have experienced the greatest growth in the Southern Hemisphere. They have grown from a handful of believers in the early 1900s to several hundred million today. Jenkins ponders, "Is it not reasonable to identify this as perhaps the most successful social movement of the past century?" (Jenkins 2002, 8)

But this is not the time for triumphalism. These tens of millions will become an indictment on the church if they are not discipled. The command Christ left with the church was not to have record attendance but to disciple through baptisms and teaching (Matthew 28: 13-20). The church should be a "kingdom of priests" (1 Peter 2:9) that participates in ministry, evangelizes their communities, and reflects their master.

One cannot assume that all who come to the altars have had a "road to Damascus" experience. Many view the walk to the altar as a symbolic act with perhaps some magical power. For others, it is only expressing interest in God, joining a church, or just responding politely to the urging of an altar worker. But even those who are not truly regenerated are expressing interest and provide an opportunity to evangelize and disciple them.

Phillip Jenkins gives a prophetic warning concerning the next generation as he reflects on the importance of training disciples:

> Historical experience suggests that fundamentalists often have good grounds to worry about their liberal grandchildren. We can speak with fair confidence about the ethnic composition of the world's Christians in fifty or a hundred years, but we must be on shakier grounds when it comes to predicting attitude to authority or orthodoxy. (Jenkins 2006, 15)

The healthy local congregation has an intentional training program to mobilize their congregation to evangelize and disciple new converts. Without this training, many who come to the altar will receive just enough Christianity to inoculate them against the real thing.

The surge toward mega churches challenges the church to be creative in how to disciple new believers en masse. Dr. Carver Yu laments that "many so-called mega churches are in fact no church but assemblies of individuals worshipping adjacent to one another" (Yu 2007, 167). The Brazilian Assemblies of God's approach to this problem is the mother church system where a central church will plant and oversee multiple smaller congregations. The smaller congregations occasionally meet together at the mother church, but their regular fellowship is a smaller group that meets closer to the members' homes.

Experience has taught that church that "no Christian will experience maximal spiritual formation in isolation from the body of Christ. Every discipleship strategy should include some type of small-group experience where people can experience ongoing support and encouragement, prayer, fellowship and accountability" (Waggoner 2008, 310). Denominational leaders and educators must be assured that the churches have adequate curriculum for Sunday school, small group studies, and new converts courses. Seldom does a local church have the ability to write these resources on its own.

Voltaire, one of history's most prominent atheists, admitted that society needed Christians who practice their faith. Although he did not want Christianity for himself, he recognized it was necessary for a rational moral life for all but the most advanced philosophers. In his own words he wrote, "I want my attorney, my tailor, my servants, even my wife to believe in God, and I think that then I shall be robbed and cuckolded less often" (Hall 1998, 21).

Training Lay Leaders

Shiphra and Puah were the two midwives who saved the lives of many Hebrew male babies, including Moses. Yancey (1999) points out the irony that God mentioned them by name but did not bother to mention the name of the Pharaoh (32). Those who serve in minor leadership levels are not overlooked in Scripture. Paul tells us of the heroics of Epaphroditus (Phil. 2:25–30) and the assistance of Euodia and Syntyche (Phil. 4:2). The apostle greets dozens of these leaders by name in his letter to the Romans (Rom. 16).

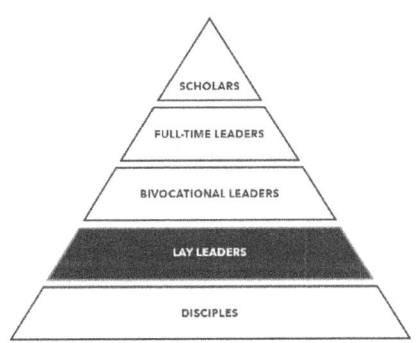

These volunteer leaders tend to be underestimated, but mobilizing them is a vital step in promoting the growth of a local church. Even though their training stresses informal and non-formal methods, it should be intentional. These volunteers teach the classes, usher the crowds, direct children's ministries, maintain the grounds, mobilize evangelism, organize church events, and schedule visits to the sick. When properly equipped and motivated, they multiply the effectiveness of a congregation. A wise pastor will not only encourage ministry at this level but will develop these leaders through a training process.

Does the church *require* intentional effort to train this level of leader? Absolutely. These leaders need to understand their task and have a strong sense of their contribution to the church. They need to be grounded in the faith and understand the philosophy of ministry of their local church. They are extensions of the full-time leadership and need to reflect the values of the church. Their example of Christianity is the face of the church. The late Derek Tan (2007) highlighted the danger of neglecting to equip this level of leadership:

> While there is still a dire need to train more clergy for the growing church, there is a neglect of the needs of equipping the laity or the community of faith. In today's church, a large slice of the ministry is carried by the laity and they need to be equipped. . . . How ironic it is that on one hand, institutions pride themselves as the protector and guardian of the right doctrine and right practice of the church and on the other hand, the obvious neglect to train those in the front line defeats their very purpose. (89)

When one out of twelve church members have some leadership role, the church transforms itself from a speaker-to-audience format to a coach-to-team emphasis. In their book *The Flight of the Buffalo*, James Belasco and Ralph Stayer give an insightful illustration of the church whose leadership is focused only on the pastor:

> In the early days of the Wild West, Native Americans killed numbers of wild buffalo by shooting the lead buffalo. Because the animals were such good followers, when the leader was killed the entire herd stopped in its tracts. Then the pursuers moved in easily for the slaughter. Organizations who want to last should rather be like geese, who rotate leaders and who work as a team. (Quoted in Nelson and Appel 2000, 105)

The task of training is the responsibility of both the academy and the church. The academy can provide the curriculum to guide the pastor with such resources as teaching manuals, lay training courses, and leadership handbooks. The pastor needs to intentionally select and prepare this team of lay leaders.

Training Bivocational Leaders

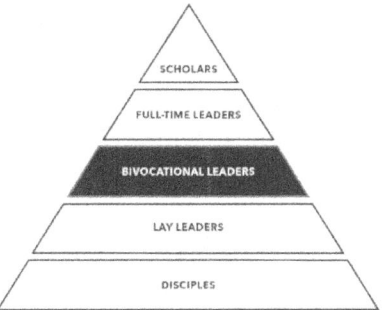

"If all you have is a hammer, everything looks like a nail." (Maslow 1966, 15). Maslow's famous quote often applies when considering approaches to training bivocational ministers at level three. Those who only appreciate the hammer—traditional forms of training—do not see the need to adapt training for the students' needs and limitations. They insist that the only valid training is done in a residential school equipped with a large physical library where the student will sit in front a teacher for fifteen weeks at a time. The student uses only qualified professional and academic textbooks, and he or she is removed from a natural ministry environment for years at a time.

Missionary John York told of an interesting reply he received when he asked an old African teacher how a curriculum was working for him. Culture would not allow the teacher to criticize it directly, so he used a personal story that implied his frustration. He shared that as a young pastor, he had never owned a pair of shoes but wanted to buy a pair to attend a major church conference. He found a pair he liked in the market, but they were too small. Undeterred, he bought them anyway. On the way to the conference, his feet hurt, so he cut out places for his little toes. By the time he got home, he had made so many holes to make the shoes comfortable that he threw them away. The moral to his story is clear: the curriculum should fit the students' needs.

The best fit for training bivocational leaders is a mixture of on-the-job informal experiences with non-formal learning that is not too rigid and inflexible. A popular axiom among missionary educators is "training *in* ministry, rather than training *for* ministry." Full-time residential living that removes leaders from their ministry, families, and the church is "Saul's armor on David" for this level. This is not the level to teach Greek, Hebrew, and exegesis. Rather, studies at this level should be need-driven and faith-oriented (Jenkins 2006, 35).

The church often tries to put all training through a college/university model, where training precedes and qualifies a person for a vocation. Liew You Kiang (2007) suggests that the traditional idea that learning must occur before a person is qualified is backwards. For him, it is better for people to prove themselves faithful in ministry before they are selected for formal training (179).

Properly implemented, this level of training not only produces candidates for degree-level training, but more importantly, it trains a multitude of leaders who do not need an advanced diploma, degree, or full-time salary to fulfill their call. These leaders can, however, benefit from intentional training through seminars, internet and typed lectures that allow them to remain in ministry while improving their skills, sharpening their understanding of the Word, and increasing their motivation to minister.

Since level-three leaders are generally self-funded and local, they are excellent candidates to serve as associate pastors, to minister in small churches, or to plant new preaching points. Just as level-two leaders are key to the growth of a local congregation, level-three bivocational leaders are key to the growth of a movement.

Most of those at this level will never move on to full-time ministry. Like Aquila and Priscilla (Acts 18:2, 3), they will continue to combine "tent making" with ministry. Others, like Timothy, will move on to full-time ministry. For training at this level, Ted Ward's classic rail fence analogy describes the ideal program that allows the student to grow in knowledge while in ministry. Ward's illustration intersperses periodic "fence posts" (seminars) connected by two horizontal "rails" (cognitive input and field experience). This basic approach combines periodic seminars with home assignments and field experience in between them. This graph is so old that it may be new to many but it is just as appropriate today as a generation ago.

Figure 3: Rail Fence Illustration (Pommerville 1973, 37)

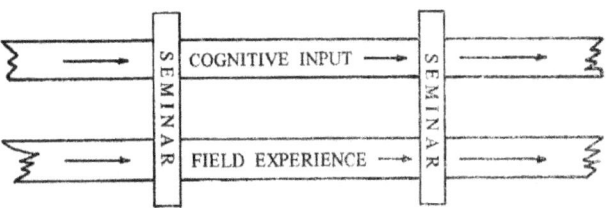

This concept dominates training in the Southern Hemisphere, but its effectiveness has a major problem: the students forget what they have learned between the fence posts. Often, the information is retained just long enough to take a test and then is forgotten before the next seminar. To encourage students to obtain and retain knowledge, Persellin and Daniels (2014) recommend these four methods:

1. Repeat and rehearse new information
2. Establish meaningful patterns to organize learning
3. Allow students time to process information
4. Find relevance in the learning (12)

Repeat and rehearse new information. An old adage advises teachers to "tell them where you are going, go there, and then tell them where you went." This is good advice for long teaching sessions. Also, reviewing concepts taught in previous sessions and integrating learning over several subjects can refresh the students' memory. For example, concepts taught in a hermeneutics course can be practiced in a class on the Synoptic Gospels.

Establish meaningful patterns to organize learning. The teacher is often a peer with a higher position than the students but not a higher level of training. The leadership of a movement or denomination would be wise to invest in a well-structured curriculum for this level of training, complete with extensive instructor's helps, clear learning outcomes, and a credible evaluation system.

Allow the student time to process the information. The student needs to use the time before the class for individual study. One of the rails between the seminar posts is cognitive input. Ideally, the students will have homework assignments before the seminar to prepare them and then have accountability on this preparation when they arrive in class.

Find relevance in their learning. At this level of training, relevance and practical application are fundamental. The students want something they can preach or teach. The content should be more practical than theoretical. Divide the students into groups and give them clearly written problems to solve, case studies to examine, or concepts to contextualize.

Earlier in this paper, it was suggested that the church needs one leader at this bivocational level for every 30 to 40 people in the church. The ratio is not meant to suggest that those with limited training cannot have large congregations, but shows the number of leaders the church needs to have trained at that level. This would include associates as well as pastors.

Most pastors who come into leadership through involvement in ministry rather than beginning with formal training do not have opportunity to travel to a distant school for years of isolated study. Their work, ministries, and families deny them that opportunity. In general, the difference between choosing to pursue a degree versus a certificate is determined more by accessibility to education rather than intellectual ability.

Those with limited training can pastor large churches and assume great responsibility, but it will be in spite of limited training, not because of it.

Full-Time Leaders

From the perspective of this paper, the more time a person spends in ministry and the more responsibility he or she assumes, the more training is needed. In most cultures full-time leaders need more formal training, such as advanced diploma and undergraduate degree. However, the diploma or degree does not certify persons for ministry; it merely enhances their capacity to serve.

Formal education is not a requirement for pastoring large congregations. Many with limited training have very large congregations. Other variables also affect the success of a leader, such as leadership ability, communication skills, interpersonal skills, management capacity, and balanced personality, as well as the sociological factors of the community where that person ministers. The primary determiners are the "spiritual life factors" such as dependence on the Holy Spirit, a sanctified life, and a passion for souls.

At the same time, experience has proven that formal training tends to greatly increase the likelihood of success and continuance in ministry. When opening or maintaining a school there are five primary factors to consider: the gatekeepers, students, faculty, curriculum, and facilities.

The Gatekeepers

Gatekeepers are those church leaders and administrators who control access to students and funding. Their support and sponsorship must be obtained before an education program is implemented. It is common to ask for permission to open a school without getting a guarantee of support. If church leadership is not willing to commit to financially support the school and to send students to study, the school will flounder. Schools at this level are long-term projects, and the leadership must be prepared to sacrifice in order to maintain them for decades.

Educators are often shocked and disappointed when their graduates are not accepted by the gatekeepers or are put on probation for a time before they are accepted into ministry. This defensive structuring by church leadership is understandable, but if it causes them to reject graduates it will negatively impact and affect the viability of a school.

When a new school opens, it is natural for the gatekeepers to feel a bit threatened—especially if it is directed by expatriates. Here are a few common reasons for their reservations:

1. Strangers or near-strangers are taking over the teaching of practice and faith. New ideas result, which may make the current leaders look dumb or errant.
2. The criteria for selecting leaders changes from selection by the authority figures to selection based on training. If the gatekeeper has come to leadership because of special gifts but does not have a degree, he may see the school as a threat to his authority.
3. Graduates tend to challenge authority and traditional methods and beliefs. A schism often forms between the older gatekeepers and younger change-agents. The school is often blamed for what is a natural product of youthful zeal and a sudden explosion of knowledge.

Much of this defensive posturing can be reduced by regular reporting, allowing key leaders a place on the school's board, and providing a way for the older ministers to train at a distance. It is also vital to integrate local church ministry into the students' curriculum.

Changes should not be rushed. There are many changes that the gatekeepers will resist for a time, but the wait is a small price to pay for their support. Some major changes must be made slowly and tactfully. Derek Tan (2007) suggested this balance:

Change must take place. But, in seeking change so as to be relevant and contemporary, we must remind ourselves not to throw away the baby with the bathwater and at the same time be aware that if we keep him in cold, soiled water, his life is in danger. (84)

The Students

In general, income from the students' tuitions and local support should provide for sustainability, as sooner or later the expatriate help will end. Help from foreign missionaries and international agencies should be limited to one-time capital expenses in facilities, libraries, and curriculum, but it should not pay salaries, nor should the teaching staff be exclusively missionary staff.

Shoki Coe cites that 70 percent of third-world theological education is still dependent on outside assistance (as quoted in Tan 2007, 83). Many institutions are handed down to the national church from missionaries and missions groups, but even if leadership is turned over to locals, the institution is not autonomous if they are dependent on financial support from the West.

The Faculty and Staff

Before starting a degree-level school or enlarging an existing school, it is necessary to calculate the number of workers needed. Are there enough local faculty with the necessary training? What are the positions and salaries needed to feed, house, and train the students? What support staff is needed?

The residential school is the most expensive and complex form of training. If the students can train while staying in ministry using the "rail fence" method, the school has the advantages of integrating ministry with training, enabling training for those who cannot leave their churches for several years, and avoiding the expense of dormitory living. Even if a school has a residential program, it can benefit from a parallel extension program. Otherwise, it will be limited to those with no family, job, ministry, or responsibilities, and most of the graduates will be 21 years old without experience in meaningful ministry.

To avoid the necessity for expatriate teachers, a missions board or the national leaders would be wise to send out local students to study abroad to prepare to assume the teaching load when missionaries are no longer available.

Ongoing faculty enrichment must also constantly take place at the local level. It is common for instructors to preach with enthusiasm but teach with lifeless monologues. Some type of teacher certification should be on the to-do list for school administrators and regional educational associations. Instructors must be taught how to alternate mini-lectures, discussions, and activities and how to involve the students in active learning. Participatory learning does not happen without intentional effort from school administrators.

The Curriculum

The curriculum of a school is more than a list of subjects and textbooks. It is all of the activities, instruction, and resources that promote learning. There are also informal aspects of curriculum, such as the culture of worship on the campus, chapels, church ministry, and prayer cells. Every planned activity, whether academic, evangelistic, or social, should match a learning outcome.

I recommend that the school board and faculty create a list of the learning outcomes that they expect to see in their students after the training is complete. These should include issues related to the heart, the hands, and the head: attitudes and beliefs in the affective domain, skills in the psycho-motor domain, and knowledge in the cognitive domain. Each expected learning outcome should then be matched to activities, courses, etc., that would achieve the goal.

Most schools do not have the size and depth of faculty to make their own curriculum, and classes based solely on instructors' notes tend to be woefully inadequate. There are excellent curriculums with examination systems such as Global

University's curriculum, the Africa's Hope Discovery Series, and the Brazilian Extension Schools of Theology Faith texts. The drawback to these is the temptation to "teach to the test." When the curricular content is alien to the culture, what is taught tends to become formalized and unrealistic and delivered in a rigid, ritualistic manner.

This prepackaged curriculum should not become a pedagogical straitjacket that does not allow for contextualization. On the other hand, simply teaching to the felt needs of the students is not adequate. There are many prescribed needs—many of which are in the Bible—that the student may not sense an urgency to study. "Real needs" are where a student's felt needs and the prescribed needs overlap.

Gangel asserts that felt needs become the "doorway to involvement" because they describe the way people understand their own needs and how willing they are to recognize those needs. (Gangel 1999, 49) Priscilla Vail labels emotion as the "on and off switch" to learning. (Persellin and Daniels 2014, 15) Taking time in class for spontaneous worship, prayer, and devotions is vital. When appropriate, truth should be presented with passion. All teaching should have a variety of inflection and draw the students into the topic.

It is better to teach less well than to practice "cognitive dumping," which leaves the students with a multitude of facts to spit back on an exam but without knowledge of how these facts relate to their own lives. The student may miss the main ideas when too many details are given or when too many ideas are presented but not developed.

One editor had a simple test for determining if a book was worth publishing: "When I finish the book, I ask, 'So what?' If I have no reply, I do not recommend it for publication." That test should determine what is taught in the classroom as well.

The Facilities

A truism says that "form follows function." Unfortunately, this is not always true when Bible school and seminary campuses are built. The buildings should be built to serve a function lest they inadvertently dictate how the school operates. In one such instance, an expensive seminary structure was built in a country that had no training program at all. The national leaders did not see a need for a degree-granting school, but once the building was complete, it had to be filled. The building was designed for residential learning, so current pastors could not attend. To fill the rooms, prospective students were offered free tuition and room and board. Many unemployed and directionless youth flocked to the school, and when they graduated, the church did not know what to do with them because they had never been chosen or vetted by the national church.

The building should result from the function. If existing structures such as churches can double as classrooms, there is no need to build extensive structures that future leadership may not be able to maintain.

The location of a school can limit or expand a school's impact. Just as the norm for buying a house is "location, location, location," so schools need to be built in locations that are assessable to the students. If no public transportation is available then administration will need to bus students or put them in dorms. If the school is not close to major metropolitan areas, few students will able to maintain ministry, families and work while attending classes.

Scholars

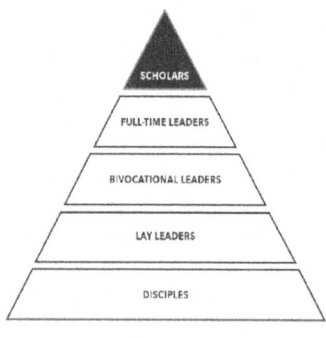

There is a proverb that says a blossom cannot be detached from its roots, for then it dies (Oden 2007, 94). In the same way, revivals may blossom with content-weak preaching, but they will not continue to thrive without strong, biblically trained leaders. The training of pastors focuses on keeping the current church stable. The training of scholars assures biblically sound orthodoxy and praxis into future generations. The scholars are the defenders of the faith. Conversely, if the scholastic level of training wanders away from Scripture, the church will follow its lead into error.

Fresh Eyes

With great revival comes an abundance of bright and talented people who could make a significant contribution to the worldwide church if they had opportunities to study at higher levels. Since travel in the West or in Europe is out of reach for all but an elite few, and extensive time away tends to remove these students from their cultures, this training is most effective when done closer to the students' home in distance and culture.

Thomas Oden, in his book *How Africa Shaped the Christian Mind*, reminds us that the church in Africa is older than the church in Europe, and African scholars dominated Christian scholarship in the second to fourth centuries:

> There is ample evidence available that the seeds of African orthodoxy have been lifted by high winds to distant northern climes. Only much later have they returned to Africa in a western guise. (Oden 2007, 72)

African scholarship was able to shape and condition virtually every diocese in Christianity (Oden 2007, 25). A major reason for this phenomenon is found in the influence of training centers that multiplied knowledge. Africa had some of the first schools of training in the Nile Valley (Alexandria) and the Madjerda Valley (Carthage). In its monastic centers, the Scriptures were copied and studied.

One can only wonder what current insights scholars in Latin America, Africa, and the Far East could offer the church if scholarly training were available in proportion to the region's growth. A current buzz phrase in my academic circles is "African hermeneutic." I do not recommend the need for churches to have regionally specific doctrines or even a locally biased approach to biblical interpretation. I do, however, applaud the motivation to have fresh eyes when studying the Scripture, which results in contextualized insights and emphasis on truth that western scholarship has overlooked.

A primary purpose for the scholar level of training is to produce men and women who can clarify and defend the faith. This defense must be appropriate to the current culture and responsive to radical changes in the cultural milieu. The North American church needs apologists to respond to a culture saturated with the fantasy of moral equivalence (the view that any assertion of truth is valid) and relativism (the view that there is no standard for assessing what is truth). The Southern Hemisphere has a similar need in a culture that is inundated with distorted perceptions of the spirit world that are promoted in traditional religions.

The radical transformation of culture due to new means of communication, urbanization, and persecution underscores a need for Christians who can think critically. In western society, Christianity has gone from "empire" to "exile" in just one century. In the Southern Hemisphere, such radical changes are accelerated. Therefore, it is paramount that a few leaders be trained to keep pace with these changes in order to guard the faith and practice of the church.

Because this level is so crucial to the church, the quality of training should be just as high in the Global South and Far East as it is in North America and Europe. Educators often try to eliminate difficulties in learning, to the students' detriment. There is a "desirable difficulty" that is necessary to challenge students toward excellence (Persellin and Daniels 2011, 5).

Often, western-trained educators patronize their students through grade inflation and less-than-standard assignments. Although many from the Southern Hemisphere come to graduate school with inadequate training on lower levels, their capacity and motivation to learn can compensate for weaknesses in earlier training. If not held to an international standard, the writers from the Global South will tend to parrot western thought and not develop their own unique message.

Three Metaphors

Ted Ward suggests three metaphors that reflect a school's or seminary's philosophy of training: filling a cup, manufacturing a product, or preparing for a life-walk (Ward 1999, 46–50). The "filling a cup" philosophy views the student as a vessel to be filled with knowledge. The learner is more acted upon than active. In this philosophy, sharing the content becomes the primary goal, and most of the learning is reduced to sharing content and testing short-term memory rather than long-term transformation.

The "manufacturing a product" approach tends to view the school like a machine that is processing a product—that is, producing a scholarly elite who can perform up to prescribed standards. In this approach, ministry and theological concerns are secondary to cognitive input and theology tends to be taught as a science rather than transforming truth. Ferris describes teaching typical of this approach:

> They can pursue ever finer strains of minutia, or they can apply new hermeneutics to the study of their fixed subject matter. Both avenues of research serve only the interest of the scholarly guild; practically, they are sterile. (Ferris 1999, 103)

Ferris (1999) warns that "theology and missiology never occur in separation. . . . When this dialogue is interrupted, whatever its confessional stance, theological education is less than Christian" (109). In both the "filling" and "manufacturing" metaphor, the core error is to stress knowing and doing over being.

The "life-walk" metaphor emphasizes being over knowing or doing. Training is not finished when the cup is full or the product has gone through a process. Students do not finish their education but graduate motivated to be self-learners, enabled to apply their learning to real life issues.

In both the filling and manufacturing metaphors, "practical experience is treated as a poor cousin to intellectual learning, and theological education is seen as preparatory to, rather than simultaneous with, ministry" (Ward 1999, 45). The life-walk metaphor sees the formal training as the beginning of the student's journey where ministry and learning happen as part of a life walk.

Maintaining a Balance

When a boat has a lot of weight in the front, it will sink lower in the water at the bow. When the weight is unevenly distributed in the rear, the front will be out of the water and the stern submerged. The center of gravity will affect how the boat sails (Nelson and Appel 2000, 78). In the same way, if a movement de-emphasizes or overemphasizes a level of training, tensions can develop between the local churches and the schools/seminaries. Two areas where lack of balance can sink training programs are friction over finances and contrasting goals in training. As illustrated by the drawing below, both result in a dichotomy of lack of integration between training and ministry and between the church and the academy.

Figure 4: A Dichotomy Between the Church and the School

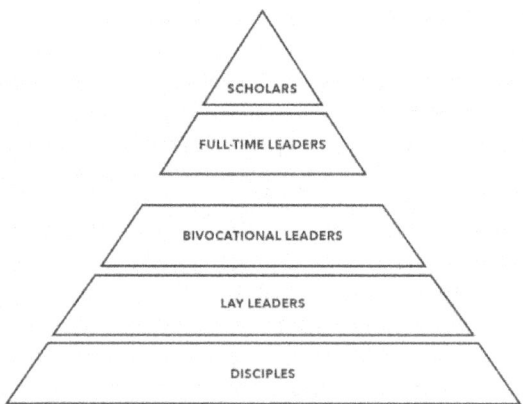

Friction Over Finances

Finances are often at the root of schisms between the churches and schools. When it comes to expense, the pyramid of training is turned upside down. It costs little to train a disciple but a great deal to train a scholar. For this reason, if is often more practical to have a region or national group finance the Bible colleges and have multiple nations with similar cultures finance the graduate level.

Often, starting graduate programs is a time of great euphoria and naïve optimism. Everyone wants the level of training, but few are willing to sacrifice in order to create and sustain it. When a mission agency or group of educators asks national church leaders if they want a Bible school, seminary, or university, they should not simply take yes for an answer. What is needed is not mere approval but a commitment to support and send students.

When finances are shared between national and expatriate stakeholders, the model should be shared resources (interdependence) rather than the expatriate entity paying the bills (dependence). In the same way, when national church leadership pays all the bills and the school administration does not share responsibility, tensions are inevitable. In this regard Mark Young (1999) suggests these questions:

> Who feels ultimate responsibility for the success of the program? To whom are the program planners and leaders ultimately accountable? Many potential problems arise when those providing resources are not proportionately involved in providing oversight and accountability for the utilization of those resources. (71)

Contrasting Goals in Training

The church leaders and the school administrators must be on the same page when it comes to the purpose and goals of the school. If the church's needs are not seriously considered and the school does not produce graduates who equip the church, a hostility toward the school can develop. Young (1999) warns that lack of accountability to the program's constituency allows planners and leaders "to develop educational forms and goals that are prime candidates for irrelevance." (72) Carver Yu describes the common complaint against schools this way:

> They are expected to train leaders; instead, they produce for the church certified professionals armed with fragmented theological ideas and lifeless Bible interpretative tools honed for critical discourse among scholars who have no interest in the Bible as the Word of God. (Carver Yu 2007, 167)

Another factor that adds tension is the perception that status in the church is earned by degrees rather than by character and ministry. It is notable that Paul's instructions to Timothy and Titus on the qualifications of an elder have few requirements dealing with knowledge and teaching and so many dealing with character. Training at any level should not have as its goal to certify a person for higher levels of status but to equip and mold him or her for servant leadership. Ted Ward laments the correlation between level of training and status in the church:

> In the church, status is earned by knowing; what is required for leadership is the possession of a magic bag of merits. These magic bags of merits are systematically dealt out only to the relatively few players in the game. The dealers are the theological seminaries. Once a magic bag of merit is in one's possession, it can be traded for honor and prestige (plus a salary) at the friendly local church, and those one maintains oneself—career and salary—more in terms of what one knows than what one is. (Ward 1999, 29)

Formal education for ministry should reflect Christian values and should not be separated from the life of the church or personal spiritual formation. This paradox can be greatly diminished by a close partnership between the churches and the schools that integrates training with ministry. This integration requires that:

- The church help academia create their goals for learning and select their students.
- The students be actively involved in ministry as a part of their curriculum.
- The school administrators and educators need to see their primary goal as transformation rather than information.

The task of intentional training at all five levels is intimidating, but if any of these five are lacking, the church must act quickly to assure that intentional training is happening. If not, the following will result:

- Without an intentional program for training disciples, that church will not maintain its character.
- Without training lay volunteers, the individual churches will not grow.
- Without training bivocational leaders, future "Timothys" will not be discovered, and new church plants and smaller congregations will lack leaders.
- Without trained pastors, churches will lack stability.
- Without some trained as scholars, the church will lack apologists to defend the faith.

An African proverb asks, "When is the best day to plant a tree?" The answer is, 20 years ago. The proverb continues, "When is the second best day to plant a tree?" The reply is, today! If any level of training is lacking in a church movement it will take time to develop, but if something is not done today, tomorrow will look like yesterday.

Bibliography

Bonino, José Míguez. *Faces of Latin American Protestantism.* Grand Rapids: William B. Eerdmans Publishing Company, 1995.

Ferris, Robert W. "The Role of Theology in Theological Education." In *With an Eye on the Future Development and Mission in the 21st Century.* Edited by Duane Elmer and Lois McKinney, 55-57. Monrovia, CA: MARC, 1999.

Gangel, Kenn. *Ministering to Today's Adults.* Nashville: Word Publishing, 1999.

Hall, Christopher A. *Reading Scripture with the Church Fathers.* Downers Grove, IL: InterVarsity Press, 1998.

Jenkins, Philip. *The New Faces of Christianity: Believing the Bible in the Global South.* New York: Oxford University Press, 2006.

———. *The Next Christendom: The Coming of Global Christianity.* New York City: Oxford Press, 2002.

Kiang, Liew Yoo. "Informal Workplace Learning and Blended Ecclesiastical Learning: Some Andragogical Reflections." In *The Pastor and Theological Education: Essays in Memory of Rev. Derek Tan.* Edited by Siga Arles, Lily Lim, Tan-Chow MayLing, and Brian Wintle, 178-205. Bangalore: Asia Theological Association, 2007.

Lwesya, Enson. *Dreaming Your Future: A Principal Approach to Leadership with an African Emphasis.* Lilongwe, Malawi: CLEAN Consult International Resources, 2003.

Maslow, Abraham. *The Psychology of Science. The John Dewey Society Lectureship Series.* New York: Harper and Row, 1966.

McKinney, Lois. *Course Manual: Educational Planning for Cross-cultural Ministries.* Wheaton, IL: Wheaton College Graduate School, 1989.

Nelson, Alan, and Gene Appel. *How to Change Your Church (Without Killing It).* Nashville: Word Publishers, 2000.

Oden, Thomas C. *How Africa Shaped the Christian Mind: Rediscovering the African Seedbed of Western Christianity.* Downers Grove, IL: IVP Books, 2007.

O'Gorman, Frances. "Are We Facilitators 'Crabbing' the Community Development Process?" In *With an Eye on the Future: Development and Mission in the 21st Century.* Edited by Duane Elmer and Lois McKinney, 169-177. Monrovia, CA: MARC, 1999.

Persellin, Diane Cummings and Mary Blythe Daniels. *A Concise Guide to Improving Student Learning: Six Evidence-Based Principles and How to Apply Them.* Sterling, VA: Stylus, 2014.

Pommerville, Paul A. *Handbook: Theological Education by Extension.* Malang, Indonesia: Assembly of God Publications, 1973.

Tan, Derek. "Theological Education in Asia: Present Issues, Challenges and Future Opportunities." In *The Pastor and Theological Education: Essays in Memory of Rev. Derek Tan.* Edited by Siga Arles, Lily Lim, Tan-Chow MayLing, and Brian Wintle, 79-94. Bangalore: Asia Theological Association, 2007.

Waggoner, Brad J. *The Shape of Faith to Come: Spiritual Formation and the Future of Discipleship.* Nashville: B & H Publishing Group, 2008.

Ward, Ted W. "Servants, Leaders, and Tyrants." In *With an Eye on the Future: Development and Mission in the 21st Century.* Edited by Duane Elmer and Lois McKinney, 27-42. Monrovia, CA: MARC, 1999.

_____ "Evaluating Metaphors of Education." In *With an Eye on the Future Development and Mission in the 21st Century.* Edited by Duane Elmer and Lois McKinney, 43-54. Monrovia, CA: MARC, 1999.

Yancey, Philip. *The Bible Jesus Read.* Grand Rapids: Zondervan Publishing House, 1999.

Young, Mark. "Planning Theological Education in Mission Settings: A Context-Sensitive Approach." In *With an Eye on the Future: Development and Mission in the 21st Century.*

Edited by Duane Elmer and Lois McKinney, 69-86. Monrovia, CA: MARC, 1999.

Yu, Carver. "Engaging the Ecclesial Dimension: Theological Education that Empowers the Church." In *The Pastor and Theological Education: Essays in Memory of Rev. Derek Tan.* Edited by Siga Arles, Lily Lim, Tan-Chow MayLing, and Brian Wintle, 166-177. Bangalore: Asia Theological Association, 2007.

KNOWLEDGE WITH ZEAL: BIBLICAL EXAMPLES OF USING A GOD-ANOINTED INTELLECT IN HIS SERVICE[1]

By Dave Johnson[2]

Introduction

In Matthew 22:37 Jesus commanded all believers to love God with all of their heart, strength, and mind, and to love their neighbor as themselves, stating that the Law and the Prophets were predicated on these two commandments. Loving God with all of one's mind can mean seeking to develop one's intellectual capacities.[3] Four men in the Bible: Moses, Ezra, Daniel, and Paul, exemplified obedience to this principle, even though three of them lived and died before Jesus ever uttered those words. With the use of non-Western narrative methodology, in this case biography, this paper will study what it means to serve God with one's intellect. Rick Nañez's repeated premise of the need for intellectual development along with spiritual passion is accepted as the basis for this paper.[4] One is compelled to agree with Donald Bowdle that "Jesus is Lord of learning . . ." as well as every other area of life.[5] Consequently, the greater weight in

---

[1] Knowledge with Zeal is an inversion of the motto of the Asia Pacific Theological Seminary in Baguio City, Philippines whose motto is "Zeal With Knowledge."
[2] This paper was originally presented at a theological consultation sponsored by the Asia Pacific Theological Association in Manduluyang City, Metro Manila, in 2006. It was later published in *Pneuma Review* and is reprinted here by permission.
[3] The need and opportunity to develop one's intellect is an underpinning premise of Rick Nañez's book, *Full Gospel, Fractured Minds?: A Call to Use God's Gift of the Intellect* (Grand Rapids: Zondervan Publishing House, 2005).
[4] Ibid.
[5] Donald N. Bowdle, "Informed Pentecostalism: An Alternative Paradigm," in *The Spirit and the Mind: Essays in Informed Pentecostalism Studies in Honor of Donald N.*

this paper will be given to the intellectual development, insofar as possible, of the lives of the biblical characters to be examined, and how that development impacted their service to God and man. These men serve as outstanding examples of combining powerful intellects with passionate piety.

Four Men Who Combined Knowledge with Zeal

There are two classes of education that are apparent in the lives of these four men. Moses and Daniel were classically educated in the liberal arts of their day while Ezra and Paul were theologically schooled in Judaism.

Moses

Moses was educated in the best tradition that ancient Egypt had to offer (Acts 7:22). Education fit for a prince would have likely included literacy, architecture, painting, astronomy, and mathematics as these were some of the strong aspects of Egyptian culture.[6] It also seems reasonable to assume that a prince would have been instructed in statecraft and law. A. W. Morton suggests Moses may have learned the duties of a scribe as part of his education and would have become literate in both Hebrew and Egyptian.[7] That he rejected the lifestyle of the palace does not suggest that he eschewed his education.

In defending the Mosiac authorship of the Pentateuch, Gleason Archer explains that there were actually two strands of Moses' intellectual development:

> He had the education and background for authorship, since he received from his ancestors that wealth of oral law which originated from the Mesopotamian cultures

---

Bowdle, eds. Terry L. Cross and Emerson B. Powery (Lanham, MD: University Press of America, 2000), 12.

[6]Taylor, William M. *Moses The Law-Giver* (Grand Rapids: Baker Book House, 1961), 24-28.

[7]Archibald. W. Morton, "Education in Biblical Times," in *The Zondervan Pictorial Encyclopedia of the Bible* 2, 206-223 (Grand Rapids: Zondervan Publishing House, 1976), 207.

back in the time of Abraham (hence the remarkable resemblances to the eighteenth century [B.C.] Code of Hammurabi), and from his tutors in the Egyptian court he received training in those branches of learning in which eighteenth dynasty Egypt excelled the rest of the ancient world. From his forebears he would naturally have received an accurate oral tradition of the career of the patriarchs and those revelations which God had vouchsafed to them.[8]

Archer's assertion regarding Mosiac authorship, however, has been contested by a number of reputable scholars, both outside and inside the evangelical community in recent decades. Because the debate itself goes well beyond the purpose of this article, I will simply state my conviction that the evidence for Mosiac authorship outweighs the arguments against it.

The Hebrew strain could have been gained from his mother but as the biblical record does not mention conclusively that she cared for him beyond the period of his weaning (Exodus 2:10), it seems most likely that he learned the traditions of his forebears during the years in the desert.

Both strands are evident in the Pentateuch. Moses was an outstanding storyteller in the oral tradition of the Hebrews. The Pentateuch reveals Moses as an experienced leader in many areas: law, tabernacle building, dietary regulations, and many other things. Concerning law, for example, E.B. Smick draws several correlations between the Mosiac law and other legal systems known in the Middle East at the time, specifically the famous law code of Hammurabi, implying that Moses was familiar with them.[9] One could argue that his knowledge of Hammurabi's Code could have come from either strand of his tradition.

The Pentateuch also reveals more than one literary style. While most of it is written in compelling narrative, certain small

---

[8] Gleason L. Archer Jr., *A Survey of Old Testament Introduction* (Chicago: Moody Bible Institute, 1974), 122.
[9] E.B. Smick, "Pentateuch," in *The Zondervan Pictorial Encyclopedia of the Bible* 4 (Grand Rapids: Zondervan Publishing Corporation, 1976), 688.

sections are poetic (i.e. Genesis 3:14-19; 4:23-24; 9:25-27; 49:1-27).[10] Also, the table of the nations in Genesis reveals that Moses had a grasp of history that went beyond that of the Egyptians and the Hebrews.

Moses' passion for God is not only reflected in the man of God and great leader that he indeed became, but also in the fact that he wrote the Pentateuch. It provided a solid history, statecraft, and numerous other things upon which Jewish society would be built.

Daniel

Daniel was taken captive by Nebuchadnezzar, most likely in the first group taken around 605 B.C. All that is known about Daniel is drawn from the Old Testament book that bears his name.[11] Nothing is known about Daniel's early life except for what is found in 1:3-4 that he was young, intelligent, handsome, part of the Jewish upper class, and showed potential for serving the king of Babylon. Daniel 1:4, 17 indicates that he and his friends were to be educated in order to serve in the court, specifically stating that they were educated in the literature, language, and wisdom of the Babylonians. The literature included writings on ethical values, aesthetic appreciation, morals, religious issues, and social attitudes.[12] Norman Porteous holds that the language they were required to learn would have either been the neo-Babylonian language spoken in the king's court or, more likely, the ancient Sumerian tongue used in their rituals and sacred myths.[13]

At the end of three years, they were to stand before the king (1:5). Being called to stand before the king could mean more than one thing. Either they would simply be presented as having

---

[10] Smick, 690-691.

[11] The issue of authorship could also be raised again. Again, the author asserts that the arguments for Daniel's authorship outweigh the arguments against it.

[12] D.J. Wiseman, "Babylonia," in *The International Standard Bible Encyclopedia* 1, rev. ed. ed. Geoffrey W. Bromily (Grand Rapids: William B. Eerdmans Publishing Company, 1982), 398.

[13] Norman W. Porteous, *Daniel: A Commentary*, The Old Testament Library (Philadelphia: Westminster Press, 1965), 27.

finished their studies and ready for service, or it could mean that he would examine them personally to see if their education was satisfactory. It appears from 1:18-21 that the latter was the case, meaning that they had additional motivation to study hard since the king held the power of life and death over them. In the case of Daniel and his friends, God gave them great favor with the king.

Their teachers were the wise men or enchanters and magicians of the land. John Goldingay gives some excellent insight into who these people were:

> The Babylonian sages combined many of the functions fulfilled by wise men, prophets, and priests in Israel, though they are to be distinguished from those cultic functionaries who were more especially concerned with the temple and its ritual. They were the guardians of the sacred traditional lore developed and preserved in Mesopotamia over centuries, covering natural history, astronomy, mathematics, medicine, myth, and chronicle. Much of this learning had a practical purpose, being designed to be applied to life by means of astrology, oneirology, hepatoscopy and the study of other organs, rites of purification, sacrifice, incantation, exorcism and other forms of divination and magic.[14]

Subjects such as astronomy, natural history, mathematics, medicine, chronicle, and perhaps myth would pose no religious conflict for the Jewish exiles, but most of the other subjects listed above represent various ways of practicing divination and were expressly forbidden by God (Leviticus 19:26, 31; 20:6). The high status of the magicians and enchanters is indicative of the depth of animistic practices in Babylon. How Daniel and his friends avoided being immersed in the occult during their three years of study is not revealed, but their later display of steadfastness of faith indicates that they must have done so (Daniel 3:1-27).

---

[14] John E. Goldingay, *Daniel*, Word Biblical Commentary, vol. 30, eds. David A. Hubbard and Glenn W. Barker (Dallas: Word Books, 1989), 16.

While most forms of divination are an abomination to God, the interpretation of dreams, known as oneiromancy, apparently is not. Because the Babylonians knew that Daniel had this gift and, therefore, was obviously in touch with a supernatural power source, they may not have been all that concerned that he did not participate in their other activities. However, the difference between Daniel and the others is that his interpretations always revealed the glory of God (cf. Daniel 2:31-45; 4:19-28), while those of other magicians tended to honor mankind.

Daniel applied his education well and spent many decades in the service of the king, holding many posts in the kingdom, including possibly becoming the top administrator in the reign of Darius the Mede (Dan. 6:2-3). That he excelled in his vocation, which would have required a substantial intellect, is abundantly clear from the biblical record. Daniel's passion to live in obedience to God's word is evident from the very beginning when he and his friends asked to be excused from eating food that was ceremonially unclean. As H.C. Leopold points out, receiving a Babylonian education and even taking on Babylonian names did not violate the consciences of Daniel and his friends. Eating the king's food, however, which was contrary to the Levitical food laws, was a different matter.[15] Abstaining from unclean food in the court of the pagan king of Babylon was not easy, but they preferred obedience to compromise (1:8-21).

Daniel's competence in his job and his piety are both revealed in Daniel 6:1-5. His enemies could find no fault with him either in reference to the execution of his responsibilities or in the area of integrity. He was both competent and faithful. The subsequent trap that his enemies laid for him was a back handed compliment to his faith. They knew that they would catch him in prayer because he was both consistent and uncompromising.

---

[15]H.C. Leopold, *Exposition of Daniel*, (Augsburg Publishing House, 1949, reprint (Grand Rapids: Baker Book House, 1969), 66.

Ezra

Ezra was a Levite who could trace his lineage all the way back to Aaron, Israel's first high priest. He was "learned in matters of the Law," (Ezra 7:1-6, 11) leaving little doubt that he was numbered among the intelligentsia of the day. How he was educated is a matter of conjecture. Most scholars believe that the institution of the synagogue was founded during the Exile as Jews could no longer worship at the temple. It may be that he was raised in a synagogue school and perhaps later trained under an individual teacher of the Law. Whatever the case, he was of such high and noble character that he even commanded the respect of the pagan king of Persia, Artaxerxes (Ezra 7:12).

Originally, the function of the scribe may have been part of the job of the Levities in the early history of Israel, and court scribes certainly served in the times of the monarchy. But scribes as a special class began to emerge in the period of the Exile, meaning that Ezra was part of a new breed (see Ezra 7:6, 11; Nehemiah 8:4, 9, 13). Ezra was trained in what is now known as Rabbinic Judaism which emphasized the study of the law—a written tradition that needed interpretation.[16] Because of his skill in interpreting the Law and his priestly lineage, Ezra symbolizes the close relationship between the priesthood and the interpretation of the Law that was common in the post-exilic period.[17] His literary skills can be seen in the book that bears his name. Many of the early church fathers also believed that he wrote the books of the Chronicles, although the evidence is not conclusive.[18] It has also been argued that he may have written all or part of the book of Nehemiah.[19]

---

[16]Frederick Carlson Holmgren, *Israel Alive Again: A Commentary on the Books of Ezra and Nehemiah*, International Theological Commentary (Grand Rapids: William B. Eerdmans Publishing Co., 1987), xv.

[17]Rainey, Anson, "Scribe, Scribes," in *The Zondervan Pictorial Encyclopedia of the Bible*, ed. Merrill C. Tenney (Grand Rapids: Zondervan Publishing Corporation, 1976), 300-301.

[18]C. F. Keil and F. Delitzsch, *Commentary on the Old Testament* vol. 3 (Peabody, MA: Hendrickson Publishers, 1986), 23.

[19]Mervin Breneman, *Ezra Nehemiah Esther: An Exegetical and Theological Exposition of Holy Scripture*. The New American Commentary (Nashville: Broadman and Holman Publishers, 1993), 37.

But Ezra was no ivory tower scholar. Not only had he served in the court of Artaxerxes, he also served as a civil leader who led a part of the Jewish remnant from Babylon back to the promised land in 458 B.C. (Ezra 7:6). Although acting in an official capacity, he surely would have understood the return of the remnant in light of Jeremiah's prophecy (Jeremiah 25:11) that the Jews would return after seventy years. Certainly he would have seen himself as part of that prophecy's fulfillment.

What he saw when he arrived in Jerusalem shocked and disturbed him. In clear and open violation of the Law of Moses, the children of the Jews who had been left behind seventy years previously had intermarried with peoples whom the Law had expressly forbidden them to marry (Ezra 9:1-2; cf. Exodus 34:15-16). His prayer in Ezra (9:6-15) is one of contrition and repentance on behalf of those that had sinned. The picture of one of the most dignified, well-educated Jews of his era sitting before God weeping with his clothes torn in repentance is most poignant (Ezra 9:5; 10:1).

As a true son of the covenant, Ezra could not be satisfied to leave things the way they were. With the encouragement of Shecaniah, Ezra began to lead the people back towards faithfulness to God (Ezra 10:2-5). Faithfulness to God demands obedience, and Ezra issued the call for them to divorce their foreign wives (Ezra 10:6-17). This proved to be a difficult task as their sin had been so rampant. While Ezra had rightly called them back to obedience, he tempered it with mercy in allotting some time to work out the issue. The melding of the intellect and piety of this marvelous man is found in Ezra 7:10 that he purposed to study, practice, and teach God's law.

Paul

Paul was from Tarsus in the province of Cilicia which was in the southeastern part of Asia Minor (Acts 21:39). As a border province and a commercial center, people from Tarsus would have not only been aware of the Hellenic culture that permeated the Roman Empire, they would have also been well aware of the religious thought to the east. E.M. Blaiklock notes that this cosmopolitan atmosphere was an ideal environment for nurturing one who would become God's messenger to the Gentiles.[20] Since God's revelation came first to the Jews, it would require the mastery of the Old Testament, but it would also require the intellectual ability to communicate that message in the thought forms of the Greek speaking world.

Tarsus was a university city, home of the renowned teacher, Athenodorus, the personal tutor of Caesar Augustus, who returned home in his later years. Unlike other cities, such as Alexandria, it was the natives of Tarsus, not those from outside, who flocked to the schools.[21] Blaiklock is surely correct in contending that it was a great learning opportunity for a brilliant mind like Paul's, and a choice place of preparation for becoming an apostle to the Gentiles.[22]

Although the Jewish enclave in Tarsus was tolerant of Hellenic culture, Philippians 3:4-11 reveals that Paul was raised in a strict Hebrew home.[23] Paul's claim to be a "son of the Pharisees" in Acts 23:6 may indicate that his father or one of his other ancestors may have been associated with the Pharisees.[24] Gerald Hawthorne notes that the phrase "a Hebrew of Hebrews," (v. 5) refers either to Paul being of completely Jewish lineage, or that he was raised to speak Hebrew in the home.[25] Perhaps both were true, although Bruce holds that Aramaic, not Hebrew, was Paul's native language.[26] Paul was most likely fluent in both of these languages as well as Greek. Paul's fluency in Hebrew would have been critical to his studies under Gamaliel, his inclusion as a member of the strictest sect of

---

[20]E.M. Blaiklock, "Tarsus," in *The Zondervan Pictorial Encyclopedia of the Bible* 5, ed. Merrill C Tenney (Grand Rapids: Zondervan Publishing Company, 1976), 599.
[21]Strabo, *Geography*, xiv. 5. 12 ff. (673ff.) in F.F. Bruce, *Paul: Apostle of the Heart Set Free* (Grand Rapids: William B. Eerdmans Publishing Company, 1977), 35.
[22]Blaiklock, 602.
[23]Ibid.
[24]F.F. Bruce, *Paul: Apostle*, 44.
[25]Gerald F. Hawthorne, *Philippians*, Word Biblical Commentary, vol 43, ed. David A. Hubbard and Glenn W. Barker, (Waco, TX: Word Publishing, 1983), 133.
[26]F.F. Bruce, *Paul: Apostle*, 43.

the Pharisees (Acts 22:3), and his ability to exegete the Old Testament in its original language.[27]

His rabbinic training under Gamaliel in Jerusalem would likely have commenced shortly after his *Bar Mitzvah*, which took place when he was thirteen.[28] Gamaliel, a prominent member of the Jewish Sanhedrin, was "an honored teacher of the law" (Acts 5:34). According to R.F. Youngblood, Gamaliel believed that the Law was divine, but tended to emphasize its human elements, calling for a more relaxed application of the Sabbath laws, and urged kindness towards the Gentiles. He was also an avid student of Greek literature.[29] Paul's knowledge of Greek literature seems to be consistent with that of his mentor, suggesting that Gamaliel's attitude may have helped to shape his own.

By far, Gamaliel's greatest influence upon Paul was in relationship to the Law of God. According to Paul's own confession, he was of the strictest sect of the Pharisees, meaning that he was passionate about the study and adherence to God's Law (Philippians 3:5). Like many others, he assumed that salvation was obtainable through obedience to the Law. Paul's Damascus Road experience resulted in a change in perspective regarding the function of the Law (Galatians 3:24), but not his desire to study and fulfill it. When Paul speaks of counting all things in his background as loss or rubbish, he was only discounting these things as a way of salvation (Philippians 3:8-9). He was not devaluing education or intellectual development. Jesus himself rightly criticized the Pharisees for many things, but the pursuit of mental acumen was not one of them.

In assessing whether Hellenism or Judaism had the greatest influence on him, one is compelled to note that Judaism held the

---

[27]R.F. Youngblood notes that while Paul normally uses the Septuagint when referring to Old Testament passages, he does use the Hebrew text in a number of places in his writings (R.F. Youngblood, "Gamaliel," in *The International Standard Bible Encyclopedia*, rev. ed. ed. Geoffrey W. Bromily (Grand Rapids: William B. Eerdmans Publishing Company, 1982), 394.

[28]R.N. Longenecker, "Paul the Apostle," in *The Zondervan Encyclopedia of the Bible*, ed. Merrill C. Tenney (Grand Rapids: Zondervan Publishing House, 1976), 625.

[29]Youngblood, 394.

stronger hand.[30] Paul's deep intellectual understanding of the Old Testament is reflected throughout his writings and in the speeches recorded (and edited) by Luke in Acts. As to his writings, the book of Romans is unsurpassed in reflecting the depth and range of his theological thinking, especially in regards to his reinterpretation of the function of the Law as a means to lead one to Christ and not as the means of salvation in itself—a radical departure from Judaism (Romans 7 and 8). Mainly didactic in nature, Merrill Tenney notes that while Romans does not contain all fields of Christian thought, "it does give a fuller and more systematic view of the heart of Christianity than any other of Paul's epistles, with the possible exception of Ephesians."[31] Romans can be described as a well articulated defense of the Christian faith.

Perhaps the clearest example of the combination of his intellect and piety is found during his time in Athens, and specifically in his sermon on Mar's Hill (Acts 17:16-34). While Athens had long passed its Golden Age, it was still the philosophical center of the Mediterranean world. In the market place, which doubled as the center for public life, Paul reasoned (v. 17 NKJV) with the philosophers of the day. John R.W. Stott suggests that Paul used the Socratic method of questions and answers, a methodology with which the Athenians would have been very familiar.[32] This means that he was well schooled in the communication patterns of his target audience and was able to communicate the gospel in thought forms known to the Greeks even if they did not understand his message. He was taken to the Areopagus, an august group of the intelligentsia of Athens, possibly involuntarily, to explain his philosophy. F.F. Bruce explains that this group had considerable authority in matters of religion and morals. Although Paul was not on trial in

---

[30]Brad H. Young, *Paul The Jewish Theologian: A Pharisee Among Christian, Jews, and Gentiles* (Peabody, MA: Hendrickson Publishers, Inc., 1997), 9.

[31]Merrill C. Tenney, *New Testament Survey* (Grand Rapids: William B. Eerdmans Publishing Company, 1961), 304.

[32]John R.W. Stott, *The Spirit, The Church, and The World: The Message of Acts* (Downer's Grove, IL: Inter-Varsity Press, 1990), 280.

a "forensic sense," he was required to give an account of his teaching.³³

One must agree with Bruce that while Paul's message presented here by Luke was likely an edited edition of the original, it is a brilliant apologetic of the gospel to educated unbelievers.³⁴ Here, his intellect and mental agility to apply what he knew are readily apparent in his message. First, he demonstrates knowledge of their history and literature in making reference to the unknown God (v. 23). Don Richardson writes that 600 years before Christ, a plague that was attributed to a curse broke out in the city of Athens. In response to an oracle, a poet philosopher named Epimenides was summoned from Crete, who called for sacrifices to an unknown deity, and the plague stopped. Several altars were built in the region to this unknown power.³⁵ While it is possible that Paul did not know the story behind the altar, it is more likely that he was familiar with it. He had read the writings of Epimenides and quotes him in 17:28.³⁶ It also seems unlikely that he would use this altar as an illustration if the background of it was unknown to him.

From the reference to this altar, Paul builds his case for Christ using linear logic and moving from the general revelation of God in nature to the specific revelation of God in Christ. Paul began with the understood concept of creation to explain the rationale for something they emphatically did not understand—the need for repentance and the reality of the coming judgment. Notably absent is any direct reference to the Old Testament, an unknown and therefore non-authoritative book to the Greeks.

As mentioned above, Paul was also familiar with the classical literature of the day, using quotes from Greek poets to

---

³³F.F. Bruce, *Commentary on the Book of Acts*, The New International Commentary on the New Testament, ed. F.F. Bruce (Grand Rapids: William B. Eerdmans Publishing Company, 1979), 352.

³⁴Ibid., 362.

³⁵Don Richardson, *Eternity in Their Hearts*, rev. ed (Ventura, CA: Regal Books, 1981), 16-19. Richardson substantiates his story by citing several classical Greek writers: Diogenes Laertius, *The Lives of Eminent Philosophers*, vol 1, 110; Plato, *Laws*; an editor's footnote on Aristotle's, *The Art of Rhetoric*, book 3, 17:10 in the Loeb Classical Library, translated by J.H. Freese; Pausanias, *Description of Greece*, vol. 1, 1:4; and Philostratus, *Appolonius of Tyana*.

³⁶Bruce, *Acts* (p. 359, footnote 49). notes that Epimenides quote was probably drawn by others from the work of Theodore of Mopsuestia.

support his argument for divine revelation.³⁷ In verse 28, he quotes from Epimenides and in verse 29 he quotes from Aratus, a native of his home province in Cilicia. Both writers referred to a Supreme Being, but not the God of the Bible. In using their writings to proclaim Christ, Bruce rightly says that Paul opened himself to the charge of misquoting their poets, but also explains that Paul's general theological position allowed him to borrow from others to the extent that what they said was in line with biblical revelation.³⁸ Stott argues that Paul's example in using the literature of his day is adequate warrant for today's believer to do the same in the intellectual debates of today for the purpose of pointing people to Christ.³⁹

But Paul's intellectual brilliance was not motivated by a desire to win an argument but to bring people to Christ (vv. 30-31). Simply stated, Paul, his mind steeped both in the Scriptures and the literature of his day, was obviously anointed by the Holy Spirit to introduce the gospel to those who had never heard it. He was a first rate apologist and evangelist.

Application and Implications for Christians Today

In assessing the lives of the men studied here, it is evident that all of them were men of great intellect and spiritual passion.

But not everything in their education was designed to lead them to God. Neither the Egyptians nor the Babylonians took the God of the Jews seriously. In Paul's case, much of what he learned in Judaism had to be jettisoned when he came to Christ. They had to critically analyze what they were taught in light of God's revelation, retaining that which was biblical or at least did not violate Scripture, while rejecting that which was unbiblical. The evidence is clear that they did so. For this they needed an intellect touched by the Holy Spirit. This is critical for modern thinkers as many of today's ideologies (and not a few theologies) are far from Christ centered. In dealing with these

---

³⁷Bruce, *Paul: Apostle*, 239.
³⁸Bruce, *Acts*, 360.
³⁹Stott, *The Spirit*, 286.

issues, one must know how to think and reason, not simply what to think.

Justification of Liberal Arts Education

The lives of Moses and Daniel reveal how they used their education to glorify God through writing the Pentateuch and through administrating government competently and honestly. Their lives provide ample justification for a Bible-based, Christ centered liberal arts education that calls for the development of a Christ like mind in every area of life including the arts, the sciences, or politics. Nañez calls for a return to studying philosophy and the sciences, pointing out that many fathers of modern science were devoted Christians and gives some outstanding examples.[40] His call is a little late, as is evidenced by the abundance of liberal arts courses in Pentecostal Bible schools and universities that predate his comments by several decades, but it is on the mark.[41]

Harry Blamires contends that everything in human experience, whether sacred or secular, can be thought about from a Christian point of view.[42] In politics, for example, William Wilberforce was an example of an outstanding Christian who used his intellectual powers for the glory of God. Serving in the English Parliament in the late eighteenth and early nineteenth century, he was one of the driving forces in outlawing slavery in the British Isles, as well as having a moralizing influence over many areas of national British life.[43]

Nañez also calls for the sanctified use of reason and logic, using these mental tools in doing theology and especially in the art of apologetics.[44] Nañez's book is culture bound, however, dealing only with issues related to Western, particularly American, Pentecostals. He advocates the reading of Western

---

[40] Nañez, 184-193.
[41] Email from Dr. Charles Harris to the author, August 18, 2007.
[42] Harry Blamires, *The Christian Mind: How Should A Christian Think?* (London: S.P.C.K., 1963), 45.
[43] John R.W. Stott, *Involvement: Being a Responsible Christian in a Non-Christian Society* (Old Tappan, NJ: Fleming H. Revell Company, 1985), 21-22.
[44] Nañez, 135-143.

philosophers, whose writings, he believes, should be studied for one's intellectual development.[45] Would he also endorse reading the Confucian classics, the sacred books of Hinduism, Buddhism, Islam, and other ideologies that are dominant in various parts of the world today? One would presume so in the interest of apologetics for those living in those cultural milieus. Knowing the ideologies of one's cultural context is important for communicating the gospel.

Maintaining Intellectual Growth and Spiritual Passion

With the possible exception of Paul's alluding to books and parchments that he had left behind (2 Timothy 4:13), the Bible, unfortunately does not reveal *how* these men continued their intellectual development. It also does not explain how they maintained a balance between the intellect and spiritual passion, but it is clear that they did so. How this can be done depends on the interests and the ability of the individual. For those who desire to get or continue a formal education, the opportunities today are endless with the advent of distance-based education. For those living in oral societies such as that of the ancient Hebrews, a wealth of information is available in the folklore, fables, and poetry that should not be ignored in seeking to understand those one is called to serve. There are no shortcuts. The words of Solomon ring true that the writing of many books is endless and the study of them is wearisome (Ecclesiastes 12:12), meaning that intellectual development is both mind stretching and exhausting.

But intellectual development is never an end in itself. It must always be held in creative tension with spiritual passion. Harold Kohl, the founding president of the Far East Advanced School of Theology in Metro Manila (now the Asia Pacific Theological Seminary in Baguio City, Philippines) argued that scholarship without spirituality is dead and barren. He also contended that spirituality that is not deeply grounded in God's word easily becomes fanaticism. True Pentecostal education

---

[45]Ibid., 172-179.

would strive for both in balance, although the challenge of holding these two ideals in creative tension is not easy.[46] Eli Javier echoed the same thoughts when he warned Bible school leaders to be wary of those who have master's degrees but no practical experience in ministry.[47] He goes on to use the metaphor of a railroad track with one rail representing the intellectual and theoretical while the other represents the practical and concrete.[48] Both rails are necessary for the train to run.

The biblical characters studied here are an excellent example. In all four cases, they sought to use their education in advancing the purposes of God in their generation. The driving force for getting an education and maintaining continued development must always be motivated by a passion for God himself and a strong desire to see his purposes accomplished in the world today.

Conclusion

This paper was written under the premise that part of fulfilling the great commandment to love God with all of one's heart, soul, and mind means to develop one's intellect. The sketch of the biblical characters revealed four men, trained in different disciplines, who used their brilliant minds in passionate service to God. Moses was a statesman, lawgiver, and gifted writer. Daniel excelled in administration, his integrity and faith known to all who worked with him. Ezra's study of the Law led him to be part of the remnant that returned and to be a leader in the spiritual renewal that followed. Paul, the disciple of Gamaliel and apostle to the Gentiles, used his gifts in articulating theology and apologetics, particularly among the Gentiles, with the goal of bringing them to Jesus Christ.

---

[46]Harold Kohl, "From the President's Desk," *BBI Gazette*, July-August, 1965, 2-12.

[47]Eli Javier, *Pursuing Excellence, Experiencing Renewal: An Agenda for AG Ministerial Training* Institutions, lectures notes at the PGCAG Bible School Faculty and Admin Staff Enrichment and Retreat, Tagaytay City, Philippines, May, 2007.

[48]Ibid.

All of them dealt with daunting challenges. Moses led the children of Israel, who were known to be hard headed and cantankerous, out of the most powerful and influential nation of the Middle East and towards the Promised Land. Daniel served a pagan king, worked with unfriendly colleagues, and spent a night with the lions because of his faith. Ezra returned to a land which had been devastated by a conqueror to serve people who had lived in violation of God's law. Paul's challenges are eloquently listed in 2 Corinthians 11:21-29. But today all are rightly remembered as men of immense intellects and passionate faith who stood faithfully for God, no matter what the circumstances.

The challenge continues today. False ideologies, errant theologies, and unbiblical worldviews are proliferating around the world, and the Asia Pacific region is no exception. This generation needs men and women who are filled with the spirit of Christ who will bend and stretch their minds to be used of God in disciplines and areas of service too numerous to elucidate here, both in the sacred and secular realms, seeking to honor Christ in all times and circumstances.

REFERENCES CITED

Archer, Gleason L. *A Survey of Old Testament Introduction.* Chicago: Moody Bible Institute, 1974.

Blaiklock, Edward M. "Tarsus." In *The Zondervan Pictorial Encyclopedia of the Bible.* Ed. Merrill C. Tenney. Grand Rapids: Zondervan Publishing House, 1976.

Blamires, Harry. *The Christian Mind: How Should a Christian Think?* London: S.P.C.K., 1963.

Bowdle, Donald. "Informed Pentecostalism: An Alternative Paradigm." In *The Spirit and The Mind: Essays in Informed Pentecostalism, Studies in Honor of Donald Bowdle.* Eds. Terry L. Cross and Emerson B. Powery. Lanham, MD: University Press of America.

Breneman, Mervin. *Ezra Nehemiah Esther: An Exegetical Commentary and Theological Exposition of Holy Scripture.* The New American Commentary. Nashville: Broadman and Holman Publishers, 1993.

Bruce, F.F. *Paul: Apostle of the Heart Set Free.* Grand Rapids: William B. Eerdmans Publishing Company, 1977.

_____. *Commentary on the Book of Acts.* The New International Commentary on the New Testament. Ed. F.F. Bruce. Grand Rapids: Zondervan Publishing Company, 1979.

Goldingay, John E. *Daniel.* Word Biblical Commentary. Eds. David A. Hubbard and Glenn W. Barker. Dallas: Word Books, 1989.

Harris, Charles. Email to the Author, August 18, 2007.

Hawthorne, Gerald. *Philippians.* Word Biblical Commentary. Vol. 43 Eds. David A.

Hubbard and Glenn W. Barker. Waco, TX: Word Publishing, 1983.

Holmgren, Frederick Carlson. *Israel Alive Again: A Commentary on the Books of Ezra And Nehemiah.* International Theological Commentary. Grand Rapids: Zondervan Publishing House, 1987.

Javier, Eli. *Pursuing Excellence, Experiencing Renewal: An Agenda For AG Ministerial Training Institutions*. Lecture notes at the PGCAG Bible School Faculty and Admin Staff Enrichment and Retreat, Tagaytay City, Philippines, May 2007.

Kohl, Harold. "From the President's Desk." *BBI Gazette* July-August, 1965.

Keil, C.F. and Delizsch. *Commentary on the Old Testament*. Vol. 3. Peabody, MA: Hendrickson Publishers, 1986.

Leopold, H.C. *Exposition of Daniel*. Augsburg Publishing House; reprint Grand Rapids:Baker Book House, 1966.

Morton, Archibald W. "Education in Biblical Times." In *The Zondervan Pictorial Encyclopedia of The Bible*. Ed. Merrill C. Tenney. Grand Rapids: ZondervanPublishing House, 1976.

Nañez, Rick. *Full Gospel Fractured Minds? A Call to Use God's Gift of the Intellect*. Grand Rapids: Zondervan Publishing House, 2005.

Porteous, Norman W. *Daniel: A Commentary*. The Old Testament Library.Philadelphia: Westminster Press, 1965.

Rainey, Anson F. "Scribe, Scribes." In *The Zondervan Pictorial Encyclopedia of the Bible*. Ed. Merrill C. Tenney. Grand Rapids: Zondervan Publishing House, 1976.

Richardson, Don. *Eternity in Their Hearts*. Rev. ed. Ventura, CA: Regal Books, 1981.

Smick, Elmer B. "Pentateuch." In *The Zondervan Pictorial Encyclopedia of the Bible*. Ed. Merrill C. Tenney. Grand Rapids: Zondervan Publishing House, 1976.

Stott, John R.W. *The Spirit, The Church, and The World: The Message of Acts*. Downer's Grove, IL: Inter-Varsity Press, 1990.

_____. *Involvement: Being a Responsible Christian in a non-Christian Society*. Old Tappan, NJ: Fleming H. Revell Company, 1985.

Strabo. *Geography*. Xiv. 5, 12ff.

Taylor, William M. *Moses The Law-Giver*. Grand Rapids: Baker Book House, 1961.

Tenney, Merrill C. *New Testament Survey*. Grand Rapids: William B. EerdmansPublishing Company, 1961.

Wiseman, Donald J. "Babylonia." In *The International Standard Bible Encyclopedia*. Ed. Geoffey W. Bromily. Grand Rapids: William B. Eerdmans Publishing Company, 1982.

Young, Brad H. *Paul The Jewish Theologian: A Pharisee Among Christians, Jews, and Gentiles*. Peabody, MA: Hendrickson Publishers, 1997.

Youngblood, Ronald F. "Gamaliel." *The International Standard Bible Encyclopedia*. Ed. Geoffrey W. Bromily. Grand Rapids: William B. Eerdmans Publishing Company, 1982.

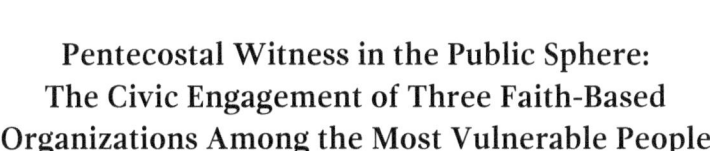

Pentecostal Witness in the Public Sphere: The Civic Engagement of Three Faith-Based Organizations Among the Most Vulnerable People in Vallejo, California

By Joel A. Tejedo[1]

Introduction

Roberto Medina, a graduate of law and a former private investigator in San Francisco, California, once became homeless and unemployed because of depression and drunkenness. But when he came to the Lord's Fellowship Church (LFC) and became a client at its Christian Help Center (CHC) in nearby Vallejo, he was transformed into a productive citizen in the community. In his emotional poem, read during the CHC's 30th anniversary celebration, he reflected on his story of crisis and transformation:

> And I had no house
> . . . and the smell from not washing
> Would sicken a mouse.
> I had one pair of shorts
> And two socks, which were gray,
> Though if washed they'd be white
> I must honestly say.

---

[1]This essay was presented at the April 16-17, 2015, International Conference on Religion and Spirituality at the University of California-Berkeley. I am delighted to offer this article in honor of Dr. John Carter, the man I deeply respect for his excellent contribution in the formation and strengthening of theological education in the Asia Pacific Region.

> *It was cold that November in 2006.*
> *Alcohol and the rules just did not mix;*
> *And it looked like I'd be walking and sore,*
> *But a guy who'd been through CHC dropped me off*
> *at their door.*
> *I felt silly and stupid, but I needed some help,*
> *I was bright, educated; I had tried it my way;*
> *But the truth of the matter popped into my head,*
> *If I didn't change something I would soon be quiet dead.*

This experimental paper reports on the civic involvement of the LFC's faith-based organizations that work among the underprivileged in Vallejo. It looks at how these organizations engage and align themselves with other social-assistance entities in creating the "common good." I examined various literature about civic engagement and used in-depth interviews and analysis to investigate whether they are social activists with respect to their doctrine and practice of ministry. My purpose was to discover how faith-based organizations translate their doctrine and values into the creation of common good in the public sphere. I hypothesized that social activism from these organizations is not limited or seen from a socialist perspective, but rather their "moral imagination" to transform society arises from the social challenges that confront them, fueled by their theological conviction and praxis of ministry. I used four case studies to elucidate further that my findings are, indeed, in line with my observations.

Religion and the Public Sphere

It has been said that "public theology" is a way of doing theology in a democratic society, because it offers a relevant and public way of doing so. Since Christianity is a minority religion, it has to negotiate its place in the public discourse, and it should embrace and promote a public sphere that is open and accessible and not dominated by any single source of power. Public theology must be done in a variety of ways and undertaken by different practitioners.² Donald McLeod, a Scottish theologian specializing in public theology, argued that there were three forces that pushed Evangelical Christians out to the far edge of public discourse. First, they have focused on the preaching the gospel and stayed out of public policy, even though it is part of their responsibility to preach the whole counsel of God.³ Second, while they believe the church is an organism that should function as salt and light, they tend to become more institutional and thus avoid the implication of Christian witness in the public sphere. And third, the increasing rise of secularism does not only seek to exclude Christian churches and organizations in the public arena, but also attempts to exclude them from getting benefits from it.⁴

Despite the fear and skepticism Christian organizations have of being engaged in the public sphere because of the possibility of compromising religious purity and co-optation, Kristin Heyer, a Catholic scholar, proposes that these organizations must disciple their adherents to become better citizens in their respective communities. Discipleship provides vision and a counter-culture, while citizenship widens the reach of Christian solidarity and provides grounds for religious claim.⁵ Heyer reminds Christians that social action and public engagement are constitutive of the gospel's call for all Christians, because it provides a larger context of community and the arenas where the Good News must be communicated and brought about.⁶ The Christian theology of creation and incarnation also shows the venue of God expressing his relationship to the world and further demonstrates that his grace touches all areas of life.⁷ Catholic theologian David O'Brien's view of discipleship and citizenship as a Christian response in the public sphere provides

---
²See Sebastian Kim, *Theology in the Public Sphere: Public Theology as a Catalyst for Open Debate*. (London: SCM Press, 2011): 256.
³Donald McLeod, "The Church in the Public Sphere," Belfast, Ireland, January 2014.
⁴Ibid.
⁵Kristin Heyer, "U.S. Catholic Discipleship and Citizenship: Patriotism or Dissent?", *Political Theology*, vol. 4. no. 2 (2003): 149-175.
⁶Ibid.
⁷Ibid.

us the "capacity to help form the church as a community of conscience loyal to the Gospel . . . and at the same time to share with others in shaping the public moral consensus that in the end governs the behavior of states and other powerful institutions."[8]

Harvard Professor Robert Putnam's provocative argument on "Bowling Alone" shows that religious groups that are least civic minded constrain interaction within organizations and eventually decrease civic engagement.[9] Religious groups, however, embed people in communities; and when they become a source of volunteerism, they increase community social capital and enhance the local quality of life.[10] Putnam's observation is based on his finding that:

> People of faith are better citizens and better neighbors; they are more apt to work on community projects, belong to voluntary associations, attend public meetings, vote in local elections, attend protest demonstrations and political rallies, and donate time and money to causes including secular ones.[11]

Though scholars like Alexander Nagel question whether faith-based organizations are efficient and better providers in delivering services to the community compared to secular organizations,[12] various researchers show that such organiza-

---

[8]David O'Brien, *From the Heart of the American Church: Catholic Higher Education and American Culture* (Maryknoll, NY: Orbis Books, 1992), 201.

[9]Robert Putnam and David Campbell, *American Grace: How Religion Is Reshaping Our Civic and Political Lives* (2010), 444. See also Robert D. Putnam, *Bowling Alone: The Collapse and Revival of American Community,* (New York: Simon & Schuster, 2000).

[10]Charles Tolbert, Thomas Lyson and Michael Erwin, "Local Capital, Civic Engagement and Socioeconomic Well-Being," *Social Forces*, vol. 77 no. 2 (1998): 401-427. See also Andrew Greeley, "Coleman Revisited: Religious Structures as a Source of Social Capital," *American Behavioral Scientist* 40: 587-94.

[11]Robert Putnam and David Campbell, *American Grace: How Religion Is Reshaping Our Civic and Political Lives* (2010), 444.

[12]Alexander Nagel, "Charitable Choice: The Religious Component of U.S. Welfare Reform: Theoretical and Methodological Reflections on Faith-Based Organizations as

tions are increasingly developing cohesive partnerships with government and other inter-governmental organizations.[13] Arthur Brooks, an American social scientist, on the topic of religious faith and charitable giving, shows that more than 90 percent of those who attend weekly worship services donate to charity and volunteer to charitable causes.[14] This is supported by other scholars who claim that active members of a church congregation are most likely to join non-religious organizations,[15] engage in community projects,[16] have a more trusting attitude toward society than those who seldom attend,[17] and have greater happiness, life satisfaction, and well-being.[18] Patrick Fagan, a religious social scientist who conducted research on the impact of religious practice on social stability, contends that:

Social Services," *Numen-International Review for the History of Religions*, vol. 53, no. 1 (2006): 78-111.

[13]World Council of Churches, "Increased Partnership Between Faith-Based Organizations, Government and Intra-Government Organizations," Statement by Faith-Based Organizations Facilitated by World Council of Churches for the UN Special General Assembly on HIV/AIDS, June 25-27, 2001. International Review of Mission, vol. XC, no. 359. Available at http://web.a.ebscohost.com/ host/pdfviewer/pdfviewer?vid=3&sid= 547b2388-7ad5-4af4-194-0f6b3168ab86%40sessionmgr4001&hid=4214 (accessed September 4, 2014).

[14]Arthur Brooks, "Religious Faith and Charitable Giving," *Policy Review 121* (Oct.-Nov. 2003): 1-13.

[15]Philip Schwadel, "Individual, Congregational, and Denominational Effects on Church Members' Civic Participation," *Journal of the Scientific Study of Religion*, vol. 44, no. 2 (2005): 159-171.

[16]Nojink Kwak, Dhiavan Shah, and Holbert Lance, "Connecting, Trusting, and Participating: The Direct and Interactive Effects of Social Associations," *Political Research Quarterly*, vol. 57, no. 4 (2004): 643-652.

[17]Michael Welch, David Sikkink, Eric Sartain, and Carolyn Bond, "Trust in God and Trust in Man: The Ambivalent Role of Religion in Shaping Dimensions of Social Trust," *Journal for the Scientific Study of Religion*, vol. 3, no. 3 (2004): 317-343. See also Mark Regnerus, Christian Smith, and David Sikkink, "Who Gives to the Poor?: The Influence of Religious Tradition and Political Location on the Personal Generosity of Americans Toward the Poor," *Journal for the Scientific Study of Religion*, vol. 37, no. 3 (1998): 481-493.

[18]Jeff Levin, "Religious Behavior, Health, and Well Being Among Israeli Jews: Findings from the European Social Survey," *Psychology of Religion and Spirituality* (November 2013): 1-11.

Regular attendance at religious services is linked to healthy stable family life, strong marriages, and well-behaved children. The practice of religion also leads to reduction in the incidence of domestic abuse, crime, substance abuse, and addiction. In addition, religious practice leads to an increase in physical and mental health, longevity, and education attainment. Moreover, these effects are inter-generational, as grandparents and parents pass on the benefits to the next generations.[19]

Pentecostals as Producers of the Common Good

In recent years, various religious and para-church organizations began to apply the concept of "social capital" in, examining the nature and impact of these groups in the larger network of society.[20] For instance, studies by Ram Cnaan, Stephanie Boddie, and Gaynor Yancey underscore the intrinsic norms of civic engagement within Christian churches, identifying that their congregations have long-held and enduring social norms. Such norms are characterized by the way in which people gather for worship and their willingness to become involved in community service.[21]

According to studies by R.S. Warner[22] and R. Wuthnow,[23] religious organizations develop a high level of social trust that results in personal involvement and the sharing of resources. Evidence indicates that the church, through collective

---

[19] Patrick Fagan, "Why Religion Matters Even More: The Impact of Religious Practice on Social Responsibility," Richard and Helen DeVos Center for Religion and Civil Society, *Heritage Foundation*, December 2006. Available at www.heritage.org (accessed, September 4, 2014).

[20] Corwin Smidt, ed. *Religious Social Capital: Producing the Common Good* (Waco, TX: Baylor University Press, 2003), 7.

[21] Ram Cnaan, Stephanie Boddie, and Gaynor Yancey, "Bowling Alone But Serving Together: The Congregational Norm of Community Involvement," in Corwin Smidt, ed. *Religious Social Capital: Producing the Common Good* (Waco, TX: Baylor University Press, 2003), 20.

[22] S.R. Warner, "Work in Progress Toward a New Paradigm for the Sociological Study of Religion in the United States, *American Journal of Sociology* 98:10: 44-93.

[23] R. Wuthnow, "*The Restructuring of American Religion: Society and Faith Since World War II* (Princeton, NJ: Princeton University Press, 1988), 23.

partnerships and networking with government and civic society, is instrumental in unmasking the social blight of the poor.[24] This notion is corroborated by studies of the Sanguaro Seminar on Civic Engagement in the U.S., which show religious organizations as being vitally important community entities that have played a central role in many of the great social and political transformations in history.[25] Putnam critically addresses the issue that religious entities can be potential tools to organize civic life and teach the values of compassion, forgiveness, fairness, altruism, and respect for the world beyond oneself.[26] In the same manner, religious organizations can be vibrant voluntary associations that teach people how to organize events, speak in public, and work together toward common ends.[27]

Studies conducted by Kevin Dougherty and his colleagues in 2005 regarding community political involvement of Pentecostals in the U.S. reveal that, in general, Pentecostals participate less in community organizations and politics than do non-Pentecostals.[28] More recent findings, however, suggest that this is changing, with such participation growing among Pentecostal people around the world.[29] Studies by Donald Miller and Tetsunao Yamamori, specializing in global Pentecostalism, show that Pentecostals are not only an emerging force in world Christianity, but through this cohesive and active actualization of their faith to the civil society, they are, in fact,

---

[24]Zizi Goschin, Daniela-Luminita Constantin, and Monica Roman, "The Partnership Between the State and the Church Against Trafficking in Person," *Journal for the Study of Religions and Ideologies*, vol. 8, no. 24 (2009): 231-256.

[25]Robert Putnam and Lewis Feldten with Don Cohen, "Religion and Social Capital," in *Better Together: Restoring the American Community* (New York: Simon & Schuster, 2003), 1.

[26]Ibid., 2.

[27]Ibid., 3.

[28]Kevin Dougherty et al., "Sidelined by Religion: Community Involvement and Political Participation of U.S. Pentecostals." Paper presented at the Symposium on Religion and Politics (Department of Sociology: Baylor University, May 2009), 3, 15. Available from: http://search.yahoo.com/search?fr=msgr-buddy&ei=UTF-8&p= Sideline %20by%20Religion (accessed 10 March 2010).

[29]Ari Pedro ORO, "Religious Politicians and Secular Politicians in Southern Brazil," *Social Compass* 2007, 54; 583. Available from http://scp.sagepub.com/cgi/content/abstract/54/4/583 (accessed 10 March 2010).

transforming local communities and individuals.³⁰ Even David Martin of the London School of Economics, observes that Pentecostals are the "little platoons of democracy—places where often very poor people learn to function democratically, elect their own officers, and develop leadership skills."³¹ Martin also acknowledged that Pentecostals "learn to participate in and run meetings, to conduct business, to handle money, to budget, to plan, to compromise, and to formulate and 'own' a course of action."³²

Civic Engagement of the Lord's Fellowship Church of Vallejo and Its Charitable Organizations: Social Context and History

Vallejo, California, once home of a notable naval base, was a thriving small city of about 117,000. Because of the naval base, business establishments were strong and growing. But with the base's closing in 1996 plus the recessions that hit the U.S.at that same time, Vallejo experienced a series of severe economic downturns that affected hundreds of families.³³ Crime, drug abuse, prostitution, and homelessness rose due to poverty and increasing unemployment,³⁴ as did the level of frustration of the many unemployed Caucasians. Promiscuity was pervasive, manifesting in sexual molestation and divorce. As a result, drug addiction victimized many children in affected families. The struggle to find adequate employment was a major social challenge for the people of Vallejo.³⁵ In fact, in 2009, Vallejo

---

[30] Donald Miller and Tetsunao Yamamori, *Global Pentecostalism: The New Face of Christian Social Engagement* (Berkley, Los Angeles, London: University of California Press, 2007): 1, 99.

[31] Centre for Development Enterprise, "Untapped Social Capital Burgeoning Under the Radar," *CDE*, March 2008. Available at http://www.cde.org.za/article.php?a_id=278 (accessed 10 March 2010).

[32] Ibid.

[33] Scott Shafer, "A City in Recovery: Vallejo After Bankruptcy," *The California Report*, March 2013.

[34] PNJ Video, "California, Hooker Capital?" Available at https://www.youtube.com/watch?v=OlUi-aq_z_s (accessed, January 23, 2015).

[35] Eva Bernardes, "Issues of Client of Global Success Center." Interviewed by the author, Mare Island, Vallejo, CA, April 20, 2014.

became the first city in California to declare economic bankruptcy.

The Lord's Fellowship Church, one of Vallejo's Pentecostal churches, is comprised of Filipinos, Caucasians, African-Americans, Hispanics, and Africans.[36] It is known locally for its engagement in the city's spiritual, social, economic, ecological, and political well-being. Founders of the church, Rey and Eva Bernardes, were products of migration, coming to the U.S. in the 1960s. After finishing high school in 1973, young Rey enlisted in the military. While serving, he became a Christian and felt called to enter Bible college.

After getting married and graduating from Bethany University in 1981, the Bernardeses started serving as assistant pastors, began home Bible studies among white Catholics, and ministered to the poor and homeless people in Mare Island, Vallejo. Through their home fellowship meetings, the couple pioneered the Lord's Fellowship Church and then the Christian Help Center, a non-government organization designed to help the city's homeless people. At the outset, the LFC and CHC rented commercial spaces both to house the new congregation and to provide temporary shelter for the homeless. Receiving a grant of $16,000 in 1983 from Mayor Curtola of Vallejo City, the CHC's rented space was renovated to create six bedrooms in order to house homeless people, even though the church continued renting its space from the First Assembly of God in Vallejo.

In 1986, as the LFC grew in numbers, it was able to rent a separate worship center and expand the CHC to 20 beds and a year later to 30 beds plus purchase its own property—a $300,000 facility in the middle of town. The church's growing social outreach resulted in more and more attendees, who were attracted to the ministry of the CHC. Then in 1989, the LFC bought a $350,000 church sanctuary that accommodated a congregation of 200. (This facility was sold in 2001 in order to transfer to its present location in Mare Island.)

---

[36] Isaac Olivarez, "Christian Help Center: A Home for the Homeless and More," *Pentecostal Evangel*, July 27, 2003. 28-29.

In 1996, the CHC was able to expand its shelter ministries to 60 beds, thanks to a $350,000 grant from Vallejo mayor Gloria Exline. The next year, the LFC received a further grant of $150,000 from the Department of Housing and Urban Development to build a center to house young people coming from foster homes and to provide character building and job referrals. Presently, the CHC is being further renovated due to a total of $1.88 million in grants, $1 million from the State of California and $880,000 from the US Federal Home Loan Bank.

In 2002, with a $1.4 million grant from the U.S. Department of Housing and Urban Development, the LFC acquired a former bar-dance hall, which they transformed into the Reynaissance Family Center (RFC) to address the needs of people with disabilities and to house victims of domestic violence. The church had prayed for fifteen years to acquire this property; as a result, the owner was converted to Christianity and sold the facility to the church. Operational since 2007 and still receiving funds from the government and other entities, the now sixteen bed RFC has provided housing for numerous domestic violence victims and has served ninety-five families of children with disabilities. Also, the LFC started in 2006 the Global Success Center (GSC) to offer life and job skills training for the unemployed, the church members donating some $100,000 to this particular outreach venture.

Doctrine and Practice of Engagement in the Public Life

The role of faith-based organizations in addressing the social blight of the poor has a strong theological basis to which Pentecostals must adhere. Pentecostal ministers like Rey and Eva Bernardes believe that the Holy Spirit, who was at work in the prophets and leaders in the Old Testament (OT) and then resident in Jesus to fulfill his messianic mission, was also transferred to the eschatological people of God to continue that mission. This empowerment enables Christian believers to proclaim the Good News to the poor while confronting the systemic evils that victimize the poor in their search for social justice and equality.[37] Quoting the Chalmers Center for Economic Development, the Bernardeses point out that in order to help the poor, "We need to have a biblically consistent framework which conceives of poverty as being rooted in the effects of the fall on the four foundational relationships that God established for each person: relationships with God, self, others, and creation."[38]

In their search to address the complex nature of poverty in Vallejo, the Bernardeses believe that "development" can be a powerful tool to reconcile relationships that manifest themselves at the spiritual, individual, community, national, and international levels.[39] It was from these challenges that the Lord's Fellowship Church and its social ministry arm—the Christian Help Center—was started so as to provide food and shelter for the homeless in Vallejo.[40] Rey said, "Helping one person helps one family."[41] It was from this community involvement that the church's members discovered for themselves the importance of serving the poor. Out of their obedience to the command of Jesus to love God and love their neighbors, they began ministering to the poor, the homeless, and other most vulnerable people in the community.

The LFC's pastors, staff, and members start each ministry day with casual greetings, welcoming new visitors, and sharing various struggles and prayers. After this, they read some Psalms and pray individually, expressing their worship in a personal way and then praying for those needs that arise from the socio-economic and political realities of the city of Vallejo. Lastly, they discuss issues of injustice and the flesh-and-blood struggles of the people they minister to and how to best help them. In the Sunday and midweek services, the members not only zealously

---

[37]Rey Bernardes, "The Role of Christian NGOs in Building a Just and Loving Society," February 16, 2013, Lecture at GMC Chapel, Asia Pacific Theological Seminary, Baguio City, Philippines.

[38]Ibid. See also The Chalmers Center for Economic Development, "Poverty Is About Broken Relationship." Available at www.chalmers.org (accessed January 21, 2015).

[39]Ibid. See also Steve Corbett, "Helping Without Hurting," the Chalmers Center for Economic Development. Available at www.chalmers.org (accessed January 21, 2015).

[40]Ibid.

[41]Ibid.

study the Bible, but also incorporate social issues in their discussions of public life. They are open to address family issues and problems they themselves are encountering, not only discussing them, but also confronting them with prayer and participation.

The political participation of the Lord's Fellowship Church is known for its active engagement in praying for Vallejo's political leaders and its participation in those civic programs that promote justice and equality. In 2012, it began sponsoring a prayer breakfast for local political, civic, and non-governmental organization leaders. This annual event has drawn the attention of these leaders to look closely at the community engagement potential of faith-based organizations and has led to their willingness to support and partner with the LFC's various programs and services.

Also known for its concern about ecological preservation and care for the earth, the church manages the Vallejo People's Garden (VPG), a 122-square-meter lot near the church, which is aimed at encouraging organic farming in order "to provide healthy food to low income and homeless people."[42] The project's goal is to promote the growing of organic vegetables in the city's many open areas and empty lots. The LFC, along with the participating volunteers from the community, grow these vegetables using compost as organic fertilizers for the garden. Established as a way of connecting with and building relationships, the VPG has served as a bridge to attract people and to make the church relevant in the community.

Social Networks and Partners

The Lord's Fellowship Church's faith-based NGOs, with their network of social engagement, are constant partners with the city of Vallejo and the Solano area in the religious, academic, economic and political arenas. For example, the church

---

[42]Sarah Rohrs, "Online Votes May Provide Seed Money for City Garden," *Times Herald*, June 6, 2010.

regularly sponsors ecumenical and political dialogues on issues and concerns of the local citizens; while its Global Success Center, partnering with Touro University, provides supportive human services to the homeless and needy. Melessa Belec, a GSC volunteer and medical student at Touro, provides this reflection on the increasing social network and volunteerism of NGOs in Vallejo, like the GSC:

> One of the things about Vallejo that I really appreciate is that everybody comes from a lot of different backgrounds, is able to set apart their differences and work toward a common goal. We might disagree about this thing and we might slightly disagree on this other political thing, but at the end of the day, everybody who's involved with the garden says, 'There's not enough access to healthy food. I want to work on that together even if we disagree about these other things.' In a lot of other places I've been, people have not been able to do that. I think that that's the coolest thing about Vallejo.[43]

GSC executive director Elvie De Leon acknowledges that the success of the local NGOs come partly through their collective partnerships with other social organizations like the Southern Solano Alcohol Council, Catholic Social Services of Solano County, and CHC.[44]

Continuum of Care

The Global Success Center teaches life skills, focusing on personal growth, communication, achievement, and employment in the global community. It is committed to behavioral and lifestyle success in terms that are broader rather than merely a

---

[43]Dianne De Guzman, "Vallejo Medical Student Works to Keep Residents Healthy," *Times-Herald News*, January 19, 2015.

[44]Elvie De Leon, "Global Success Center: A Journey from Corporate to the Non-Profit Sector," *Examiner*, April 17, 2010. Available at www.examiner.com/article/global-center-for-success-getting-bigger-one-shoe-at-a-time (accessed January 23, 2015).

financial measure. Further, it exhibits a high respect for those seeking help and conducts itself in a manner that is not only legal but also fair and morally correct. Rey Bernardes pointed out that, "We are trying to address the overall picture of a person's life. Homelessness is a mufti-dimensional issue. It could be marriage issue, an emotional issue, money management, literacy, or a lack of skills."[45]

The GSC's assistance starts with experienced case managers conducting assessment interviews to determine their clients' need for supportive services. The clients then attend training classes and support groups for a period of two to three weeks.[46] Upon completion of the required classes and support group participation, they receive a certificate of completion at ceremonies held throughout the year at Mare Island. In 2005, out of 431 unduplicated clients served, seventy-four graduated from the program.[47]

The GSC was given an award in March 2012 by the office of the mayor of Vallejo City for its efforts to improve the quality of life by providing housing and food for the homeless and disabled through the Christian Help Center and Reynaissance Family Center. It also provides clothing, educational and health care support, and job readiness programs for the unemployed. These three faith-based entities work to close the "gap of need" of their clients.

The GSC collaborates with other faith-based organizations to identify issues of concern in the community. One goal of this effort is to unite the body of Christ to become a practical expression of Jesus to the most vulnerable people and to serve as a witness to the community. It also facilitates a Mayor's Breakfast for political and religious leaders in order to strengthen

---

[45] Rey Bernardes, Interviewed by the author, April 22, 2014, Mare Island, Vallejo, CA.

[46] Anonymous, "Global Center Upgrades on Mare Island Allow School to Offer More Classes," Vallejo Forum, November 27, 2011. Available at www.topix.com/forum/city/vallejo-ca/ TDEK64PEA3FS08ML5, (accessed January 23, 2015).

[47] Elvie De Leon, "Global Center for Success," Interview by the author, April 21, 2014, Mare Island, Vallejo City, CA. For the overview of the program and advocacy of GSC, see www.youtube.com/watch?v=0g8 YFysY2mo. (Accessed January 23, 2015).

the cohesion and solidarity between these leaders and Christian organizations.

Community Impact

The Lord's Fellowship Church and its related faith-based NGOs have been instrumental not only in proclaiming the Good News to the underprivileged, but also in serving as agents of social justice and equality.

The Christian Help Center is known throughout the city of Vallejo as a key provider of housing for the homeless. Statistics provided by its administrative staff show that, in some thirty years of operation, it has housed 26,200 homeless, served over one million meals to the hungry, clothed 250,000 of Vallejo's poor, and helped find employment for 35-40% of those who graduated from the GSC.[48]

The Reynaissance Family Center, recognized by the U.S. Internal Revenue Service as a charitable organization, is known for its advocacy for the victims of domestic violence. Over the last eight years, it has helped at least 100 families to cope with disabilities. In addition, in collaboration with the CHC and GSC, the RFC provides to its residents such services as case management, counseling, computer literacy, General Educational Development (GED) preparation, recovery support, parenting classes, and spiritual support. Former resident Ruth Watkins, now of Sacramento, CA, testified:

> Once again I returned back to the Christian Center with my husband and I brought my shattered pieces of life with me. We were accepted into the shelter and given 30 days to do the best we could do with what we had. I still remember until this day one of the helpers saying each and every day, 'you only have 30 days'. This stuck in our heads all the way up until our 30 days were up and on that 30 day mark the door of the Reynaissance Center were open. We became tenants and assistant

---

[48]Ibid.

managers at the Reynaissance Center where we continued to stay on for 10 months . . . we moved back to Sacramento where we are currently on-site managers at the apartment complex we live.[49]

The Global Success Center has become instrumental in the creation of jobs and life-skills development that have resulted in productive citizens in the city of Vallejo. Through these efforts, it has bettered the lives of many of the poor by fostering in them the character formation and changes that helped make the difference.[50] In 2012, Osby Davis, the mayor of Vallejo, in honoring the Lord Fellowship Church as the Faith-Based Community Volunteer of the Year, said:

> In recognition of your consistent and dedicated effort to improve the quality of life for citizens of Vallejo by providing housing and food for the homeless and disabled through the Christian Help Center and Reynaissance Family Center, clothing, educational and health care support, through job readiness programs for the unemployed through the Global Center for Success for those who are most vulnerable and in need. Thank you for your compassion, generosity and commitment to improving the quality of life of all Vallejoans. We are better city because of your willingness to fill the "Gap of Need." Thank you on behalf of the City of Vallejo, the Vallejo City Council and myself. Your efforts make a difference in the lives of so many of the citizens of Vallejo.[51]

The impacts and influence of these faith-based organizations were both noted and "seconded" by the community's other

---

[49]Ruth Watkins, "Reflection on the Impact of Christian Help Center," Working Brochure of CHC, 2008.

[50]Rey Bernardes, "Community Impact of TLF and Its Ministries," Interviewed by the author, Los Angeles, CA, April 4, 2014.

[51]Osby Davis, "Mayor's Faith-Based Community Volunteer-of-the-Year Award," City of Vallejo, November 16, 2012.

social entities who have long recognized their efforts in helping to build a just society.[52] (Sadly, some "fake" organizations have tried to use faith-based NGOs like GSC to recruit and raise support from the people of Vallejo.[53])

Assessment of the Organizational Issues and Benchmarks for Success

In order to assess the organizational issues that impact and define the ministry effectiveness of the CHC, RFC, and GSC, the author elicited responses from the 15 persons who run and/or otherwise serve these entities. The following are their responses from which, upon analysis, are used to identify the benchmarks for success.

Issue 1. Regarding organizational mission, nine of the fifteen staff members strongly agreed and six agreed that each of the entities has a sharply focused and clear mission statement, that they personally are deeply committed to these organizations and that their "calling" is being fulfilled in working within these ministries. A number of staffers, however, did express the importance of "revisiting" the mission statements at least every two years.

Issue 2. As to the challenges and needs of the community they are serving, the staff was asked if there was a system of addressing these needs and tracking the community's shifting demographics. *Responses.* Ten strongly agreed and five agreed that the LFC's three NGOs not only have a clear picture of those needs, but also the staff themselves have developed a system of addressing the complex issues of their clients.

Issue 3. Assuming that running an organization is to be a collective partnership and a product of team effort, the staffers

---

[52]Mare Island Health and Fitness Academy, "Full-Service Community." Available at http://mihfa-vcusd-ca.schoolloop.com/FSC, (Accessed January 23, 2015). See also Recology Vallejo, "Global Success," *Recology Newsletter*, April 26, 2014. Available at www.recologyvallejo.com/pdf/vallejo_views_commercial_ summer_2014.pdf (accessed January 23, 2015).

[53]A Concerned Vallejo Citizen, "Presence of the H. Marting Foundation in Vallejo...Stealing Our Identity," October 15, 2009. Available at http://ibvallejo.com/docs/concerned.pdf. (accessed January 23, 2015).

were asked if leadership and responsibilities are being shared. *Responses.* Nine strongly agreed and six agreed that leadership within these organizations is, in fact, a team effort; eight strongly agreed and seven agreed that leadership demonstrates its commitment to building effective teams; nine strongly agree that the leadership team is informed, engaged, and interested in sharing leadership responsibilities in the organizations; nine strongly agreed and six agreed that the team has the capacity to make an outstanding contribution to the organization; and eight strongly agreed and six agreed that they are free to disagree with the leadership.

Issue 4. Assuming that shared vision is important to developing cohesiveness and solidarity within the organization, staff was asked if they are collectively part of the vision of their organizations. *Responses.* Seven strongly agreed and eight agreed that they share a common vision; seven strongly agreed and eight agreed that each person can describe the future impacts of their particular organization; ten strongly agreed and five agreed that they are enthusiastic about their organization's future; nine strongly agreed and five agreed that their vision is becoming clearer and attainable; and seven strongly agreed and five agreed that people outside their organizations are aware and familiar with their vision.

Issue 5. Assuming that designing a program within the organization is pivotal in encouraging staff and volunteers to work for the common goal, staff was asked if their roles and responsibilities are clear. *Responses.* Eight strongly agreed and seven agreed that organizational roles, authorities, and responsibilities are clear; seven strongly agreed that they know what they are supposed to do and eight of them agreed that they know what they are doing; eight strongly agreed and seven agreed that their organization supports each person with the necessary resources; ten strongly agreed and five agreed that all programs fulfill their organization's mission; and seven strongly agreed and eight agreed that their organization's structure supports clear communication and role delineation.

Issue 6. Assuming that evaluating program performance is not only necessary but also provides feedback helpful to running a faith-based entity to its full potential, staff was asked if their organizations have effective measures for each person's performance evaluation. *Responses.* Fourteen strongly agreed that effectiveness is measured by the performance of the person through evaluation; eight strongly agreed and seven agreed that clear and reasonable goals and objectives have been established; nine strongly agreed and six agreed that their gifts and talents are matched with program opportunities; and eight strongly agreed and seven agreed that people are affirmed for their performance.

Issue 7. Staff was asked if they believe in the effectiveness of their programs. *Responses.* Eight strongly agreed and seven agreed that they can measure the degree of effectiveness; five strongly agreed and ten agreed that often they make changes to their programs due to feedback from those whom they served; ten of them recognize the importance of collecting information from the clients to know if they are being effective; and five also believe that the inputs of the staff members are important for measuring their effectivity.

Issue 8. Assuming program efficiency is also a factor in measuring an organization's success, staff was asked if their feedback is sought from the management on how their entity's planning and budgeting processes might be improved. *Responses.* Nine strongly agreed and six agreed that taking feedback seriously can benefit the budgeting process (in fact, many suggested "participatory budgeting"); eight strongly agreed and seven agreed that their financial report, which is published on each organization's website, is accurate and provides an adequate picture; eight strongly agreed and seven agreed that checks-and-balances are in place to ensure that the staff members are being good stewards of the organizational resources; and nine of the staff strongly agreed that, to ensure transparency, they frequently compare their programs with other organizations in terms of cost-benefit analysis.

Conclusions

Rarely do we find Pentecostal churches who are heavily involved in the public square, but rather they, along with many faith-based organizations, remain on the sideline of social and political engagement. The model of the Lord's Fellowship Church and its charitable NGOs demonstrates the fact that religious entities, when aligned and seeking partnership with other social organizations can be instrumental in advancing the common good and social justice. The ability of faith-based NGOs to be agents of change when it comes to such issues as homelessness, domestic violence, and economic poverty serves as signposts that "religion" can be a vital prayer in creating a better society. Advocacy by these organizations should be fueled by their conviction that our God is a God of hope and thus that they are mandated to translate their love for God into loving their neighbors.

Bibliography

A Concerned Vallejo Citizen. "The Presence of the H. Marting Foundation in Vallejo . . . Stealing our Identity," October 15, 2009, Available at http://ibvallejo.com/docs/concerned.pdf (Accessed January 23, 2015).

Anonymous. "Global Center Upgrades on Mare Island Allow School to Offer More Classes," Vallejo Forum, November 27, 2011, Available at http://www.topix.com/forum/city/vallejo-ca/TDEK64PEA3FS08ML5 (Accessed January 23, 2015).

Bernardes, Eva. "Issues of Client of Global Success Center" Interview by the author, Mare Island, Vallejo, California, April 20, 2014.

Bernardes, Rey. Interview by the author, April 22, 2014, Mare Island, Vallejo City, CA.

_____. "The Role of Christian NGOs in Building a Just and Loving Society," February 16, 2013, Lecture at GMC Chapel, Asia Pacific Theological Seminary, Baguio City.

_____. "Community Impact of TLF and Its Ministries," Interview by the author, Los Angeles, California, April 4, 2014.

_____. "Global Center for Success," Interview by the author, April 21, 2014, Mare Island, Vallejo City, California. For the overview of the program and advocacy of GSC, see https://www.youtube.com/watch?v=0g8YFysY2mo (Accessed, January 23, 2015).

Brooks, Arthur C. "Religious Faith and Charitable Giving," *Policy Review* 121 (October-November 2003): 1-13.

Centre for Development Enterprise. "Untapped Social Capital Burgeoning under the Radar," *CDE*, March 12, 2008; available at: http://www.cde.org.za/article.php?a_id=278 (Accessed 10 March 2010).

Cnaan, Ram A., Stephanie C. Boddie and Gaynor I. Yancey. "Bowling Alone But Serving Together: The Congregational Norm of Community Involvement," in Corwin Smidt, ed. *Religious Social Capital: Producing the Common Good*, Waco, TX: Baylor University Press, 2003.

Corbett, Steve. "Helping without Hurting," The Chalmers Center for Economic Development, Available at www.chalmers.org (Accessed, January 21, 2015).

Davis, Osby. "Mayor's Faith Based Community Volunteer of the Year Award" City of Vallejo, 16th of November, 2012.

De Guzman, Dianne. "Vallejo Medical Student Works to Keep Residents Healthy," *Times-Herald News*, January 19, 2015.

De Leon, Elvie. "Global Success Center: A Journey from Corporate to the Non-Profit Sector," *Examiner*, April 17, 2010 Available at http://www.examiner.com/article/global-center-for-success-getting-bigger-one-shoe-at-a-time (Accessed, January 23, 2015).

Dougherty, Kevin D. et al. "Sideline by Religion: Community Involvement and Political Participation of U.S. Pentecostals," Paper presented at 2009 Symposium on Religion and Politics (Department of Sociology: Baylor University, May 12, 2009), 3, 15; available from: http://search.yahoo.com/

search?fr=msgr-buddy&ei=UTF-8&p=Sideline%20by%20Religion (Accessed 10 March 2010).

Fagan, Patrick F. "Why Religion Matters Even More: The Impact of Religious Practice on Social Responsibility," Richard and Helen DeVos Center for Religion and Civil Society, *Heritage Foundation*, December 18,2006; Available at heritage.org (Accessed, September 4, 2014).

Greeley, Andrew. "Coleman Revisited: Religious Structures as a Source of Social Capital," *American Behavioral Scientist*, Vol. 40, Number 5 (March 1997):587-94.

Goschin, Zizi., Constantin, Daniela-Luminita and Roman, Monica "The Partnership between the State and the Church against Trafficking in Person," *Journal for the Study of Religions and Ideologies*, Vol. 8, No. 24 (2009): 231-256.

Heyer, Kristin. "US Catholic Discipleship and Citizenship: Patriotism or Dissent? *Political Theology*, May 2003, Vol. 4. Issue 2: 149-175.

Kim, Sebastian. *Theology in the Public Sphere: Public Theology as a Catalyst for Open Debate*. London: SCM Press, 2011.

Kwak, Nojink., Dhiavan V. Shah and Holbert R Lance, "Connecting, Trusting, and Participating: The Direct and Interactive Effects of Social Associations," *Political Research Quarterly* 57, No. 4 (December 2004): 643-652.

Levin, Jeff . "Religious Behavior, Health, and Well Being among Israeli Jews: Findings from the European Social Survey," *Psychology of Religion and Spirituality*, (November 2013):1-11.

Mare Island Health and Fitness Academy. "Full Service Community," Available at https://mihfa-vcusd-ca.schoolloop.com/FSC (Accessed, January 23, 2015). See also, Recology Vallejo, "Global Success," *Recology Newsletter*, Summer (April 26, 2014). Available at http://www.recologyvallejo.com/pdf/vallejo_views_commercial_summer_2014.pdf (Accessed January 23, 2015).

McLeod, Donald. "The Church in the Public Sphere," Belfast, Ireland, January 30, 2014.

Miller, Donald and Tetsunao Yamamori. *Global Pentecostalism: The New Face of Christian Social Engagement*, Berkley, Los Angeles, London: University of California Press, 2007.

Nagel, Alexander Kenneth. "Charitable Choice: The Religious Component of US-Welfare-Reform-Theoretical and Methodological Reflections on Faith Based Organizations as Social Services" *Numen-international Review for The History of Religions*, vol. 53, no. 1 (2006): 78-111.

O'Brien, David J. *From the Heart of the American Church: Catholic Higher Education and American Culture* Maryknoll, NY: Orbis Books, 1992.

ORO, Ari Pedro. "Religious Politicians" and "Secular Politicians" in Southern Brazil, *Social Compass* 2007; 54; 583; available from http://scp.sagepub.com/cgi/content/abstract/54/4/583 (Accessed 10 March 2010; Ahn Bersten. "Pentecostalism in South Africa and its Potential Social and Economic Role," A Comprehensive Research Report of Centre for Development and Enterprise (Johannesburg, South Africa, March 2008) available from http://search.yahoo.com/search:_ylt=A0oGkxVDkZdLweYAZZFXNyoA?p=Under+the+Radar%3A+Pentecostalism+in+South+A (Accessed 10 March 2010).

Olivarez, Isaac. "Christian Help Center: A Home for the Homeless and More" *Pentecostal Evangel*, July 27, 2003. 28-29.

Pentecostal and Charismatic Research Initiative. "Research Questions" *University of Southern California*, available from http://crcc.usc.edu/initiatives/pcri/ (Accessed 05 February 2010.

Petersen, Douglas and Magali Negron Gil. "Pentecostals and Social Capital in Nicaragua and Costa Rica," Unpublished Paper, Judkins Institute for Leadership Studies, Vanguard University of Southern California, Costa Mesa, CA.

PNJ Video, "California, Hooker Capital? Available at https://www.youtube.com/watch?v=OlUi-aq_z_s (Accessed January 23, 2015).

Putnam, Robert and David Campbell. *American Grace: How Religion Is Reshaping Our Civic and Political Lives,* (2010), 444.

____.and Lewis L. Feldten with Don Cohen. "Religion and Social Capital" in *Better Together: Restoring the American Community,* New York: Simon & Schuster, 2003.

Regnerus, Mark D., Christian Smith and David Sikkink. "Who Gives to the Poor? The Influence of Religious Tradition and Political location on the Personal Generosity of Americans toward the Poor," *Journal for the Scientific Study of Religion* 37, No. 3 (September 1998): 481-493.

Rohrs, Sarah. "Online Votes May Provide Seed Money for City Garden," *Times Herald,* Sunday June 6, 2010.

Schwadel, Philip. "Individual, Congregational, and Denominational Effects on Church Members Civic Participation," *Journal of the Scientific Study of Religion* 44, No. 2 (June 2005):159-171.

Shafer, Scott. "A City in Recovery: Vallejo after Bankruptcy," *The California Report,* March 22-24, 2013.

Smidt, Corwin. ed. *Religious Social Capital: Producing the Common Good,* Waco, TX: Baylor University Press, 2003.

The Chalmers Center for Economic Development. "Poverty is about Broken Relationship," Available at www.chalmers.org (Accessed January 21, 2015).

Tolbert, Charles M., Thomas A. Lyson and Michael D. Erwin. "Local Capital, Civic Engagement and Socioeconomic Well-Being," *Social Forces* Dec 98, Vol. 77 Issue 2: 401-427.

Warner, S.R. "Work in Progress toward a New Paradigm for the Sociological Study of Religion in the United States. *American Journal of Sociology* (98:10)44-93.

Welch, Michael R., David Sikkink, Eric Sartain and Carolyn Bond, "Trust in God and Trust in Man: The Ambivalent Role of Religion in Shaping Dimensions of Social Trust," *Journal for the Scientific Study of Religion* 43, No. 3 (September 2004): 317-343.

World Council of Churches. "Increased Partnership Between Faith-Based Organizations, Government and Intra-Government Organizations," Statement by Faith-Based Organizations Facilitated by World Council of Churches for the UN Special General Assembly on HIV/AIDS June 25-27, 2001. International Review of Mission, Vol. XC No. 359 Available at http://web.a.ebscohost.com/ehost/pdfviewer/pdfviewer?vid =3&sid=547b2338-7ad5-4af4-a194-0f6b3168ab86%40sessionmgr4001&hid=4214 (Accessed September 4, 2014).

Wuthnow, R. "*The Restructuring of American Religion: Society and Faith Since World War II*, Princeton, NJ: Princeton University Press, 1988.

APTS Press Monograph Series Book 3 — New from APTS Press

UNDERSTANDING THE IGLESIA NI CRISTO

What They Really Believe and How They Can Be Reached

ANNE C. HARPER

A Theology of the Spirit in Doctrine and Demonstration

Essays in Honor of Wonsuk and Julie Ma

Edited by
Teresa Chai

APTS Press Monograph Series Book 1

Theology in Context

In this book, Dave Johnson discusses a biblical response to Folk Catholicism in the Philippines. Specific topics include what the Bible says about:
- All Saint's Day and the dead returning to their gravesites
- How Filipinos have been transformed by the power of God within their own cultural setting
- Praying to Mary and the saints
- Demon Possession
- Town Fiestas
- Sickness and Healing
- And much more!

About the Author

Dave Johnson, D.Miss. has been an Assemblies of God (USA) missionary to the Philippines since 1994 and has conducted extensive research on lowland Filipino culture. He is also the author of *Led by the Spirit: The History of the American Assemblies of God Missionaries in the Philippines* and is the managing editor of the *Asian Journal of Pentecostal Studies*, the theological journal of the Asia Pacific Theological Seminary in Baguio City, Philippines. He can be contacted at www.apts.edu or through his own website, www.daveanddebbiejohnson.com.

Now available at:

ICI Ministries
2909 Raffles Corp. Center
Emerald Ave., Ortigas Center
Pasig City
Tel. (632) 914 9800

ICI Distribution Center, Valenzuela
BBC Compound, Gov. I Santiago St.
Malinta, Valenzuela City
Tel. (632) 292-8509/
294-6137/444-9139

APTS Bookstore
444 Ambuklao Road

APTS Press Monograph Series Book 2

LEAVE A LEGACY
Increasing Missionary Longevity

Russ Turney

In this second volume of the new APTS Press Monograph Series, Dr. Russ Turney presents a compelling case study of why some missionaries leave the field far too soon. Normal attrition occurs because of health problems, retirement, or the obvious call of God to go elsewhere. However, Turney notes that far too often missionaries leave due to interpersonal conflicts with their colleagues or nationals, problems with authority and other issues that, Turney contends, could be significantly reduced. He then presents an excellent strategy for dealing with these and other issues, enabling missionaries to continue in their calling long term and finish well.

This strategy will help equip not only missionaries and mission leaders from both the West and the Majority World, but also pastors and church members who love and support missionaries and who want to learn how to strengthen them better through prayer and action. Anyone who shares the warm hearted conviction that missionaries can and should leave a legacy will benefit from this book.

Now available at: **Jet Bookstore**   **ICI Bookstore**

A HISTORY AND COMPONENTS
OF PENTECOSTAL THEOLOGICAL EDUCATION[1]
by Paul W. Lewis

The role of theological education for ministers has been a major point of discussion for centuries within the church. Since the advent of the modern Pentecostal movement over a hundred years ago, this topic has been typified by various positions and, at times, analytical neglect.[2] More often than not, a philosophy of theological education was presupposed or assumed without examination or scrutiny. The endeavor to either analyze previous philosophies of Pentecostal theological

---

[1] This essay is a revised version of my earlier essay, Paul Lewis "Explorations in Pentecostal Theological Education" *Asian Journal of Pentecostal Studies* 10 No. 2 (2007), 161-176 (used by permission); and a portion of this essay was in an earlier form, Paul Lewis, "Some Theological Considerations on Pentecostal Theological Education," in *Reflections on Developing Asian Pentecostal Leaders: Essays in Honor of Harold Kohl,* ed. A. Kay Fountain (Baguio, Philippines: APTS Press, 2004), 305-321. It is also strongly dependent on Paul Lewis, "Reflections on a Hundred Years of Pentecostal Theology," *Cyberjournal of Pentecostal-Charismatic Research* 12 (2003).

[2] For a look at the changes of Pentecostal theology and theological education over the last century see M. Paul Brooks, "Bible Colleges and the Expansion of the Pentecostal Movement," *Paraclete* 23 No. 2 (1989), 9-17; Jeffrey Hittenberger, "Toward a Pentecostal Philosophy of Education," *Pneuma* 23 No. 2 (2001), 217-44; idem., "Education," in *Encyclopedia of Pentecostal and Charismatic Christianity,* ed. Stanley Burgess (New York, NY: Routledge, 2006), 158-162; Paul Lewis, "Reflections on a Hundred Years of Pentecostal Theology," *Cyberjournal of Pentecostal-Charismatic Research* 12 (2003); Wonsuk Ma, "Biblical Studies in the Pentecostal Tradition: Yesterday, Today, and Tomorrow," in *The Globalization of Pentecostalism,* eds. Murray Dempster, Byron Klaus and Douglas Petersen (Irvine, CA: Regnum Press, 1999), 52-69; Frank Macchia, "The Struggle of Global Witness: Shifting Paradigms in Pentecostal Theology," in *The Globalization of Pentecostalism,* 8-29; and Lewis Wilson, "Bible Institutes, Colleges, Universities," in *Dictionary of Pentecostal and Charismatic Movements,* eds. Stanley Burgess and Gary McGee (Grand Rapids, MI: Zondervan, 1988), 57-65.

education or give a detailed proposal for such a philosophy is beyond the scope of this essay.[3] Rather, the goals are: first, to look at a brief history of Christian (and Pentecostal) theological education in general; next, to delineate some pertinent elements relating to the nature of theological education, especially in reference to Pentecostal theological education; and then to discuss issues relating to Pentecostal theological education and aspects of a model of theological understanding from a Pentecostal perspective, leading to appropriate conclusions.

In this essay, by "Pentecostal" I mean to refer to the modern (i.e., Classical) Pentecostal movement. As such, it includes all of those elements of that tradition which express themselves as part of the Pentecostal tradition.[4] Meanwhile, this does not exclude the applicability of these same ideas or implications to other branches of Orthodox Christianity.

By "theological education," I am referring to formal institutions of higher education whose purpose is providing ministerial and/or church lay-person training for ministry. This does not mean to imply anything related to non-formal or informal education, to Christian education in other venues (e.g., Christian liberal arts colleges)[5], or to prior education levels. The focus here is on the intentional training of persons for the growth in and work of the Lord, whether for potential ordained ministers or informed lay persons. Further, I am focusing mainly

---

[3] On this, see Jeffrey Hittenberger, "Toward a Pentecostal Philosophy of Education," *Pneuma* 23 No. 2 (2001), 217-44, and the issue dedicated to the topic, "Pentecostal Education," *Asian Journal of Pentecostal Studies* 3 No. 2 (2000).

[4] have described this (as a "Pentecostal paradigm") in more detail elsewhere; see Paul Lewis, "The Baptism in the Holy Spirit as Paradigm Shift" *Asian Journal of Pentecostal Studies* 13 No. 2 (2010), 301-344; and idem., "Toward a Pentecostal Epistemology: The Role of Experience in Pentecostal Hermeneutics," *The Spirit & Church*. 2 No. 1 (2000), 95-125. Three other helpful works along this line are: Simon Chan, *Pentecostal Theology and the Christian Spiritual Tradition*, Journal of Pentecostal Theology Supplement 21 (Sheffield, UK: Sheffield Academic Press, 2000); Stephen Land, *Pentecostal Spirituality*, Journal of Pentecostal Theology Supplement 1 (Sheffield: Sheffield Academic Press, 1994); and Douglas Petersen, "Pentecostals—Who Are They?" in *Missions as Transformation*, eds. Vinay Samuel and Chris Sugden (Oxford, UK: Regnum Press, 1999), 76-111.

[5] As emphasized in Arthur Holmes' monumental work, *The Idea of a Christian College*, rev. ed. (Grand Rapids: Eerdmans, 1987). But how this is played out has variations; see Robert Benne, *Quality with Soul: How Six Premier Colleges and Universities Keep Faith with their Religious Traditions* (Grand Rapids: 2001).

on the role of "accredited" Bible schools or seminary-level institutions. So, in this essay I will assume this understanding of theological education.⁶

A Brief History of Christian and Pentecostal Theological Education⁷

From the early church, the education of clergy originally embraced the Greek concept of *paideia* at its root. *Paideia* was an emphasis on character or personal formation, persons of *habitus* (habits of the heart). However, it was also tied to *arete* or virtue (e.g., Aristotle's *Nicomachean Ethics*), which was related to the *polis* or city-state. So the Greeks would be trained in Homer's classics (poetry) and athletics as well as in other traditions, culture, and literature. Within the early church, *paideia* was the foundational concept of education or training, with the goal being the formation of character, albeit the foundations of that formation were different (e.g., Christocentric).⁸ This was clearly articulated in the First Epistle to Rome by Clement and in the writings of Origen and the Cappadocian Fathers.⁹

The Reformation period, while following the *paideia* model of character formation, further emphasized the importance of *sola scriptura*. This, plus the Renaissance's influence of going

---

⁶This is not necessarily the standard perception by Pentecostals concerning theological education, see Brooks, "Bible Colleges and the Expansion of the Pentecostal Movement," 11-12; Macchia, "The Struggle of Global Witness," 9; and Wilson, "Bible Institutes, Colleges, Universities," 61.

⁷I would like to express my gratitude for the several pointers and insights on this section, especially related to the Reformation, by Dr. Gregory Miller of Malone University, Canton, OH, interviewed by author, July 5, 2007. For a helpful historical summary of the development of education that preceded the modern American model, see Christopher J. Lucas, *American Higher Education: A History*, 2nd ed. (New York: Palgrave Macmillan, 2006), 3-100.

⁸Werner Jaeger, *Early Christianity and Greek Paideia* (London, UK: Oxford University Press, 1961); idem., *Paideia: The Ideals of Greek Culture*, 3 vols. (New York, NY: Oxford University Press, 1939-63); David Kelsey, *Between Athens and Berlin* (Grand Rapids: Eerdmans, 1993), 6-11; and idem., *To Understand God Truly* (Louisville, KY: Westminster/John Knox Press, 1992), 64-72.

⁹Rowan Greer, "Who Seeks for a Spring in the Mud? Reflections on the Ordained Ministry in the Fourth Century," in *Theological Education and Moral Formation*, ed. Richard John Neuhaus (Grand Rapids: Eerdmans, 1992), 22-55; and Werner Jaeger, *Early Christianity and Greek Paideia* (London: Oxford University Press, 1961).

back to the original resources, laid the foundation by which a strong study of the Bible (particularly in the original languages) was necessary. The Word and the Spirit were coupled in that both are intertwined—the Word being understood/enabled by the Spirit and the Spirit being known through the Word while self-authenticating the Word (especially noted by John Calvin). Further, the belief in the "priesthood of all believers" had, and has, educational implications for all believers.[10] Thus, literacy and the Bible in the vernacular were condoned and emphasized; and the "calling" of those to vocation was broadened, although (at least for Huldrych Zwingli) the "calling" of the clergy was unique or special.[11] Thereby the training for those in ministry was deemed as necessary for learning the Bible (including the languages); and rhetoric, *contra* medieval emphasis on logic, was promoted in the guise of preaching.[12] Also due to the Reformers' criticisms of Roman Catholic priestly education, the Council of Trent of 1545-1563 mandated establishment of a seminary for clergy training in each diocese (or at least jointly between dioceses due to finances).[13]

---

[10]Noted in Alister McGrath, "Theological Education and Global Tertiary Education: Risks and Opportunities," *Journal of Adult Theological Education* 14 No. 2 (2006), 20; and highlighted within the Pentecostal perspective, see Miguel Alvarez, "Distinctives of Pentecostal Education" *Asian Journal of Pentecostal Studies* 3 No. 2 (2000), 281-93, especially 287-8, and Benjamin Sun, "The Holy Spirit: The Missing Key in the Implementation of the Doctrine of the Priesthood of Believers," in Wonsuk Ma and Robert Menzies, eds. *Pentecostalism in Context,* JPT Supplement Series 11 (Sheffield: Sheffield Academic Press, 1997), 173-94.

[11]Eric Gritsch, "Vocation," in *The Oxford Encyclopedia of the Reformation,* vol. 4 (Oxford: Oxford University Press, 1996), 245-6; Wolfgang Klausnitzer, "Ordination," in *The Oxford Encyclopedia of the Reformation,* vol. 3 (Oxford: Oxford University Press, 1996), 177-9; and J. Philip Wogaman, *Christian Ethics: A Historical Introduction* (Louisville, KY: Westminster/John Knox Press, 1993), 110-3, 120-2;.note that the evolution of the printing press likewise influenced literacy by providing cheap copies of books and the Bible in particular.

[12]Preaching with baptism and the Lord's Supper became part of the *de mediis salutis* (i.e., means of salvation), showing the elevation of preaching from the medieval Roman Catholic Church; see Jürgen Moltmann, *The Church in the Power of the Spirit,* trans, Margaret Kohl (San Francisco, CA: HarperCollins, 1991), 199-204.

[13]Especially noted by Dr. Gregory Miller, interviewed by author, July 5, 2007. A detailed account of the "nuts and bolts" of education in the Reformation period is by Jo Ann Hoeppner Moran (Cruz), "Education," in *The Oxford Encyclopedia of the Reformation,* ed. Hans Hillerbrand (Oxford: Oxford University Press, 1996), 19-28, esp. 24; note the importance of the Jesuits in this educational development.

Martin Luther, following the medieval tradition of *lectio divina* (or "divine reading"), noted the order of theological inquiry (highlighted in his work on Psalm 119), which should be instilled in the students. These are: *oratio, meditatio* and *tentati—oratio* (or "prayer") meaning an attentive listening; *meditatio* meaning a time of reflection, which includes questioning and judgments reached; and *tentatio* (or "wrestling") meaning the appropriation of those judgments in practice and life.[14] So there was the active participation of the learner in listening, reflection, and appropriating into practice as part of the learning process.

Initially through late Medieval Nominalism and later much more pronounced by Protestant Scholasticism and the Enlightenment, the study of theology became divorced from the study of spirituality. Thus, the study of theology was based on the idea "Theology [as] a science became linked to the belief that science could generate value-free knowledge. This pointed theology towards a position of isolation from context or personal feeling." [15] There became a bifurcation between "spirituality" as a discipline and "theology" itself. John Wesley, the Pietists (e.g., August Francke, Philip Spener), Jonathan Edwards, and their adherents were the notable exceptions, in that the study of Wesley's theology, for example, "is an exercise in daily practical spiritual maturation."[16] However, in Protestantism as a whole, "spirituality" became divorced from "theology" (especially where theological education took place), although Wesley *et al.* were interested with both the spiritual and practical sides of theology.

The next major change in theological education was inspired by the Napoleon conquest of Prussia. As a reaction to their

---

[14]Highlighted in Charles Wood, *An Invitation to Theological Study* (Valley Forge, PA: Trinity International Press, 1994), 7-8; and idem., *Vision and Discernment* (Eugene, OR: Wipf and Stock, 1985), 27-29.

[15]Philip Sheldrake, *Spirituality and Theology: Christian Living and the Doctrine of God* (Maryknoll, NY: Orbis Press, 1999), 45; see also Edward Farley, *Theologia: The Fragmentation and Unity of Theological Education* (Philadelphia, PA: Fortress Press, 1983), 34-48, which also highlights the difference between the University Divinity School and the Protestant Seminary.

[16]Thomas C. Oden, *John Wesley's Scriptural Christianity* (Grand Rapids: Zondervan, 1994), 21.

defeat, the Prussians sought to revamp their educational system. Friedrich Schleiermacher was one of the three-person committee constituted for the purpose of rethinking and reshaping the university system, in particular the University of Berlin. The realignment was to be more in the order of Enlightenment Principles—i.e., scientific method and rationalism. As such, Schleiermacher emphasized two elements of theological education. The first was the *wissenschaft* or the critical research of theology. So as a part of the university, the minister in his training must learn how to do research—methods, techniques, ordering, etc. Academic freedom was therefore of tantamount importance. The second element was that theological education must include "professional" training. In other words, the minister must learn the skills and have practical instruction in order to become a minister. So the minister would be trained professionally like the doctor or lawyer.[17]

For Pentecostal theological education history, the Bible school movement's emergence in the 1880s was very influential. It developed mainly through the instigation of D.L. Moody, A.B. Simpson, and others interested in education to emphasize social change and individual formation as well as to oppose "liberal" theology, which was perceived as happening in North American Protestant schools (especially seminaries). The main curriculum was the study of the Bible, which in the U.S. was in English, and the skills/abilities for evangelism and missions.[18] In the years 1910 through 1915, teachers wrote a collection of essays called *The Fundamentals: A Testimony to the Truth* (later simply *The Fundamentals*), with an emphasis on the basic beliefs of Christianity (e.g., the virgin birth of Christ, the bodily resurrection of Christ). The resulting theology tended to be reductionistic (and

---

[17]On Schleiermacher and his theological educational scheme, see Kelsey, *Between Athens and Berlin*, 12-19; Kelsey, *To Understand God Truly*, 78-100; and Wood, *Vision and Discernment*, 1-19.

[18]On this movement, see Virginia Lieson Brereton, *Training God's Army: The American Bible School, 1880-1940* (Bloomington, IN: Indiana University Press, 1990); and Richard Flory, "Bible Schools," in *Encyclopedia of Fundamentalism*, ed. Brenda Brasher (New York: Routledge, 2006), 57-61. For a broader understanding of higher education in the U.S., see Lucas, *American Higher Education*, 103-283.

dispensational).[19] Thus, within these theological institutions, *The Fundamentals* and related textbooks were taught, and the theology articulated in the classroom was a summation of doctrinal statements with no emphasis on analysis.[20]

Pentecostals such as the Assemblies of God (AG) USA followed the Bible school movement. The Missionary Training Institute, established by A.B. Simpson in Nyack, New York, was the *alma mater* of many key early leaders of the AG in the U.S., such as Frank M. Boyd and William I. Evans, and overseas in the missionary work of such men as Victor Plymire and W.W. Simpson.[21] Following in the footsteps of the Bible schools movement, the Pentecostal Bible schools tended to emphasize both short-term training anywhere up to two years (partially for eschatological reasons) and pastoral (including church planting and evangelism) and missionary skills with Pentecostal spiritual life. Also, the tendency was to establish many smaller schools rather than a few key schools. Noteworthy was that, after a short time many of these schools were closed or merged with others. The training tended to be basic Pentecostal indoctrination; while ministerial training, personal formation, and education were collapsed into each other.[22] Further, from the strong influence of fundamentalism, the textbooks tended to be non-Pentecostal or even anti-Pentecostal, such as Henry Thiessen's *Lectures in Systematic Theology*. All of these traits were likewise transplanted overseas with missionary-instigated Bible schools.[23]

---

[19] Ronald Nash, *The New Evangelicalism* (Grand Rapids: Zondervan, 1963), 23-9; see also Flory, "Bible Schools," 57-9.

[20] Macchia, "The Struggle of Global Witness," 8-10; and Wilson, "Biblical Institutes, Colleges, Universities," 61.

[21] See Gary McGee, *This Gospel Shall Be Preached*, vol. 1 (Springfield, MO: Gospel Publishing House, 1986), 62-63; and C. Nienkirchen, "Christian and Missionary Alliance," in *Dictionary of Pentecostal and Charismatic Movements,* eds. Stanley Burgess and Gary McGee (Grand Rapids: Zondervan, 1988), 163-6.

[22] See Brooks, "Bible Colleges and the Expansion of the Pentecostal Movement," 11-18; Lewis, "Reflections on a Hundred Years of Pentecostal Theology"; and Wilson, "Bible Institutes, Colleges, Universities," 58-61.

[23] McGee noted the early development of Bible schools in the Assemblies of God missionary efforts; see McGee, *This Gospel Shall Be Preached*, vol. 1, 98, 140-141, 166-167, etc.; and idem., *This Gospel Shall Be Preached*, vol. 2 (Springfield: Gospel Publishing House, 1989), 34-37, etc. Naturally these missionaries would follow the models that they worked in and were familiar with.

Toward a Pentecostal Theological Educational Model

David Kelsey in his work, *Between Athens and Berlin*, has argued that there has developed a tension between the "scientific" (objective) and the "formative" (subjective) parts of theological inquiry and thus in theological education. This tension developed over the primacy of the formation element of theological education (ala *paideia* of Athens) compared to the *wissenschaft*/professional element (ala Berlin). As such, Kelsey further articulates that, since then, the major works on theological education have tended to lean toward either the "Athens" model or the "Berlin" model.[24] The question, "How might this tension be mediated?" is fundamentally tied to the question, "What is excellence in theological education?" How a school or person answers the latter will determine where they are on the Athens-Berlin continuum.[25]

From the Berlin model, which Edward Farley calls "the Encyclopedic Movement,"[26] is the articulation of the four-fold theological education curriculum model—Bible, theology, history, and practical theology. This has, Farley argues, led to the fragmentation of theological education and the distancing of theory from practice[27] and has created, or at least exacerbated, a bifurcation in schools between theology courses and ministry courses.

---

[24]See Kelsey, *Between Athens and Berlin* (Grand Rapids: Eerdmans, 1993). E.g. of 'Athens', see John Henry Newman, *The Idea of a University* (New York: Chelsea House, 1983); Edward Farley, *Theologia* (Philadelphia: Fortress Press, 1983); and idem., *The Fragility of Knowledge* (Philadelphia: Fortress Press, 1988). E.g. of 'Berlin', see Niebuhr, *The Purpose of the Church and its Ministry* (New York: Harper & Row, 1956). E.g. of an attempt of a synthesis, see Charles Wood, *Vision and Discernment*, and idem., *An Invitation to Theological Study*.

[25]A primary yet problematic question noted in Samuel Carnegie Calian, *The Ideal Seminary: Pursuing Excellence in Theological Education* (Louisville: Westminster John Knox Press, 2002), esp. 19-26.

[26]Farley, *Theologia*, 73-98.

[27]See Farley, *Theologia*; and idem., *The Fragility of Knowledge*, especially 104-106.

A History and Components of Pentecostal Theological Education

As to what a school of theology needs to provide, Charles Wood suggests that training needs to take place for the student in three areas—formation, understanding the faith, and equipping for ministry.[28] Formation is set up in the school for the purpose of *paideia* through such avenues as small groups, chapel, and the like. Understanding the faith is developed through the courses, readings, and conversations that should be indicative of the school. Equipping for ministry is the practical experience with supervision, which is important in a theological training situation. Further, Wood writes, "Theological education is something we do through the whole curriculum and through life together as a community."[29] The implications are the role of the community is dominant in theological education and curriculum is more than just a set of certain course offerings. Students in this setting should come to know themselves better, to know others and their hearts, and to understand and implement Christian faith and tradition.[30] Or as Virginia Samuel Cetuk notes:

> Theologically educated persons are in touch with societal trends and technology; have a thorough and intimate knowledge of themselves as thinking, feeling, embodied, and spiritual beings; and evidence deep and firm commitments to a faith tradition that is at once rooted in the past, relevant to the present, and linked to the future.[31]

One could say that the focus of theological education is to develop students' beliefs, skills, and attitudes. Whereas beliefs and skills take a predominate amount of curricular planning and development, attitudinal formation or transformation has been

---

[28] Wood, *Invitation to Theological Study*, 3.
[29] Ibid.
[30] Ibid., 16-19.
[31] Virginia Samuel Cetuk, *What to Expect in Seminary: Theological Education as Spiritual Formation* (Nashville, TN: Abingdon Press, 1998), 102.

noted but typically is less developed.[32] It is apparent that, while attitudes are the hardest to train or evaluate, frequently a school's reputation is dependent on the attitudes of its graduates (alumni). Further, since attitudes are more time-consuming to develop, the current move to shorten theological educational programs and create "fast track" systems can only be seen either as making allowances for those who do not need this formational guidance or that attitudinal development is not a priority at such schools.[33] So attitudinal training and formation, like belief and skill formation, must be intentional within the curriculum if an "Athens" model or a balanced model is to be implemented.[34]

The theological model noted here emphasizes a holistic approach to Christian life and, by implication, theological education. This approach incorporates the three elements into a holistic package—*orthodoxy* (right belief); *orthopraxis* (right action); and *orthopathy* (right experience, affections, or passion). All three are needed for a fully coherent Christian life. *Orthodoxy* sets the boundaries for experience and work; *orthopraxis* supplies action to belief, experience, and passion; and *orthopathy* grants the heart and life to belief and work.[35]

---

[32]This is a key concern for Everett McKinney, "Some Spiritual Aspects of Pentecostal Education: A Personal Journey." *Asian Journal of Pentecostal Studies* 3 No. 2 (2000), 253-279; see also Jon Mark Ruthven, "Are Pentecostal Seminaries a Good Idea?," *Pneuma* 26 No. 2 (2004): 339-45.

[33]Richard F. Brogden, Jr., in his doctoral dissertation specifically highlights the importance of abiding in Jesus as part of the ministerial-missionary life and work, which just takes time; see Brogden, "Abiding Mission: Missionary Spirituality and Disciple-Making Among the Muslim Peoples of Egypt and Northern Sudan" (Ph.D. diss., Assemblies of God Theological Seminary, 2014).

[34]Ralph Tyler, *Basic Principles of Curriculum and Instruction* (Chicago: University of Chicago Press, 1949), 75-79.

[35]Stephen Land, *Pentecostal Spirituality*; Lewis, "Toward a Pentecostal Epistemology: The Role of Experience in Pentecostal Hermeneutics," *The Spirit & Church* 2 No. 1 (2000), 102-3; Theodore Runyon, "The Importance of Experience for Faith," in *Aldersgate Reconsidered*, ed. Randy Maddox (Nashville: Kingswood Books, 1990), 93-107; idem., "A New Look at 'Experience'," *Drew Gateway* 57 No. 3 (1987): 44-55; Samuel Solivan, *The Spirit, Pathos and Liberation: Toward an Hispanic Pentecostal Theology*, Journal of Pentecostal Theology Supplemental 14 (Sheffield: Sheffield Academic Press, 1998); and R. Paul Stevens, "Living Theologically: Toward a Theology of Christian Practice," *Crux* 30 (1994), 36-44; c.f. Gregory Clapper's usage of the term *orthokardia* instead of *orthopathy*, Clapper, *John Wesley on Religious Affections* (Metuchen, NJ: Scarecrow Press, 1989).

This *orthopathy* has both the Godward "affections" (ala Land) and the outward passion for others, including the poor and marginalized (ala Solivan). From this triad, it is understood that there is a resulting circle of learning—theory (and belief) leads to practice which leads to theological reflection (cognitive, experiential, verificational, and emotive) which, in turn, leads to new practice and so on. A revised form of the hermeneutical circles would appear as follows. The Bible leads to theology which (through theological reflection of the person in community that mediates between cognitive, experiential and practical strands) leads to *praxis* and then back to the Bible.[36]

This process can also be described as the interrelationship of *theoria, poesis,* and *praxis*—*theoria* being the speculative or theoretical knowledge; *poesis* the creative capacity or ability to make; and *praxis* the active or practical knowledge.[37] Further, this should include the *yada* relational knowledge as emphasized in the Hebrew Old Testament.[38] All these need each other for a balanced and adequate understanding of the Christian life. The epistemological avenues of *theoria, poesis, praxis,* and *yada* lead one to *orthodoxy, orthopathy,* and *orthopraxis.*[39] The balanced Christian life includes all elements of "knowing" and Christian faith.

There are some implications concerning the *orthodoxy-orthopraxy- orthopathy* triad. First, within graduate theological education, *orthodoxy,* or its study, would tend to take the form

---

[36]On theological reflection, see Kathyrn Tanner, "Theological Reflection and Christian Practices," in *Practicing Theology: Beliefs and Practices in Christian Life,* eds. Miroslav Volf and Dorothy Bass (Grand Rapids: Eerdmans, 2002), 228-42; see also from a Pentecostal perspective on related subjects Cheryl Bridges Johns, *Pentecostal Formation,* Journal of Pentecostal Theology Supplemental 2 (Sheffield: Sheffield Academic Press, 1994).

[37]Max Stackhouse, *Apologia: Contextualization, Globalization, and Mission in Theological Education* (Grand Rapids: Eerdmans, 1988), 84-135.

[38]Thomas Groome, *Christian Religious Education* (San Francisco: Harper, 1980), 139-51; Jackie David Johns and Cheryl Bridges Johns, "Yielding to the Spirit: A Pentecostal Approach to Group Bible Study," *Journal of Pentecostal Theology* 1 (1992): 109-34; and Jackie David Johns, "Yielding to the Spirit: The Dynamics of a Pentecostal Model of Praxis," in *The Globalization of Pentecostalism,* eds. Murray Dempster, Byron Klaus and Douglas Petersen (Oxford: Regnum, 1999), 70-84; see also Michael Polanyi, *Personal Knowledge.* Corrected ed. (Chicago: University of Chicago Press, 1962).

[39]Stevens, "Living Theologically," 39-40; see also Stackhouse, *Apologia,* 84-135.

of the theology, Bible, and church history courses. There would be an emphasis on the proper hermeneutics of the biblical text, the awareness of church history, and the parameters and internal coherence of systematic theology and historical theology. Academic rigor can also assist in theological reflection (e.g., What does the Bible mean to me in my context?) and by helping put boundaries on *praxis* and a foundation for *poesis*. This endeavor is especially important in determining and discerning various heretical or cultic theological positions from Christian orthodox stances.

Within the seminary environment, the students have opportunity to develop in the area of *orthopraxy*. First, this takes place by the mentors/teachers having extensive "practical" experience (e.g., a pastor with 20 years of experience). The students, coming from, or currently in, a ministerial role are able to bring questions of a practical nature to class, and all benefit from this interaction. The seminary must also balance the practical parts of the curriculum, such as "practicum" or "field education," with the ongoing role that the students should have in the local church or in chapel. It can be within the *praxis*-oriented classes where the academic rigor can be given the focus of maintaining a theology for the "person in the pew."

Probably one of the hardest aspects of seminary life is the development of *orthopathy*. This is more difficult to quantify than the previous two, but that still does not diminish its importance. The need for a spiritual emphasis, both individually and corporately (e.g., chapel), is vital. However, the seminary is not solely responsible for establishing the spiritual disciplines, which should have been already learned from and used in the home church.[40] Classes and studies can help guide students into a deeper experience, but ultimately students must set aside times for theological reflection, meditation on the Word, and consistent devotions. The seminary should not be viewed as the

---

[40]See Joseph L. Castleberry, "Pentecostal Seminaries are Essential to the Future Health of the Church," *Pneuma* 26 No. 2 (2004), 346-54, especially 348-9; and Miroslav Volf, "Teachers, Crusts and Toppings," *Christian Century* 113 No. 5 (1996), 133-5; see also Richard Dresselhaus, "What Can the Academy Do for the Church?," *Asian Journal of Pentecostal Studies* 3 No. 2 (2000): 319-23.

place where the spiritual disciplines are learned but rather the place where these disciplines are refined and deepened.[41] The students' personal development can likewise be guided by mentors, but accountability to mentors (and to others) has a primary role in the development of the students' experiences.

Issues in Pentecostal Theological Education

With regard to the nature of Pentecostal theological education, the implications are clear—formation includes theological, spiritual, and moral formation. As such, the need for small groups and related activities for personal growth are essential for moral development and integration; chapel and personal devotions are necessary for spiritual growth; courses (including readings) and life with fellow students and teachers within a community of faith assist in the understanding of the faith. Yet, the goal is not just *formation* but *transformation*, which takes an encounter with God.[42] It is important to remember that, as Pentecostals, "understanding of the faith" must include both "the faith" broadly as Christians and narrowly as Pentecostals. The tendency is to overemphasize one or the other. Our own tradition is important as a corporate voice for the betterment of Christianity as a whole. Further, equipping for ministry includes the Ephesians 4:11 list, so the equipping is not just for pastors or teachers but is necessary for all potential ministers. Yet the formation, understanding of the faith, and equipping must all be within the context of a community. A vital, vibrant community aids students in moral growth, developing

---

[41] L. Gregory Jones compares the traditional model as the 'baton' model in which the church trains in basic discipleship, then seminary trains at the next level, and then the student returns to the church as a leader to train the next generation. This is different from the "pilgrimage" model, which is more organic, and the church and seminary work closely together. L. Gregory Jones, "Beliefs, Desires, Practices and the Ends of Theological Education," in *Practicing Theology*, 185-188.

[42] See David Daniels, "Live So Can Use Me, Anytime, Lord, Anywhere:" Theological Education in the Church of God in Christ, 1970-1997," *Asian Journal of Pentecostal Studies* 3 No. 2 (2000), 295-310, especially 308-9; and Jones, *Transformed Judgment: Toward a Trinitarian Account of the Moral Life* (Notre Dame, IN: University of Notre Dame Press, 1990), esp. 2-5, 73-86.

theological acumen and discernment, and comparative spiritual maturity.[43]

Pentecostal spirituality presupposes the ongoing work of the Holy Spirit in individuals' lives, so they need to be open and sensitive to the Spirit's leading. Further, traditionally, Pentecostals have highlighted the imminence of Christ's return.[44] As such, Pentecostal theological education should foster these two concepts into an atmosphere or *ethos* within their institutions that the Spirit can break into at any time in praise, *charismata*, etc. and we live in light of His imminent return.

The faculty members set the tone, teaching through the classroom and chapel, and modeling through life, the fully integrated Pentecostal. The role of the faculty is immeasurable, so selection of faculty is very important. Good Pentecostal faculty cannot be based on academic or experiential qualifications alone, but also on the spiritual and moral qualities needed to model and present an integrated ministry and life.[45] This is also why chapel is important, not only as a time and place for spiritual growth, but also as a place where good ministerial practices (e.g. good hermeneutics, preaching, worship leading) are modeled and where the appropriate dealing with problematic issues (e.g., moral issues in the school, inappropriately used *charismata*, proper spiritual discernment) are demonstrated.[46]

However, as Jeff Hittenberger has noted, among the reasons for the lack of Pentecostal dynamics and philosophy of

---

[43]Dietrich Bonhoeffer, *Life Together/Prayerbook of the Bible,* Dietrich Bonhoeffer Works Vol. 5 (Minneapolis, MN: Fortress Press, 1996), especially 1-140.

[44]Although it should be noted that, contrary to previously held common perspectives, contemporary Pentecostals have also highlighted that we should plan as if He may return in the distant future. See also McKinney, "Spiritual Aspects of Pentecostal Education," 253-79; Alvarez, "Distinctives of Pentecostal Education," 281-93; and Edgar Lee, "What the Academy Needs from the Church?" *Asian Journal of Pentecostal Studies* 3 No. 2 (2000): 311-8, especially 315.

[45]See Merle Strege, "Chasing Schleiermacher's Ghost: The Reform of Theological Education in the 1980s," in *Theological Education and Moral Formation,* 124.

[46]This is why I believe that chapel should be carefully prepared for and led. It should not be a place where worship songs are selected at the last minute or a person with no experience leads chapel. (This is not to say that students should not play a role, but they should take it seriously and have good supervision and modeling.)

education is the "reliance upon pedagogical and philosophical models that are more Evangelical (or fundamentalist) than Pentecostal. . . . [and] written resources on educational philosophy and pedagogy authored by Pentecostals for Pentecostal educators are lacking, especially for higher education."[47] So part of the reason for this lacunae is reliance on Evangelical models in the classroom and even in the Bible schools (via the Bible schools movement) and through Evangelical textbooks and institutional models that may not (and often do not) reflect a Pentecostal philosophy, *pathos,* or *ethos.*

Several issues arise from the above *orthodoxy-orthopathy orthopraxy* model. One of the common problems in theological education today is the bifurcation between theology and ministry (e.g., curriculum, attitudes). Of course, it is noted that many seminaries have been or are actively attempting to address this issue. The problem within Pentecostal circles revolves around an assumption that theology is impractical and will only distort the student. The primary values are placed upon *"real* ministry." The danger of such a bifurcation between theology and ministry is that it separates the work of the Kingdom from the study of the Kingdom *orthopraxy* from *orthodoxy.* In reality, theology and ministry should supplement and complement each other.[48] Theology helps guide students (and their further ministerial roles) into a deeper understanding of the Bible and its ramifications for us today, while practical theology or ministry courses help them "flesh out" their theology in the marketplace or on the street. Both are necessary. The proper interaction brings vibrancy and vitality to the students' current and future ministries.

It has been sometimes stated within Pentecostal circles that theological studies and classes are not necessary; only

---

[47]Hittenberger, "Toward a Pentecostal Philosophy of Education," 226, 230; see also Lewis, "Reflections on a Hundred Years of Pentecostal Theology."
[48]Some noted discussions of this are Craig Dykstra, *Growing in the Life of Faith* (Louisville: Geneva Press, 1999); idem., "Reconceiving Practice," in *Shifting Boundaries: Contextual Approaches to the Structure of Theological Education,* eds. Barbara Wheeler and Edward Farley (Louisville: Westminster/John Knox Press, 1991), 35-66; and the essays in Miroslav Volf and Dorothy Bass, eds., *Practicing Theology: Beliefs and Practices in Christian Life* (Grand Rapids: Eerdmans, 2002).

ministerial classes are needed. First, it needs to be understood that everyone has a theology, whether it is analyzed or not. Second, bad theology can lead to a poor witness (e.g., being obnoxious in the name of Christ), to harmful church practices, or even to death.[49] Therefore, it is important to demonstrate and teach the necessity of the interrelationship of theology and ministry within the courses and through life.

Another issue within Pentecostal theological education is confusion about the purpose of such education. One fundamental difference between seminary-level training and non-credit or undergraduate training is that these latter tend to emphasize indoctrination into doctrinal positions or basic Christian stances (i.e., "what to think"), whereas the seminary-level training emphasizes the analysis and process deriving and discerning various positions (i.e., "how to think"). For some, theological education, even at the graduate level, is indoctrination. It is often assumed within Pentecostal circles that all theological education, even at the graduate level, is interested in teaching "what to think," with an emphasis on denominational positions. The reason why this issue is important is due to the students' future goals. If students become a teacher in a Bible college, a pastor of an influential church, or a denominational official, then they will come in contact with aberrant beliefs, cult practices, and various philosophies. If they are not taught analytical skills, they may not be able to deal with these erroneous positions appropriately.

The lack of theological training to analyze various positions can and has undermined the very foundations of a church. Theological indoctrination only gives "what to think" and the parameters of past belief. Contemporary or future issues can be outside the "experiential box" and will confuse the minister who does not have the tools to deal with new issues.[50] Further, those

---

[49] An example is the graduate from a Bible school in Asia who thought if he would pray and fast enough, his church would grow; since the church did not grow, he fasted more and more only to starve himself to death.

[50] This is analogous to the person who studies a specific computer language (e.g., COBOL); but when it is outdated and no longer in use, he either has to keep teaching an old language that no one uses or completely learn a new one. However, he has never acquired the tools needed on how to go about it, or how to change.

A History and Components of Pentecostal 195
Theological Education

who are only indoctrinated will not have the tools or abilities by which to discern truth from error. Instead, they will look to others for this discernment. But how are these resources tested? The tendency can be to look to popular books considered to be acceptable and truthful; however, the authors or their positions are often not analyzed, just accepted. A key purpose of theological education should be development of the critical tools within the student by which to rightly discern the Word, and to be able to spot aberrant, and cultic beliefs and practices.

Another common problem is the collapse of *orthopathy* into *orthopraxy*. Or put another way, there is confusion between spiritual experience and passion with the practical application. This issue is also found within the curriculum issue that places *pathos* or spirituality-type classes (e.g., "Christian spirituality," "prayer") under ministerial courses. As such, experience is then considered to be an extension of practical theology or, on the other hand, a subject purely under cognitive analysis. Further, the above noted triad is reduced to a theology-ministry dyad with spirituality neglected. Ultimately, reflective spirituality is neglected within the seminary experience (except possibly in chapel) as well as the tools of fostering proper *pathos* and the ability to sort through the appropriate interaction between these.

An integrated curriculum would offer some theology and ministerial classes in which not only the spiritual disciplines and Christian spirituality are studied, but also spiritual *pathos* is fostered and mentored as a passion for God and for others (including the poor). Further, times of prayer, devotion, meditation, etc. are actively promoted by the school (e.g., Dietrich Bonhoeffer at Finkenwald)[51] for a proper *pathos* experience and its related *praxis* understanding.

Ultimately, the goal must be an *orthodox-orthopraxy-orthopathy* integration and growth within the life of the students. The teachers are thereby "pilgrims" on the same journey but just further along, guiding those behind them on the same way. So the necessity of a "radical discipleship" is foundational for the

---

[51]Dietrich Bonhoeffer, *Life Together/Prayerbook of the Bible*, Dietrich Bonhoeffer Works Vol. 5 (Minneapolis: Fortress Press, 1996), especially 81-92; and idem., *Meditating on the Word* (Nashville: Abingdon Press, 1987).

school,[52] in that teachers teach, model, and with intentionality, guide in practice (i.e., show, teach, supervise, send, and debrief). Many who came from traditional Pentecostal roots (and their anti-intellectualism, [53] especially in North America) frequently saw graduate studies as the context whereby students became "liberal" or "cold" to the work of the Lord. Frequent jokes about the "seminary" being a "cemetery" were proclaimed, and the seminary was seen as "killing the faith" of its students.[54] Those statements have more to do with that part of the century when those sayings originated and the "liberal" climate at many seminaries at the time (i.e., early 1900s)[55] and less to do with the role of the seminary itself. Unfortunately, these have been confused. Further, often students in graduate education studied certain commonly held beliefs only to find that some of those beliefs were not true or accurate, biblically or historically.[56] However, when these seminary graduates try to bring this to light in their churches, they are branded as "liberal." Although this has been changing, at times it is still apparent.

Pentecostal theological education should incorporate the rigors of academia with a commitment to the Word and being

---

[52]Ibid. The importance of "radical discipleship' is highlighted in the work of Bonhoeffer and Jürgen Moltmann, for example, in Bonhoeffer's *The Cost of Discipleship*, rev. ed. (New York: Macmillan, 1963), and Moltmann's "Political Discipleship of Christ Today," in *Communities of Faith and Radical Discipleship*, edited by G. McLeod Bryan (Macon, GA: Mercer University Press, 1986), 13-31.

[53]See Rick Nañez, *Full Gospel, Fractured Minds?* (Grand Rapids: Zondervan, 2005); Roger Olson, "Pentecostalism's Dark Side," *Christian Century* 123 No. 5 (2006), 27-30; and Russell Spittler in "Three Leaders Talk Frankly about Pentecostalism," *Christianity Today* 50 No. 4 (2006), 38-41 (41). This is more typical of American Pentecostalism; see William Menzies, *Anointed for Service* (Springfield, MO: Gospel Publishing House, 1984), 141; and Vinson Synan, *The Holiness-Pentecostal Tradition*, 2nd ed. (Grand Rapids: Eerdmans, 1997), 207.

[54]See Jones, "Beliefs, Desires, Practices and the End of the Theological Education," 186-187.

[55]See Lewis, "Reflections of a Hundred Years of Pentecostal Theology;" and Macchia, "The Struggle of Global Witness," 8-29.

[56]An example is "what 'authorized' means for the KJV Bible?" Whereas "authorized" did not originally have any spiritual connotation, it came to mean the official translation of the Bible (for which there is no official evidence) into English endorsed and supported by the King. However, many now assume (of which I have personally heard stated) that "authorized" has a spiritual meaning; see S.L. Greenslade, "English Versions of the Bible, 1525-1611," in *The Cambridge History of the Bible*, ed. S.L. Greenslade (Cambridge: Cambridge University Press, 1963), 164-168.

led by the Spirit. Yet it should be noted that there is also an important element that many students tend to grow in "knowledge" but unfortunately do not learn "wisdom" or how to use that "knowledge." Both are important in the ministry. Further, the goal is in the interaction between the church, the school, and the student to provide the best possible Pentecostal theological education. Although the seminary must be aware of, and self-critical about its role, if students leave "liberal" or "cold," it may have more to do with their preparation or background prior to coming to the school or not having been properly "traditioned" into Pentecostal Christianity.[57]

Perhaps one of the greatest tensions in graduate theological education for students is that between academic rigor and the need for time to reflect or pray. In any graduate program, there is a problem of balancing time for other things with the time for study. Further, it is a usual problem within the world of ministry that there is never enough time. On the one hand, if students cannot be stretched to work through these issues and find time for prayer and reflection within their schedules, then their ministerial experiences will likewise be distorted. On the other hand, there is also a responsibility for the administration/faculty to oversee the spiritual growth of the students and ultimately to make sure that they are not overloading themselves in order to graduate too quickly without proper time to reflect and pray. This sense of haste many students have frequently demonstrates their interest to receive a degree rather than to obtain an education. The integration of *orthodoxy, orthopraxy,* and *orthopathy* must be mirrored within the life of the graduate, and times of reflection are necessary for this to take place.

There is little doubt that Pentecostalism has direct implications concerning the nature of its own theological

---

[57]On Pentecostal "traditioning", see Simon Chan, *Pentecostal Theology and the Christian Spiritual Tradition,* Journal of Pentecostal Theology Supplemental Series 21 (Sheffield: Sheffield Academic Press, 2000). Thomas C. Oden makes it clear that, although there are "liberal" seminaries, there are other legitimate ones that are orthodox (tradition laden) in Oden, *Requiem: A Lament in Three Movements* (Nashville: Abingdon Press, 1995); see note No. 32. See also Jones' discussion of the various critical and self-critical works by the academy and the church in Jones, "Beliefs, Desires, Practices and the End of Theological Education," 186-7.

education. Pentecostal doctrinal distinctives are not the only inclusions into a curriculum. Rather, the whole atmosphere, *ethos*, and integration of *orthodoxy, orthopathy,* and *orthopraxy* are all necessary for a Pentecostal theological educational philosophy. Although not the final word, it is my hope that this essay will help further the goal of focusing on the Pentecostal theological education—"what it means" and "where to go from here."

Tongues as a Sign: Reconciling Luke and Paul
By Robert P. Menzies[1]

I am delighted to be able to contribute to this work honoring Dr. John Carter and his wife, Bea. John and Bea have blessed my family and me in numerous ways. I served at Asia Pacific Theological Seminary (APTS) under Dr. Carter during his tenure as the academic dean, and then later was privileged to teach as an adjunct professor while he was the president of this fine institution. Through the years I have grown to appreciate Dr. Carter as a capable and committed missionary educator and also as a friend. John and Bea share a passion for training Christian leaders. They have encouraged many to serve the cause of Christ by following the call to be a teacher, and I am one of them.

Not long ago while I was writing a book on Pentecostal identity and how its core elements are rooted in Luke's narrative, I began to consider a question. It is a question of significance for Pentecostals, but it is one that, to my knowledge, has not been seriously addressed. Shortly after I completed my writing project, yet while this question was still fresh in my mind, I received a note from an Assemblies of God pastor. He raised, in a slightly different form, the question that I had been pondering, "How do we reconcile Luke's positive emphasis on speaking in tongues as a sign that serves to strengthen and encourage the Christian community and that may, in special instances, have apologetic value as well (Acts 2:1-22, 33; 10:44-46; 19:1-7; cf. Luke 11:9-13) with Paul's disparaging comments about tongues as a "negative" sign in 1

---

[1] Robert P. Menzies (Ph.D., University of Aberdeen) is the Director of Synergy, a rural service organization located in Kunming, China.

Corinthians 14:20-25?'" Of course, our answer to this question carries with it very practical and important implications. How we answer this question, as my pastoral colleague perceived, will impact our understanding of "order" in church services. It will dictate, to a large extent, the contexts in which we might encourage people to seek to be baptized in the Holy Spirit (Acts 1:8; 2:4), since the biblical model for this experience includes glossolalia. Indeed, if we accept a literal reading of Paul over and against Luke at this point, then we would not allow any expression of tongues in our church services without interpretation.[2] Of course, this is precisely what many non-Pentecostal (and perhaps not a few Pentecostal) churches do. However, these questions must be asked: "Is this really fair to Luke? Does it do justice to the full canon of Scripture? Cannot Luke and Paul be reconciled in a manner that actually does justice to the intention of both inspired authors?" These are the questions that this essay shall seek to address.

Speaking in Tongues: Overview and Definitions

The phenomenon of speaking in tongues was well known and widely practiced in the early church. References or allusions to speaking in tongues are scattered throughout the New Testament and the phenomenon is specifically described in numerous passages.[3] In 1 Corinthians 12-14 Paul refers to the gift of tongues (γλώσσαις)[4] and uses the phrase λαλέω γλώσσαις to designate unintelligible utterances inspired by the Spirit.[5] The fact that this gift of tongues refers to unintelligible utterances rather than known human languages is confirmed by the fact that Paul explicitly states that these tongues are directed

---

[2] Presumably, this would exclude expressions of glossolalia in corporate praise and prayer, such as "singing in tongues."
[3] See 1 Cor. 12-14; Acts 2:4, 10:46, 19:6; note also Mark 16:17 and Romans 8:26-27. More general references to charismatic activity that might include speaking in tongues include: 2 Cor. 5:4; Eph. 5:19, 6:18; Col. 3:16; and 1 Thess. 5:19.
[4] 1 Cor. 12:10; 12:28; 13:8; 14:22, 26.
[5] 1 Cor. 12:30; 13:1; 14:2, 4, 6, 13, 18, 23, 27, 39.

to God (1 Cor. 14:2) and must be interpreted if they are to be understood (1 Cor. 14:6-19, 28; cf. 12:10, 30).[6] In Acts 2:4, 10:46, and 19:6 Luke also uses the phrase λαλέω γλώσσαις to designate utterances inspired by the Spirit. In Acts 10:46 Peter and his colleagues hear Cornelius and his household "speaking in tongues and praising God."[7] Acts 19:6 states that the Ephesian disciples "spoke in tongues and prophesied." The literary parallels between the descriptions of speaking in tongues in these passages and 1 Corinthians 12-14 are impressive. All of these texts associate speaking in tongues with the inspiration of the Holy Spirit, utilize similar vocabulary (λαλέω γλώσσαις), and describe inspired speech associated with worship and prophetic pronouncements. Additionally, since 1 Corinthians 12-14 clearly speaks of unintelligible utterances and there is no indication in either Acts 10:46 or 19:6 that known languages are being spoken–indeed, there is no apparent need for a miracle of xenolalia in either instance–most scholars interpret the occurrences of λαλέω γλώσσαις in these texts as referring to glossolalia.

In Acts 2:4 we read that the disciples at Pentecost were "filled with the Holy Spirit" and began "to speak in other tongues" (λαλεῖν ἑτέραις γλώσσαις). Here "speaking in tongues" refers to a miraculous occurrence of xenolalia, for the disciples are enabled to declare the wonders of God in the various languages (or mother-tongues) of those present (Acts 2:5-12).[8] The fact that the actual phenomenon described in Acts

---

[6] I define glossolalia as "an utterance inspired by the Holy Spirit that typically is unintelligible to both the human speaker and hearer, that is not in a known human language, and that is directed to God as a form of prayer and praise." For a similar definition see Gordon D. Fee, *God's Empowering Presence: the Holy Spirit in the Letters of Paul* (Peabody, Mass: Hendrickson Publishers, 1994), pp. 172-73, 217-19. Glossolalia is thus different from xenolalia, which I understand as "an utterance in a human language that the speaker has not previously learned."

[7] All quotations from the Bible are taken from the NIV unless otherwise noted.

[8] It is certainly possible to interpret the "tongues" of Acts 2:4 as referring to glossolalia. According to this reading, the miracle that occurs at Pentecost is two-fold. First, the disciples are inspired by the Spirit to declare the "wonders of God" in a spiritual language that is unintelligible to human beings (i.e., glossolalia). Second, the Jews in the crowd who represent a diverse group of countries are miraculously enabled to understand the glossolalia of the disciples so that it appears to them that the disciples are speaking in each of their own mother-tongues. Although Jenny Everts demonstrates that this view is plausible and has merit, the xenolalia reading still appears to be the most natural. See

2:4 (xenolalia) is different from that which is narrated in Acts 10:46 and 19:6 (glossolalia) highlights the significance of the literary connections that Luke makes by designating all of these as instances of "speaking in tongues" (λαλέω γλώσσαις). Luke consciously seeks to link these events and thus he describes them with essentially the same terms. Why this is the case will prove to be the focal point of our next section.

Tongues as a Sign: Luke's Perspective

One of the striking features of Luke's narrative in Acts is the conspicuous role played by speaking in tongues. Speaking in tongues is associated with prophecy and presented as a significant sign in each of the three passages which describe this phenomenon in Acts. The stage is set in Acts 2.

The Sign Defined (Acts 2)

In Acts 2:17-18 (cf. Acts 2:4) speaking in tongues is specifically described as a fulfillment of Joel's prophecy that in the last days all of God's people will prophesy. The strange sounds of the disciples' tongues-speech, Peter declares, are in fact not the riotous babbling of inebriated men and women; rather, they represent prophetic utterances issued by God's end-time messengers (Acts 2:13, 15-17). The meaning of the symbolism of the speaking "in other tongues," which enables "the Jews from every nation under heaven" to hear the message in their "own language" (Acts 2:5-6), is clearly explained. It marks this group as members of Joel's end-time prophetic band and indicates that the "last days" and the salvation associated with it have arrived. Thus, Luke narrates Peter's powerful declaration concerning Jesus, "Exalted to the right hand of God . . . he [Jesus] has poured out *what you now see and hear*" [author's emphasis] (Acts 2:33). "Therefore," Peter declares, "let all Israel

---

Jenny Everts, "Tongues or Languages? Contextual Consistency in the Translation of Acts 2," *JPT 4* (1994), pp. 71-80 and my assessment in Robert Menzies, *The Language of the Spirit: Interpreting and Translating Charismatic Terms* (Cleveland, TN: CPT Press, 2010), 99-103.

be assured of this: God has made this Jesus, whom you crucified, both Lord and Christ" (Acts 2:36).

The logic of the narrative is transparent: Since the Spirit of prophecy is only given to the "servants" of God (Acts 2:18)—that is, the true people of God, the heirs of the promise God made to Israel (Joel 2:28-32)—and, since the disciples of Jesus are those who are now receiving this gift, it follows that Jesus is Lord (Acts 2:33) and that his disciples constitute the true people of God. In Acts 2 speaking in tongues, then, serves as a sign that both validates the disciples' claim that Jesus is Lord and confirms their status as members of Joel's end-time prophetic band.[9]

None of this should surprise us, for Luke anticipates this outpouring of the Spirit of prophecy earlier in his narrative. In Luke 10:1-16, Luke describes Jesus' sending of the Seventy, a passage unique to Luke's gospel.[10] The number seventy is rooted in the OT narrative and has symbolic meaning. The background for the reference to the "seventy" is to be found in Numbers 11:24–30.[11] This passage describes how the Lord "took of the Spirit that was on [Moses] and put the Spirit on the seventy elders" (Num. 11:25). This resulted in the seventy elders, who had gathered around the Tent, prophesying for a short duration. Two other elders, Eldad and Medad, did not go to the Tent; rather, they remained in the camp and they continued to prophesy. When Joshua heard of this, he rushed to Moses and

---

[9]So E. Schweizer concludes that the phrase "and you will receive the gift of the Holy Spirit" (Acts 2:38) should be interpreted as a promise that the Spirit shall be "imparted to those who are already converted and baptized" (Schweizer, "πνεῦμα," *TDNT*, vol. 6, p. 412). Note also the judgment offered by S. Brown: "Surely it is preferable to interpret the passage in accordance with all the other texts which we have considered and to understand the words 'you shall receive' to point to an event subsequent to baptism" ("'Water-Baptism' and 'Spirit-Baptism' in Luke-Acts," *ATR* 59 [1977], 144).

[10]Some translations, such as the NIV, list the number as "seventy-two." The manuscript evidence is divided: some manuscripts read "seventy" and others, "seventy-two." As a matter of convenience, we will list the number as "seventy." For a discussion of this question and how the manuscript tradition supports my reading of the text, see Robert Menzies, "The Sending of the Seventy and Luke's Purpose," in Paul Alexander, Jordan D. May, and Robert Reid, eds., *Trajectories in the Book of Acts: Essays in Honor of John Wesley Wyckoff* (Eugene, OR: Wipf & Stock, 2010), 87-113.

[11]See Menzies, "The Sending of the Seventy," 87-113 for arguments that support this conclusion.

urged him to stop them. But Moses replied, "Are you jealous for my sake? I wish that all the Lord's people were prophets and that the Lord would put his Spirit on them!" (Num. 11:29).

The reference to the Seventy thus evokes memories of Moses' wish that "all the Lord's people were prophets," and, in this way, points ahead to Pentecost (Acts 2), where this wish is initially fulfilled. Of course this wish, as we shall see, continues to be fulfilled throughout the narrative of Acts. This reference to the Seventy, then, foreshadows the outpouring of the Spirit on all the servants of the Lord and their universal participation in the mission of God (Acts 2:17–18; cf. 4:31).[12] According to Luke, every follower of Jesus is called and promised the requisite power to be a prophet.

It is important to note that the ecstatic speech of the elders in Numbers 11 constitutes the backdrop against which Luke interprets the Pentecostal and subsequent outpourings of the Spirit.[13] This is the sign that signifies that they too have a share of Moses' prophetic anointing. It would appear that Luke views every believer as (at least potentially) an end-time prophet, and that he anticipates that they too will issue forth in Spirit-inspired ecstatic speech.[14] This is the clear implication of his narrative, which includes repetitive fulfillments of Moses' wish that reference glossolalia. For the Pentecost account in Acts 2, which highlights the fact that the inspired tongues of the disciples serve as a significant sign, is merely the beginning.

The Meaning of the Sign Affirmed (Acts 10)

The sign-value of tongues is highlighted once again in Acts 10:42-48. In the midst of Peter's sermon to Cornelius and his

---

[12]Keith F. Nickle, *Preaching the Gospel of Luke: Proclaiming God's Royal Rule* (Louisville: Westminster John Knox Press, 2000), 117: "The 'Seventy' is the church in its entirety, including Luke's own community, announcing the in-breaking of God's royal rule throughout the length and breadth of God's creation."

[13]Gordon Wenham describes the prophesying narrated in Numbers 11:24-30 as an instance of "unintelligible ecstatic utterance, what the New Testament terms speaking in tongues" (Wenham, *Numbers* [Downers Grove, IL: InterVarsity Press, 1981], 109).

[14]With the term, "ecstatic," I mean "pertaining to or flowing from an experience of intense joy." I do not wish to imply a loss of control with this term. While glossolalia transcends our reasoning faculties, the experience does not render them useless (cf. 1 Cor. 14:28, 32-33).

household, the Holy Spirit "came on all those who heard the message" (Acts 10:44). Peter's colleagues "were astonished that the gift of the Holy Spirit had been poured out even on the Gentiles, for they heard them speaking in tongues and praising God" (Acts 10:45-46). It is instructive to note that the Holy Spirit interrupts Peter just as he declares, "He [Jesus] commanded us to preach to the people and to testify that he is the one whom God appointed as judge of the living and the dead. *All the prophets testify about him* [author's emphasis] that everyone who believes in him receives forgiveness of sins through his name" (Acts 10:42-43).

In view of Luke's emphasis on prophetic inspiration throughout his two-volume work and, more specifically, his description of speaking in tongues as prophetic speech in Acts 2:17-18, it can hardly be coincidental that the Holy Spirit breaks in and inspires glossolalia precisely at this point in Peter's sermon. Indeed, as the context makes clear, Peter's colleagues are astonished at what transpires because it testifies to the fact that God has accepted uncircumcised Gentiles. Again, the connection between speaking in tongues and prophecy is crucial for Luke's narrative. In Acts 2:17-18 we are informed that reception of the Spirit of prophecy (i.e., the Pentecostal gift) is the exclusive privilege of "the servants" of God and that it typically results in miraculous and audible speech.[15] Speaking in tongues is presented as one manifestation of this miraculous, Spirit-inspired speech (Acts 2:4, 17-18). So, when Cornelius and his household burst forth in tongues, this act provides demonstrative proof that they are in fact part of the end-time prophetic band of which Joel prophesied. They too are connected to the prophets that "testify" about Jesus (Acts 10:43). This astonishes Peter's colleagues, because they recognize the clear implications that flow from this dramatic event: since Cornelius and his household are prophets, they

---

[15]Of the eight instances where Luke describes or refers to the initial reception of the Spirit by a person or group, five specifically allude to some form of inspired speech as an immediate result (Luke 1:41; 1:67; Acts 2:4; 10:46; 19:6) and one implies the occurrence of such activity (Acts 8:15, 18). In the remaining two instances, although inspired speech is absent from Luke's account (Luke 3:22; Acts 9:17), it is a prominent feature in the pericopes that follow (Luke 4:14, 18f.; Acts 9:20).

must also be "servants" of the Lord (that is, members of the people of God). How, then, can Peter and the others withhold baptism from them? (Acts 10:47-48).

The importance of this connection in the narrative is highlighted further in Acts 11:15-18. Here, as Peter recounts the events associated with the conversion of Cornelius and his household, he emphasizes that "the Holy Spirit came on them as he had come on us at the beginning" (Acts 11:15) and then declares, "God gave them the same gift as he gave us . . ." (Acts 11:17). The fact that Jewish disciples at Pentecost and Gentile believers at Caesarea all spoke in tongues is not incidental to Luke's purposes; rather, it represents a significant theme in his story of the movement of the gospel from Jews in Jerusalem to Gentiles in Rome and beyond. Once again, speaking in tongues serves as an important sign that identifies God's end-time prophets (Acts 10:46-47) and bears witness to Jesus' lordship (Acts 10:42-43).

The Meaning of the Sign for Luke's Readers (Acts 19)

In Acts 19:6 this pattern is repeated. The connection between prophecy and speaking in tongues is explicitly stated. When Paul laid hands on the Ephesian disciples, the Holy Spirit "came on them, and they spoke in tongues and prophesied." Here, again, tongues serves as a significant sign. Paul's prior question posed to the Ephesian "disciples," "Did you receive the Holy Spirit when you believed?" (Acts 19:2), implies another question, "How would we know?" Of course the pattern and literary connections that Luke has created enable us to answer this question and anticipate the outcome that follows.

All of this demonstrates that Luke has carefully crafted his narrative in order to highlight the connections between Acts 2:4, 10:46, and 19:6. Luke creates this literary linkage by presenting, in each instance, "speaking in tongues" as the definitive and expected sign for reception of the Spirit of prophecy promised by Joel. This sign confirms that the disciples are the true people of God and also validates their proclamation that Jesus is Lord.

It should be noted that of the four instances in the book of Acts where Luke actually describes the initial coming of the Spirit, three explicitly cite glossolalia as the immediate result (Acts 2:4; 10:46; 19:6) and the other one (Acts 8:14-19) strongly implies it.[16] This is the case even though Luke could have easily used other language—particularly in Acts 2, which speaks of xenolalia rather than glossolalia—to describe what transpired. The Acts 8 passage has various purposes. However, when it is viewed in the context of Luke's larger narrative, there can be little doubt in the reader's mind concerning the cause of Simon's ill-fated attempt to purchase the ability to dispense the Spirit. The motif is transparent; Luke's point is made: the Pentecostal gift, as a fulfillment of Moses' wish (Num. 11:29) and Joel's prophecy (Joel 2:28-32), is a prophetic anointing that enables its recipient to bear bold witness for Jesus *and, this being the case, it is marked by the ecstatic speech characteristic of prophets* (i.e., glossolalia).[17] This reading, then, explains why Luke presents tongues-speech as a sign—a sign that confirms that the disciples of Jesus are God's promised end-time prophets and that validates their proclamation. I would add that this sort of apologetic suggests that Luke's readers routinely experienced this sign themselves. If "speaking in tongues" was relatively unknown to Luke's readers, this message—that tongues validated their proclamation and standing before God—would carry little encouragement. However, if they too experienced glossolalia, then the dialogue in Luke's narrative takes on fresh meaning.[18] Peter's declaration that "They have received the Holy Spirit just as we have" (Acts 10:47) speaks directly to Luke's readers and reminds them of

---

[16]Paul's experience of the Spirit is not actually described (Acts 9:17-19); rather, it is implied.

[17]It is interesting to note that Luke does not share the angst of many modern Christians concerning the possibility of false tongues. Luke does not offer guidelines for discerning whether tongues are genuine or fake, from God or from some other source. Rather, Luke assumes that the Christian community will know and experience that which is needed and good.

[18]Robert C. Tannehill notes that Peter, in his sermon recorded in Acts 2, "appeals to his hearers' own experience, to what they themselves know, see, and hear (2:22, 29, 33), which can be an especially convincing basis for an argument" (*The Narrative Unity of Luke-Acts: A Literary Interpretation*, vol. 2 [Minneapolis: Fortress Press, 1990], 41). Tannehill does not seem to consider that this appeal to experience might also be directed to Luke's readers.

the apostolic calling and power that is also theirs. Paul's question, "Did you receive the Holy Spirit when you believed?," encourages Luke's readers to reflect on their experiences of Spirit-inspired rapture and recognize that their own expressions of tongues-speech mark them as end-time prophets, people called and empowered to bear witness for Jesus.

The Significance of the Sign for the Church (Luke 11)

This suggestion, that Luke's readers routinely experienced tongues, finds further support in Luke's redaction of Jesus' teaching on prayer, recorded in Luke 11:13, "If you then, though you are evil, know how to give good gifts to your children, how much more will your Father in heaven give the Holy Spirit to those who ask Him!" The parallel passage in Matthew's gospel contains slightly different phrasing; "good gifts" rather than "the Holy Spirit" (Matthew 7:11). It is virtually certain that Luke has interpreted the "good gifts" in his source material with a reference to the "Holy Spirit."[19] Luke, then, provides us with a Spirit-inspired, authoritative commentary on this saying of Jesus. Since this promise is addressed to disciples/Christians and not realized until Pentecost, it is evident that Luke highlights the relevance of this saying for his post-Pentecostal readers. Luke's usage elsewhere coupled with the fact that this saying is directed to Christians, suggests that Luke has a prophetic enabling in mind.

What sort of prophetic activity did Luke anticipate would accompany this bestowal of the Spirit? Certainly a reading of Luke's narrative would suggest a wide range of possibilities: joyful praise, glossolalia, visions, bold witness in the face of persecution, to name a few. However, several aspects of Luke's narrative suggest that glossolalia was one of the expected outcomes in Luke's mind and in the minds of his readers.

---

[19]Reasons for this conclusion include: (1) the fact that the reference to the Holy Spirit breaks the parallelism of the "good gifts" given by earthly fathers and "the good gifts" given by our heavenly Father; (2) Luke often inserts references to the Holy Spirit into his source material; (3) Matthew never omits or adds references to the Holy Spirit in his sources.

First, Luke's narrative indicates that glossolalia typically accompanies the initial reception of the Spirit. Furthermore, as we have noted, Luke highlights the fact that glossolalia serves as an external sign of the prophetic gift. These elements of Luke's account would undoubtedly encourage readers in Luke's church, like they have with contemporary readers, to seek the prophetic gift, *complete with its accompanying external sign.*

Second, in view of the emphasis in this passage on asking (v. 9) and the Father's willingness to respond (v. 13), it would seem natural for Luke's readers to ask a question that again is often asked by contemporary Christians, "How will we know when we have received this gift?" Here we hear echoes of Paul's question in Acts 19:6. Of course, Luke provides a clear answer. The arrival of prophetic power has a visible, external sign, glossolalia. This is not to say that there are not other ways in which the Spirit's power and presence are made known. This is simply to affirm that Luke's narrative indicates that a visible, external sign does exist and that he and his readers would naturally expect to manifest this sign.

I would add that this sign must have been tremendously encouraging for Luke's church as it is for countless contemporary Christians. It signified their connection with the apostolic church and confirmed their identity as end-time prophets. I find it interesting that so many believers from traditional churches today react negatively to the notion of glossolalia as a visible sign. They often ask, "Should we really emphasize a visible sign like tongues?" Yet these same Christians participate in a liturgical form of worship that is filled with sacraments and imagery, a form of worship that emphasizes visible signs. Signs are valuable when they point to something significant. Luke and his church clearly understood this.

Finally, the question should be asked, "Why would Luke need to encourage his readers *not to be afraid* of receiving a bad or harmful gift (note the snake and scorpion of vv. 11-12)?"[20] Why would he need *to encourage* his church to pursue this gift

---

[20]It is perhaps significant that Luke's comparisons feature dangerous objects ("snake" and "scorpion," Luke 11:11-12), whereas Matthew's comparisons include one that is simply useless ("stone" and "snake," Matthew 7:9-10). This suggests that Luke was consciously seeking to help his readers overcome their fear.

of the Spirit? If the gift is quiet, internal, and ethereal, why would there be any concern? However, if the gift includes glossolalia, which is noisy, unintelligible, and has many pagan counterparts,[21] then the concerns make sense.[22] Luke's response is designed to quell any fears. The Father gives good gifts. We need not fret or fear.

In short, through his skillful editing of this saying of Jesus (Luke 11:13), Luke encourages his readers, post-Pentecostal disciples, to pray for a prophetic anointing, an experience of spiritual rapture that will produce power and praise in their lives, an experience similar to those modeled by Jesus (Luke 3:21-22; 10:21) and the early church (Acts 2:4; 10:46; 19:6). The reader would naturally expect glossolalia to be a normal, frequent, and anticipated part of this experience.[23]

We may summarize our discussion by noting that Luke presents us with a formidable resume for speaking in tongues. Luke expected that tongues would continue to play a positive role in his church and ours, both of which are located in "these last days." In Luke's view, every believer can manifest this spiritual gift. So, Luke encourages every believer to pray for prophetic anointings (Luke 11:13), experiences of Spirit-inspired exultation from which power and praise flow—experiences similar to those modeled by Jesus (Luke 3:21-22; 10:21) and the early church (Acts 2:4; 10:46; 19:6). Luke believed that these experiences would typically include glossolalia which he considered a special form of prophetic speech. More specifically, Luke presents speaking in tongues as a powerful and edifying sign—a sign that reminds us of our calling as end-time prophets and that testifies to the majesty and exalted status of Jesus.

---

[21] For Jewish and pagan examples of ecstasy and inspired utterances see James D.G. Dunn, *Jesus and the Spirit* (London: SCM Press, 1975), 304-5.

[22] Note that the Beelzebub controversy immediately follows (Luke 11:14-28). Some accused Jesus of being demon-possessed (Luke 11:15). The early Christians were undoubtedly confronted with similar charges. It is thus not surprising that Luke "takes pains to show [that] Christianity [is] both different from and superior to magic" (Richard Vinson, *Luke* [Macon, GA: Smyth & Helwys Publishing, 2008], 380; cf. Acts 8:9-24; 16:16-18; 19:11-20).

[23] For more on Luke's perspective on tongues and the work of the Holy Spirit more broadly, see Robert Menzies, *Pentecost: This Story is Our Story* (Springfield, MO: Gospel Publishing House, 2013).

Tongues as a Sign: Paul's Perspective

This analysis of Luke's perspective calls us to reconsider Paul's attitude towards speaking in tongues, and particularly his perspective on tongues as a sign. Perhaps it is worth noting, at the outset, that Paul has a relatively high view of glossolalia and its place in Christian experience. In 1 Corinthians 12-14 Paul refers to glossolalia as one of the gifts God grants to the church. A thorough reading of these chapters reveals that, in spite of the Corinthian's misunderstanding and abuse of this gift, Paul holds the private manifestation of tongues in high regard.[24] Although Paul is concerned to direct the Corinthians towards a more mature expression of spiritual gifts "in the assembly"—and thus he focuses on the need for edification and the primacy of prophecy over uninterpreted tongues in the corporate setting— Paul never denigrates the gift of tongues. Indeed, Paul affirms that the private manifestation of tongues is edifying to the speaker (1 Cor. 14:5) and, in an autobiographical note, he thanks God for the frequent manifestation of tongues in his private prayer-life (1 Cor. 14:18). Fearful that his instructions to the Corinthians concerning the proper use of tongues "in the assembly" might be misunderstood, he explicitly commands them not to forbid speaking in tongues (1 Cor. 14:39). With reference to the private manifestation of tongues, Paul declares, "I would like every one of you to speak in tongues. . ." (1 Cor. 14:5).

The Problem at Corinth

Nevertheless, it is evident that 1 Corinthians 12-14 is polemical. Here Paul is attempting to correct problems in the Corinthians' understanding and use of tongues. At least some of the Corinthians appear to have viewed tongues as an expression of a superior level of spirituality. Thus, they valued tongues above other gifts and, in the context of corporate meetings, their spiritual elitism often found expression in unintelligible

---

[24]So also Gordon D. Fee, *The First Epistle to the Corinthians* (NICNT; Grand Rapids: Eerdmans, 1987), 659.

outbursts that disrupted meetings and did not build up the church.[25] This basic reconstruction of the problem at Corinth has found widespread acceptance. However, one matter is less clear. Were all of the Corinthians caught up in this elitist form of spirituality (and thus standing in opposition to Paul) or was the church itself divided over the issue? The former position has been advocated by Gordon Fee, the latter by Christopher Forbes.[26]

Max Turner, following closely the lead of Forbes, suggests that at Corinth the gift of tongues was exercised by some to establish or reinforce their position as a member of the spiritual elite. The exercise of tongues was, then, a part of the "power games" that divided the church at Corinth.[27] This being the case, we can see that Paul seeks to correct the Corinthians' misunderstanding: he highlights the variety and origin of God's gracious gifts (1 Cor. 12, esp. vss. 4-6), that everyone has a role to play (1 Cor. 12:11-27), and that edification is the key goal (1 Cor. 12:7). Specifically, with reference to tongues, he insists that in the assembly, unless tongues are interpreted, they do not edify the church and thus prophecy is to be preferred (1 Cor. 14:2-5). In the context of his argument that prophecy is greater than tongues in the assembly, Paul also states that the private manifestation of tongues is edifying to the speaker and, furthermore, it is not limited to an elite group, but rather available to all (1 Cor. 14:5, 18). In other words, just as Paul notes he is no stranger to tongues and thus qualified to speak of the gift's significance (perhaps here he bests the Corinthians at their own game of elitist claims; 14:18), so also Paul seeks to undermine the Corinthians' improper sense of superiority with his comments concerning the universality of the gift.

Fee, on the other hand, suggests that we should see the entire church standing in opposition to Paul. The church as a whole was caught up in these elitist ideas and felt that their

---

[25]Max Turner, "Tongues: An Experience for All in the Pauline Churches?," *Asian Journal of Pentecostal Studies* 1 (1998), 235-36.

[26]Fee, *First Corinthians*, 4-15; Christopher Forbes, *Prophecy and Inspired Speech in Early Christianity and its Hellenistic Environment* (Tübigen: Mohr, 1995), 14-16, 171-75, 182-87, 260-64.

[27]Turner, "Experience for All," 237.

exercise of tongues displayed their superior wisdom and spirituality in relation to Paul.[28] Regardless of the specific makeup of the elitist faction, all are agreed that the key problem at Corinth with reference to tongues was the abuse of the gift "in the assembly" (that is, when the church gathered together; cf. 1 Cor. 12:28; 14:4-6, 9-19). We can envision the elitist group reveling in their *public display* of tongues, even though others likely exercised the gift in private as did Paul (1 Cor. 14:18).[29] The elitists viewed this public display of "speaking mysteries" (14:2) as a sign of their special knowledge and position, and superior to any private usage. Of course, with this flawed thinking, Paul cannot agree.

Paul's Response to the Problem

So, Paul seeks to correct the immature thinking, attitudes, and actions of the elitist group at Corinth. In addition to challenging the basis for these elitist views as noted above, Paul specifically challenges the Corinthian's exercise of tongues at two key points. First, he admonishes the church at Corinth to limit the public expression of tongues in a given meeting to two or three speakers, and these messages in tongues must be interpreted (1 Cor. 14:28). "If there is no interpreter," Paul declares, "the speaker should keep quiet" (1 Cor. 14:28). Second, Paul counters the Corinthian understanding of tongues as a sign. Here we must grapple with a passage of critical importance for our present study, 1 Corinthians 14:20-25.

The structure of 1 Corinthians 14:20-25 is rather straightforward, although its meaning is much more difficult to ascertain. The structure may be outlined as follows:

1. Exhortation (v. 20), "Brothers, stop thinking like children..."

---

[28]Fee, *First Corinthians*, 4-15.
[29]The contrast between 1 Cor. 14:18 ("I thank God I speak in tongues more than you all") and 14:19 ("But, in the church . . .") indicates that Paul's autobiographical comments in 14:18 refer to the private exercise of tongues.

2. Argument (vs. 21-25)
   a. Quotation (v. 21), "'Through men of strange tongues . . . I will speak to this people, but even then they will not listen to me,' says the Lord."
   b. Assertion 1 (v. 22a), "Tongues, then, are a sign, not for believers, but for unbelievers." Assertion 2 (vs. 22b), "Prophecy, however, is for believers, not for unbelievers."
   c. Illustration 1 (v. 23), "So if . . . everyone speaks in tongues . . . will they not say that your are out of your mind?" Illustration 2 (v. 24), "But if . . . while everybody is prophesying . . . he will fall down and worship God, exclaiming, 'God is really among you!'"

This passage is widely acknowledged to be one of the most difficult to fathom in all of Paul's writings.[30] The key problem centers in v. 22, and involves its relationship to the Old Testament (OT) quotation that precedes (vs. 21) and to the illustrations that follow (v. 23-25). The illustrations of vs. 23-25 appear to contradict the assertions of v. 22. How can tongues be a sign for unbelievers, when they cause the unbelievers to declare that the Christians who utter them are "out of [their] minds?" How can prophesy not be a sign for unbelievers, when it results in them declaring, "God is really among you!"

Pondering these and related problems have caused more than one pastor to lose considerable sleep, and for good reason. Chrysostom stated it well, "The difficulty at this place is great, which seems to arise from what is said."[31] In spite of the considerable challenges posed by this text, most scholars agree that Paul's position is most clearly seen in the illustrations of vs. 23-25. The critical appraisal of tongues as an evangelistic tool and the positive assessment of the impact of prophecy contained in these verses seem to square well with the general tenor of Paul's argument in 1 Corinthians 12-14. How all of this

---

[30]S.J. Kistemaker notes that "this text has been problematic for every interpreter" (Kistemaker, *1 Corinthians* [Grand Rapids: Baker, 1993], 500).

[31]Chrysostom, *1 Cor. Hom.*, 36:2 (as cited in Anthony Thiselton, *The First Epistle to the Corinthians* [Grand Rapids: Eerdmans, 2000], 1122).

relates to the OT quotation (v. 21) and the assertions of v. 22 is another matter.

Two answers to this vexing question appear to commend themselves. One response, that offered by Fee and a host of others, suggests that the problem lies in how we understand the word "sign."[32] The OT quotation, we are told, indicates that the term "sign" carries with it a negative sense; it is a negative sign, one that signals a hardness of heart and God's judgment. Thus, tongues, which are not understood by the unbelievers, serve as a sign, albeit a negative one, for them—a sign of judgment. Prophecy, on the other hand, is presented as a positive sign, one that leads to belief. Although this is undoubtedly one of the better solutions offered for this riddle, it is not without its flaws. It does require that we understand the term "sign" to function in different ways when applied to tongues and prophecy respectively, even though these terms appear in the same sentence.

A better solution, I believe, has been advanced by B. C. Johanson.[33] Johanson argues that in this passage Paul utilizes a rhetorical device known well among the ancient Greeks, the diatribe. Thus, after offering a rather loose paraphrase of Isa. 28:11-12,[34] Paul has an imaginary opponent voice his view in the form of a rhetorical question. The rhetorical question is actually an inference drawn from the preceding quote from Isaiah, "Are tongues, then, meant as a sign not for believers but for unbelievers?" (v. 22a).[35] It should be noted that in Johanson's view, this is not Paul's perspective. It is rather the perspective of

---

[32]Fee, *First Corinthians*, 676-88.
[33]Bruce C. Johanson, "Tongues, a Sign for Unbelievers?," *NTS* 25 (1979), 180-203.
[34]Ibid., 182, 193.
[35]Changing punctuation is not a problem since the earliest manuscripts contain hardly any punctuation. The question mark, in particular, was not used until the ninth century. See Bruce Metzger, *The Text of the New Testament* (New York, 1964), 27. On the grammatical feasibility of this proposal, see Johanson, "Tongues, a Sign for Unbelievers?," 189, 193. David Garland argues that Johanson's view "fails to take into account the οὖν in 14:23," which he sees as pointing to the consequences of v. 22 (*1 Corinthians* [Grand Rapids: Baker, Academic, 2003], 649). However, as Dr. George Flattery II pointed out to me in an email message, ou}n can be used with an adversative sense ("but" or "however") or, I would add, even to express certainty ("certainly" or "to be sure"; cf. 1 Cor. 3:5), both of which would fit with Johanson's view. See W. Bauer, *A Greek-English Lexicon of the New Testament* (Chicago: University of Chicago Press, 1979), 593.

Paul's opponents. In the opponents' minds, the question should be answered with a resounding "yes."

This reading, then, offers a coherent explanation of the relationship between the paraphrase from Isaiah 28:11-12 and the opponents' inference (v. 22). Johanson notes that Paul's paraphrase, which deviates from both the Masoretic Text (MT) and the Septuagint (LXX), omits the intelligible message spoken by the "Lord" (MT) or "they" (LXX) to which "this people" refuse to listen. Thus, in Paul's version, the hearers refuse to listen to the unintelligible speech of the "foreigners" rather than the intelligible message from God offered in the MT and LXX. This suggests that the quotation either stems from the Corinthian glossolalists or was tailored by Paul to reflect their views. Whichever approach is taken (Johanson opts for the latter view),[36] the essential meaning of the quotation from Isaiah 28:11-12 remains the same; the "people" of v. 21 refers to believers and the point of the quotation (as understood by Paul's opponents) is to say that tongues, although ineffective for instructing Christians, serve as an authenticating, apologetic sign for unbelievers.

After this reference to tongues as a sign for unbelievers ("Are tongues, then, meant as a sign not for believers but for unbelievers . . ."), Paul then has his imaginary opponent blunder on by saying: ". . . while prophecy is meant as a sign not for unbelievers but for believers?" (v. 22b). It may well be that there were two factions at Corinth, both of which were vying for authority and power in the church: one emphasized the gift of prophecy; the other, the gift of tongues. Indeed, Johanson asserts that "the evidence . . . points strongly in the direction that there was in particular a confrontation between prophets and glossolalists in Corinth."[37] He points out that while Paul seems to strengthen the hand of the prophets, he is not totally uncritical of their behavior as well. Paul censures both groups (e.g., 1 Cor. 13:2, 8-9; 14:28-33a, 37-40).

Johanson's reading of 1 Cor. 14:20-25, particularly his thesis that v. 22 gives voice to the Corinthian glossolalists' view, finds

---

[36]Johanson, "Tongues, a Sign for Unbelievers?," 193.
[37]Ibid., 196.

support in one other previously overlooked piece of historical evidence. It should be noted that in the New Testament the term "sign" (σημεῖον) is utilized in conjunction with speaking in tongues in three texts: Mark 16:17 ("these signs will accompany those who believe . . . they will speak in new tongues"); Acts 2:19; and 1 Cor. 14:22. The points of connection between Mark 16:9-20 and Luke's narrative are particularly striking.[38] Mark and Luke both highlight Mary Magdalene's role as a witness to the resurrection and note how the other disciples did not believe her testimony (Mark 16:11; Luke 24:11). Mark and Luke also refer to Jesus' post-resurrection encounter on the road with two disciples (Mark 16:12-13; Luke 24:13-35). Mark and Luke both emphasize the fact that the resurrected Jesus appeared to the eleven while they were eating and rebuked them for their lack of faith (Mark 16:14; Luke 24:40-45).[39] Mark and Luke both present Jesus' commissioning of the disciples for their future mission, which includes a reference to special "signs" which will mark their ministry (Mark 16:15-20; Luke 24:45-49 and Acts 1:4-8; 2:1-4,14-21). Mark and Luke also describe Jesus' ascension to "the right hand" of the Father (Mark 16:19; Luke 24:51 and Acts 1:9-11; 2:33). Finally, and particularly significant for our purposes, Mark and Luke specifically speak of speaking in tongues as one of the signs that will mark the disciples of Jesus (Mark 16:17; Acts 2:4, 15-21). These texts from Luke-Acts and "the long ending" of Mark clearly bear witness to early, underlying tradition. They also indicate that this early tradition included the idea that tongues serve as a positive, authenticating sign within the Christian community.[40] It seems evident that this tradition was known by, and influenced, Christians in the church at Corinth. Paul's instruction in 1 Corinthians 12-14

---

[38]Whether or not one accepts "the long ending" of Mark as the inspired word of God, the historical value of Mark 16:9-20 cannot be questioned. This text was composed at the very latest in the early second century and bears witness to the faith and practice of the early church.

[39]Note how Luke highlights the disciples' inability to understand the prophecies concerning Jesus; see Luke 24:6-8, 25-27, 44-49.

[40]Contra James A. Kelhoffer, who notes the connections between Mark 16:9-20 and Luke-Acts, but claims that only Mark presents tongues as an ongoing sign for believers beyond the apostles (*Miracle and Mission: The Authentication of Missionaries and their Message in the Longer Ending of Mark* [WUNT 2.112; Tübingen: Mohr Siebeck, 2000], 141-47, 281).

indicates that at least some of these Christians had taken this idea (i.e., that tongues serve as a positive sign), rooted in the tradition, and applied it in extreme and destructive ways for self-centered reasons. Nevertheless, 1 Corinthians 14:22 also bears witness to the existence and relatively wide dissemination of this tradition in the early church. Of course, the existence of this tradition makes Johanson's thesis all the more plausible.

However we read 1 Corinthians 14:20-25, it appears that there was a group at Corinth that viewed tongues as a positive sign (this is clearly the case if Johanson is correct). In spite of the immature, selfish, and divisive nature of their outlook, this group did see tongues as a positive and encouraging sign of their community's (perhaps too narrowly defined) connection to the calling and power of the apostolic church. Additionally, as our analysis of 1 Cor. 14:20-25 reveals, they also felt that tongues served an evangelistic purpose. They viewed glossolalia as an authenticating sign and, as such, a sign with apologetic value. Of course, given what we read in Acts 2 and also Mark 16:17, we can understand how this view developed in the early church. In fact, it would appear that there were others, in addition to this faction at Corinth, that held to similar views–that is, others who viewed tongues as a positive and significant sign, both for believers in the community (it was a mark of their identity as end-time prophets and a testimony to Jesus' exalted status) and, in some instances, for non-believers outside the community (as at Pentecost, tongues might validate the proclamation of the gospel). Many in the communities represented by the Gospel of Luke and the Gospel of Mark must have held to similar views.

This brings us back to our central question. How do we reconcile these differing views? How do we understand Paul's polemical thrust, where he challenges this positive appraisal of tongues as a sign, when at the same time we see evidence for it in the book of Acts (and the Gospel of Mark)? I believe the answer to this problem is to be found in a careful analysis of Paul's argument and, in particular, his underlying motives. To this analysis we now turn.

Tongues as a Sign: Paul's Concerns

Our analysis of Paul's argument above highlights with clarity one important fact; Paul was addressing a specific problem at Corinth. This is an important observation, one that should impact how we understand and apply Paul's instructions to the church at Corinth. Because Paul is addressing a specific problem, we should be cautious about making sweeping judgments concerning normative rules for church order. This is particularly the case when we cannot define with certainty the exact nature of the problem.

A good, cautionary example for us is found in 1 Corinthians 14:34, ". . . women should remain silent in the churches." Is this a principle that should guide the practice of every church? Or, as I believe to be the case, is Paul here addressing a problem specific to the church at Corinth?[41] In other words, would Paul have laid down this guideline in every church he encountered or were there elements unique to the congregation at Corinth that called for this very special, specific rule? As we assess Paul's guidelines for the use of tongues in corporate gatherings at Corinth, we should consider carefully whether here too we need to distinguish between transcendent, universally applicable principles and rules that are contextually specific. This is particularly the case given the fact that Paul clearly sees value in the private manifestation of tongues in other passages in the New Testament; most notably those in the book of Acts bear witness to a fuller, more complex view. All of this calls us to take another look at Paul's perspective, particularly his motives.

A review of Paul's argument reveals that he has two overriding concerns with the manner in which tongues were being exercised in the church gatherings at Corinth. First, Paul was clearly upset with the lack of concern for intelligibility in church. This concern comes to the forefront time and time again in 1 Cor. 14. After noting that the one who speaks in tongues "utters mysteries" (1 Cor. 14:2) and does not edify others

---

[41]For a discussion of the hermeneutical issues, see Paul Elbert, *Pastoral Letter to Theo: An Introduction to Interpretation and Women's Ministries* (Eugene, OR: Wipf & Stock, 2008).

(1 Cor. 14:4), Paul declares, "he who prophesies is greater than one who speaks in tongues, unless he interprets" (1 Cor. 14:5). Paul queries, "unless you speak intelligible words with your tongue, how will anyone know what you are saying?" (1 Cor. 14:9). Finally, he admonishes them to "stop thinking like children" (1 Cor. 14:20). Tongues should not, Paul declares, take the place of proclamation or instruction–the intelligible messages found in prophetic utterances (1 Cor. 14:23-25). Indeed, Paul concludes by laying down the law, "If anyone speaks in a tongue . . . someone must interpret" (1 Cor. 14:27).

On this reading of the evidence, it would appear that Paul's concern is not specifically with tongues or even the expression of tongues in the corporate setting. His concern is with the abuse of tongues, or more precisely, the overuse of tongues in the corporate setting. It is apparent, as we read Paul's directives, that at Corinth tongues were taking the place of intelligible messages, whether for the edification of believers or for the purpose of evangelizing non-believers. Notice how in the illustration in 1 Cor. 14:23 Paul refers to "everyone" speaking in tongues with the result being that others do not understand. The implication is that tongues were taking the place of, or totally eclipsing, intelligible proclamation. The abuse was so great that Paul felt that strict guidelines had to be put in place.

When we recognize that in 1 Corinthians 12-14 Paul is dealing with a problem specific to the church at Corinth and that Paul's primary concern has to do with the manner in which tongues were eclipsing intelligible utterances, then we read his guidelines on church order with fresh eyes. We wisely become more cautious concerning an overly rigid application of these guidelines in our contemporary settings. We consider the situation in our church services and ask, "Are our meetings dominated by unintelligible utterances in tongues? Is their little time for intelligible proclamation of the gospel or instruction in the ways of God?" I think the answer to this question is sadly all too evident for the vast majority of our churches. Unbridled enthusiasm is probably not the primary problem with which we must grapple. In other words, we have little to fear when it comes to this concern of Paul.

However, I would note that Paul's polemic clearly issues from a second and perhaps more significant concern. Paul was disturbed by the fact that a group in the church at Corinth was speaking in tongues as a means of establishing their superior status in relation to other believers. In this way, they were also vying for power and authority in the church. Paul seeks to correct this immature, childish, and destructive behavior. He does so by highlighting the rich variety and origin of God's gracious gifts (1 Cor. 12, esp. vss. 4-6). He emphasizes that in the assembly everyone has a role to play (1 Cor. 12:11-27) and that edification is the key goal (1 Cor. 12:7). Ultimately, he declares, "If I speak in tongues . . . but have not love, I am only a resounding gong or a clanging cymbal" (1 Cor. 13:1). Yet, once again, we must be careful to identify Paul's real concern. Here, I would suggest, it is imperative that we distinguish between Paul's disapproval of twisted motives and the actions produced by these improper motives. In other words, Paul's imperatives concerning church order appear to be largely influenced by the twisted motives that governed at least one faction's exercise of tongues. It is debatable, given a different setting with a more mature group of Christians, whether Paul would lay down similar guidelines.[42]

In short, I would suggest that Paul's attitude towards tongues as a sign might not be so different from Luke after all. Once we recognize the polemical nature of Paul's words in 1 Cor. 12-14 and the underlying concerns that shape his argument and related imperatives, we find that Paul may be more appreciative of the sign-value of tongues than is often recognized. Paul clearly recognizes the edifying nature of glossolalia for the individual. Would this not include the fact

---

[42]Here I think particularly of the manner in which Paul restricts the expression of tongues, even when interpreted, to two or three speakers, presumably in a single service (1 Cor. 14:27). I would also note that in 1 Cor. 14:2, when Paul states that "anyone who speaks in a tongue does not speak to men but to God," he is simply highlighting the fact that tongues are unintelligible to other people. For this reason, I do not believe that Paul intends with these words to define or restrict the content of messages delivered through tongues and interpretation exclusively to praise or prayer (directed to God) as opposed to words of exhortation or encouragement (directed to people). Additionally, Dr. George Flattery II noted to me that the "unless" clause of 1 Cor. 14:5 suggests that tongues with interpretation, in Paul's view, may function in the same manner as prophecy.

that tongues call us to recognize our connection with the apostolic church?[43] Would not Paul affirm that tongues serve to remind us that we are end-time prophets empowered to bear witness for Jesus?[44] Would he not agree that Spirit-inspired language, which finds its ultimate source in the Spirit-baptizer, testifies to Jesus' true identity?[45] Since Paul probably refers with approval to "singing in tongues" and appears open to various forms of Spirit-inspired prayer and praise,[46] I think that most likely Paul would recognize the value of uninterpreted tongues in corporate worship as long as it is expressed communally, such as in concert prayer or praise, and not as the focal point of an isolated event. In other words, if our expression of tongues in the context of corporate worship does not disrupt or eclipse intelligible forms of address, such as proclamation, instruction, or prophecy, then I find it hard to believe that Paul would object. Paul might even affirm the value of tongues in an evangelistic setting, if they are expressed in conjunction with intelligible proclamation and not disruptive of it. After all, it was Paul who declared, "my message and my preaching were not with wise and persuasive words, but with a demonstration of the Spirit's power" (1 Cor. 2:4). As in so many matters, for Paul the underlying motive was crucial. If tongues are expressed in love and not out of self-seeking motives, then their potential value increases exponentially.

Conclusion: Reconciling Luke and Paul

I have suggested that Luke's and Paul's respective attitudes towards tongues, particularly tongues as an edifying or positive sign, are not so different after all. In fact, when Paul's argument in 1 Cor. 12-14 is understood against the backdrop of the situation at Corinth and his primary concerns, Paul's references to speaking in tongues take on fresh meaning. Indeed, when the specific rules that Paul lays down for order in worship are

---

[43]See 1 Cor. 2:2-5; 1 Thess. 5:19.
[44]See 1 Cor. 1:2, 4-9; 2 Tim. 1:6-8.
[45]See 1 Cor. 12:3, which has points of similarity with Luke 11:13; Rom. 8:23, 26; 2 Cor. 5:1-4.
[46]See Eph. 5:19; 6:18; and Col. 3:16.

evaluated in the light of this larger context and his concerns, a rigid application of these imperatives in our contemporary settings appears to be quite misguided. I would like to summarize the implications of our study for the life of the church in catechetical fashion—that is, with a series of questions and answers.

Question 1: Can tongues serve as an evangelistic tool?

Yes, but this appears to be very rare. The account of the Pentecostal outpouring of the Spirit in Acts 2 is the only biblical record of this taking place. It should be noted that here speaking in tongues takes the special form of xenolalia. Thus, "Jews from every nation under heaven" (Acts 2:5) understood the tongues of Acts 2. Nevertheless, numerous instances of similar phenomenon in more recent times have been recorded by credible scholars.[47] It is certainly possible that God may choose to work in this manner today. It is also possible that unintelligible tongues (glossolalia) might be used in conjunction with proclamation to arrest the hearer's attention and authenticate the message. However, there is also the very real danger that, as Paul's words in 1 Cor. 14:23-25 attest, tongues may be exercised in a disruptive and inappropriate way. Indeed, they may hinder evangelism. Thus, Paul forbids this evangelistic use of tongues as the normal practice in the assembly. I would suggest that only in very special cases, certainly not as the normal practice of the church, and only in conjunction with intelligible witness should tongues be exercised with an evangelistic purpose in view.

Question 2: Should tongues be banned from our church services unless they are interpreted?

No, I believe that an overly rigid application of Paul's imperatives in 1 Cor. 14:27-28 misunderstands Paul's underlying concern and purpose. Paul appears to be quite open to various

---

[47]See Jordan May, *Global Witness to Pentecost: The Testimony of "Other Tongues"* (Cleveland, TN: Cherohala Press, 2013).

forms of Spirit-inspired prayer and praise (Eph. 5:19; 6:18). Additionally, Luke's record in Acts suggests that tongues were edifying and encouraging in various corporate contexts. With this mind, I believe that both Paul and Luke call us to recognize the value of uninterpreted tongues in corporate worship as long as they are expressed communally, such as in concert prayer or praise, and not disruptive of proclamation, instruction, or prophecy.

> Question 3: Is it appropriate during our corporate gatherings (generally, but not necessarily, at the conclusion) to call people to collectively seek God's empowering, complete with manifestations of tongues?

By all means, yes! Our churches desperately need to establish times when we come together for the purpose of prayer and to collectively seek all that God has for us. This will inevitably lead to experiences of spiritual rapture, those moments when various individuals are baptized in the Holy Spirit and burst forth in glossolalic praise (Acts 2:4). This was the practice and experience of those early Pentecostal pioneers as well as the early church (Acts 1:14; 2:1-4).

Luke, in particular, emphasizes that in these moments, tongues serve as a powerful sign, both to the individual and to the community. It is a sign that reminds us of our calling as end-time prophets and that testifies to the majesty and exalted status of Jesus. I am confident that with this Paul would agree.

Is Servant Leadership Effective in Motivating Volunteers?
By Stephen Fogarty

Introduction

Christian leaders typically acknowledge the example of Jesus the servant leader as being pertinent to their own leadership roles. He represents an ideal of serving and acting in the best interests of others, and of engaging in personal sacrifice. While acknowledging that the example of Jesus is a noble ideal, the question arises as to whether it represents leadership that is effective in achieving desired organisational outcomes. Most churches and related organisations have visions and missions and related outcomes that they are seeking to bring to fruition. Christian leaders normally face the challenge of motivating volunteers, and a minority of paid employees, to achieve such desired outcomes.

The question that this study addresses is whether servant leadership is an effective style for motivating volunteers to higher levels of commitment and performance in order to bring about desired organisational outcomes. The study compares the impact of servant leadership on volunteer motivation within church congregations with the impact of transformational leadership and transactional leadership. It also compares the effect of the three leadership styles on volunteer trust in and value congruence with the leader.

Jesus the Servant Leader

The example of Jesus as a servant leader should be a core consideration in any understanding of a Christian leadership style. A key biblical text relating to the servant leadership of Jesus is the christological hymn in Philippians 2:5-11, which is used by the apostle Paul to encourage his Philippian readers to maintain unity within the church. In Philippians 2:1-4 Paul appeals to his readers to avoid division and divisiveness within the community. It seems that in the face of external persecution (1:27-30) internal dissension was occurring within the church. The apostle recognises that the church can only survive external pressure when its members are "standing firm in one spirit, striving side by side with one mind for the faith of the gospel" (1:27). He therefore urges them to "be of the same mind, having the same love, being in one accord and of one mind" (2:2). Practically, this means that each member should "look not to your own interests, but to the interests of others" (2:3). Barth (1962) comments, "each is to climb down from the throne on which he sits, and to mind and seek after the one end, which is then also that of the others and in which all must find their way to unity" (50). Unity is produced through practicing mutuality. Paul refers to such behavior as "humility" which regards "others as better than yourselves" (2:3). The supreme example of such behavior is Jesus Christ who is the subject of Philippians 2:5-11.

Paul uses the life of Jesus Christ as the model for Christian behavior and community. As Thurston and Ryan (2005) point out, "our wholeness and unity as a community come through renunciation of the natural, selfish state and the appropriation of Jesus' self-giving, to which God responded positively" (90). Paul apparently felt that the Philippians were engaging in behavior that was selfish and ambitious. Such behavior has no place in the Christian community. Thurston and Ryan (2005) suggest, "it is only through chosen acts of self-emptying, only through looking to others' welfare as well as our own (2:4) that we are brought into the sphere of Jesus, his life and his power" (91). Witherington (1994) suggests, "Christ becomes the ultimate example of one who did not pursue his own interests or selfishly take advantage of rights, privileges, or status that were properly his, but rather 'emptied himself'" (66). To live as a follower of Jesus is to act in status-rejecting ways and to be prepared to suffer for others.

Witherington (1994) points out that Paul's advice to the Philippians has social implications because it cuts across "the distinction usually made between those of greater and lesser status" (63). Such social hierarchies are undermined by everyone serving and considering the interests of others. All human thoughts of the exaltation of self are critiqued by Jesus Christ. Leaders become "at most exemplary or head servants" (Witherington, 1994, 65). When one has as a model a servant leader one willingly takes on a much lower status and undertakes servile roles. Fee (1995) points out that Christ's actions reveal the character of God: "Here is the epitome of God-likeness: the pre-existent Christ was not a 'grasping, selfish' being, but one whose love for others found its consummate expression in 'pouring himself out,' in taking the role of a slave, in humbling himself to the point of death on behalf of those so loved" (197). God is not an acquisitive being, but self-giving for the sake of others. To follow Christ is therefore to engage in servant-hood and self-sacrifice for the sake of others.

Jesus epitomizes the servant leader and Paul presents him as an example for the Philippians. Jesus set aside his own rights for the sake of others to the point of laying down his life (c.f. John 15:13). Peter, reflecting later on the example of Jesus, writes "For to this you have been called, because Christ also suffered for you, leaving you an example, so that you should follow in his steps" (1 Peter 2:21). Paul uses the example of Jesus in the same way as Peter in an effort to inspire his readers to become servant leaders themselves.

Servant Leadership

While the concept of servant leadership has a long tradition in Christian thinking, it has been introduced to business and organisational theory in recent decades through the work of Robert Greenleaf and subsequent writers. Greenleaf (1977) coined the term "servant leadership" which he thought commenced "with the natural feeling that one wants to serve, to serve first." He posited that service to followers is the primary responsibility of leaders and the essence of ethical leadership.

His test of leadership effectiveness was, "Do those served grow as persons? Do they . . . become healthier, wiser, freer, more autonomous, and more likely themselves to become servants?"

Servant leadership encompasses nurturing, defending, and empowering followers. A servant leader is concerned for the needs of his or her followers and seeks their well-being along with the well-being of the organization. A servant leader empowers followers rather than dominating them. Such empowerment occurs directly through the leader mentoring and training followers, and indirectly by providing support and concern as well as an ethical and a transparent working environment (Farling, Stone, & Winston, 1999; Laub, 1999; Patterson, 2003; Barbuto & Wheeler, 2006; Liden, Wayne, Zhao, & Henderson, 2008; Van Dierendonck, 2011; Winston & Fields, 2015).

Winston and Fields (2015) have devised a reliable measurable set of servant leadership behaviors (Table 1). The 10 item Essential Servant Leadership Behaviors table is the result of extensive testing and refinement of previous sets of servant leadership behaviors.

Table 1: Servant Leadership Behaviors

A Servant Leader	
1	Practices what he or she preaches
2	Serves people without regard to their nationality, gender, or race
3	Sees serving as a mission of responsibility to others
4	Is genuinely interested in followers as people
5	Understands that serving others is most important
6	Is willing to make sacrifices to help others
7	Seeks to instil trust rather than fear or insecurity
8	Is always honest
9	Is driven by a sense of higher calling
10	Promotes values that transcend self-interest and material success

Greenleaf believed that followers of servant leaders are inspired to become servant leaders themselves. The results of servant leadership include higher ethical standards within organizations, safe and strong working relationships, and greater value placed on human worth. Servant leaders oppose social injustice and treat the weak and marginal members of society with respect and appreciation.] (Patterson, 2003; Liden, et al, 2008; Andersen, 2009; Van Dierendonck, 2011).

Servant Leadership and Transformational Leadership

Servant leadership is similar to and often contrasted with transformational leadership. Both approaches to leadership are viewed as being ethical and focused on the well-being of those impacted by leadership behavior. Sendjaya, Sarros, and Santora (2008) maintain that servant leadership is conceptually distinct from transformational leadership for two reasons.

First, servant leaders are more likely than transformational leaders to demonstrate the natural inclination to serve marginalized people. Bass (1985) argued that transformational leaders seek to empower and elevate followers rather than keep followers weak and dependent. However, the effects of that increased motivation and commitment will not necessarily benefit followers, as "there is nothing in the transformational leadership model that says leaders should serve followers for the good of followers" (Graham, 1991, 110). On the other hand, servant leadership requires that leaders lead followers for the followers' own ultimate good.

Second, servant leaders are more likely than transformational leaders to prioritise their leadership focus as followers first, organization second, and their own needs last (Graham, 1991). Barbuto and Wheeler (2006) point out that the role of servant leaders is to serve followers, whereas the role of transformational leaders is to inspire followers to pursue organizational goals. Hence, the focus of servant leadership, first and foremost, is on individual followers, and takes precedence over organizational objectives. The rationale behind this deliberate focus on followers is well summarized by Stone, Russell, and Patterson (2004, 355) who assert, "organizational goals will be achieved on a long-term basis only by first facilitating the growth, development, and general well-being of the individuals who comprise the organization." The difference in emphasis between servant and transformational leadership is demonstrated by comparing the servant leadership behaviors in Table 1 with the transformational leadership behaviors from the Multifactor Leadership Questionnaire in Table 2.

Table 2: Transformational Leadership Behaviors

A Transformational Leader	
1	Goes beyond self-interest for the good of the group
2	Acts in ways that build followers' respect
3	Talks about their most important values and beliefs
4	Specifies the importance of having a strong sense of purpose
5	Talks optimistically about the future
6	Articulates a compelling vision of the future
7	Re-examines critical assumptions to question whether they are appropriate
8	Seeks differing perspectives when solving problems
9	Spends time teaching and coaching
10	Treats people as individuals rather than just as members of a group

Transformational leadership is focused on inspiring others to perform beyond expected levels of commitment and contribution. Transformational leaders inspire followers by serving as idealised role models, by providing a clear and attractive vision of the organisation's future, by encouraging innovation and creative problem solving, and by coaching and mentoring (Avolio and Bass, 2004; Judge and Bono, 2000; Riggio et al., 2004). Whereas the primary focus of transformational leadership is inspiring followers to performance beyond expectations, the *sine qua non* of servant leadership is followers' holistic moral and ethical development.

Servant Leadership and Transactional Leadership

Both servant leadership and transformational leadership focus on motivating followers through inspiration. In contrast, transactional leadership seeks to motivate followers through a process of exchange (Bass, 1985; Riggio et al., 2004). Transactional leaders also seek to motivate followers by providing an adequate exchange of valued resources for follower support and by monitoring performance and taking corrective action.

The difference in emphasis between servant and transactional leadership is demonstrated by comparing the servant leadership behaviors in Table 1 with the transactional leadership behaviors from the Multifactor Leadership Questionnaire in Table 3. Transactional leadership focuses on followers' performance to expectation in exchange for adequate reward, and lacks the emphasis of servant leadership on followers' well-being and development.

Table 3: Transactional Leadership Behaviors

A Transactional Leader	
1	Provides followers with assistance in exchange for their efforts
2	Discusses in specific terms who is responsible for achieving performance targets
3	Makes clear what can be expected when performance goals are achieved
4	Expresses satisfaction when expectations are met
5	Focuses attention on irregularities, mistakes, and deviations from standards
6	Concentrates on dealing with mistakes, complaints, and failures
7	Keeps track of all mistakes
8	Directs followers' attention toward failures to meet standards

Volunteer Motivation

Volunteers are individuals who provide unpaid help in an organised manner to parties with regard to whom the volunteer has no obligations (Millette and Gagné, 2008; Snyder and Omoto, 2004; Wilson and Janoski, 1995). They are eagerly sought after because they add value to organisations and endeavours (Wilson and Musick, 1997), and are typically employed in non-profit organisations including churches and charities (Phillips and Phillips, 2010, 2011). Because volunteers do not receive direct personal tangible gains such as a salary, non-profit organisations must find other ways to motivate volunteers to work well and to continue in volunteer activity, and by doing so retain the knowledge and skill resources of the organisation (Millette and Gagné, 2008). Maintaining volunteer motivation at levels that result in sustained and productive voluntary service is critical to the effectiveness of non-profit organisations in fulfilling their stated missions.

Volunteer motivation can be conceptualised using self-determination theory (Deci and Ryan, 2000, 2008), which posits that people are motivated to satisfy their innate psychological needs for autonomy, competence, and relatedness. Autonomy refers to the desire to control one's own behavior and activities in order to experience personal integration and freedom. Competence is one's propensity to be effective in dealing with the environment while attaining valued outcomes within it. Relatedness refers to one's desire to be connected to others. According to Deci and Ryan, the satisfaction of all three of these needs is "essential for ongoing psychological growth, integrity, and well-being" (2000, 229).

Self-determination theory connects the needs for autonomy, competence, and relatedness to levels of motivation, from extrinsic to intrinsic. Extrinsic motivation refers to engaging in an activity for instrumental reasons, such as acquiring a reward or avoiding a penalty, where the primary motivators are external to the volunteer. By contrast, intrinsic motivation refers to engaging in an activity for its own sake, because one finds it enjoyable and interesting, where the primary motivators are internal to the volunteers as they seek to fulfil their needs for autonomy, competence, and relatedness. Extrinsic motivation has been demonstrated to predict lower quality task performance and shorter volunteer tenure, whereas intrinsic motivation predicts higher quality task performance and longer volunteer tenure (Deci and Ryan, 2008; Millette and Gagné, 2008). It is advantageous to churches and non-profit organisations if they are able to stimulate and maintain intrinsic motivation within volunteers.

Leadership Style and Volunteer Motivation

Fogarty (2013) found that transactional leadership predicted extrinsic motivation, whereas transformational leadership predicted intrinsic motivation. Similarly to transformational leadership, servant leadership is likely to produce intrinsic motivation in volunteers. Volunteers in both leadership styles are motivated by their personal identification with the leader and their accompanying commitment to the mission of the organisation articulated by the leader (Winston & Fields, 2015). This personal identification and commitment is internally driven and volunteers are likely satisfying the needs of autonomy, competence, and relatedness. Therefore, a leader's exercise of servant leadership behaviors is likely to stimulate volunteer intrinsic motivation.

Leadership Style and Volunteer Trust and Value Congruence

The effective exercise of leadership is based upon leader–follower relationships that incorporate followers' trust in, and value congruence with, the leader (Yukl, 2006). Trust in a leader is "faith in and loyalty to the leader" (Podsakoff et al., 1990, 113). Value congruence with a leader is belief that the follower's personal values are congruent with and aligned with those of the leader (Posner, 2010). Fogarty (2013) found that transformational leadership predicted trust and value congruence, but that transactional leadership did not.

Similarly to transformational leadership, servant leaders are likely to increase followers' trust and value congruence by developing their skills and confidence to perform tasks and assume responsibility, by providing support and encouragement when necessary in the face of obstacles, difficulties, and fatigue, and through their own role modeling of desirable behavior and willingness to engage in sacrifice in order to achieve the organisational vision (Winston & Fields, 2015; Bass and Avolio, 1990; Yukl, 2006). Therefore, the practice of servant leadership behaviors is likely to increase volunteers' trust in the character and competence of the leader. It also is apt to produce change in volunteers' values and to increase their value congruence with the leader.

Study Hypotheses

The following hypotheses were tested:

H_1: The servant leadership behaviors of senior pastors will be positively related to volunteer intrinsic motivation.

H_2: The servant leadership behaviors of senior pastors will be positively related to volunteer trust in, and value congruence, with the leader.

Sample

The sample for this study was drawn from volunteers attending and participating in twenty eight different Australian Christian Church (ACC) congregations in Australia. The sample consisted of 790 subjects who served in a voluntary capacity within their congregation and who rated the leadership behaviors of their senior pastor. The selection of twenty eight different ACC congregations was designed to provide responses from volunteers within each of five congregational size categories that ACC recognises. ACC, also known as the Assemblies of God in Australia, is a fellowship of autonomous churches which had 1,087 registered churches throughout Australia as of May 17, 2010 (ACC, 2010). These congregations represent 2.6% of the total number of ACC congregations. ACC conducts an annual census of all congregations in May. The census collects data on various church activities, including weekend attendance which is measured as the total number of attendees at all services from Friday evening to Sunday evening on one weekend in May each year. ACC categorises congregational sizes into five categories: (a) under 100 attendees, (b) 100-199 attendees, (c) 200-499 attendees, (d) 500-999 attendees, and (c) 1000 and more attendees. In 2010, the average size of an ACC congregation was 208 attendees. [This reader would find it useful to have a breakdown of the number of participants in each of the previous groups.]

Measures

The survey questionnaire employed 66 items to measure: (a) volunteers' assessment of the senior pastor's practice of servant, transformational, and transactional leadership behaviors, (b) volunteers' self-assessment of their motivation, and (c) volunteers' self-assessment of their trust in, and value congruence, with the senior pastor. The sixty-six items consisted of the ten item Essential Behaviours of Servant Leaders scale (Winston & Fields, 2015) to measure volunteers' assessment of the senior pastor's practice of servant leadership behaviors (scale reliability $\alpha = .63$); twenty items adapted from the Multifactor Leadership Questionnaire (MLQ-5X; Bass and Avolio, 2000) to measure volunteers' assessment of the senior pastor's practice of transformational leadership behaviors (scale reliability $\alpha = .86$); twelve items adapted from the Multifactor Leadership Questionnaire (MLQ-5X; Bass and Avolio, 2000) to measure volunteers' assessment of the senior pastor's practice of transactional leadership behaviors (scale reliability $\alpha = .69$); six items adapted from Millette and Gagné (2008) to measure volunteers' intrinsic motivation (scale reliability $\alpha = .74$); six items adapted from Millette and Gagné (2008) to measure volunteers' extrinsic motivation (scale reliability $\alpha = .76$); six items adapted from Podsakoff et al. (1990) to measure volunteers' trust in the senior pastor (scale reliability $\alpha = .76$); and six items adapted from Posner (1992, 2010) and Posner et al. (1985) to measure volunteers' value congruence with the senior pastor (scale reliability α = .78).

Results

Correlation analysis was used to detect one-to-one correlations between the independent and dependent variables. The mean scores and standard deviations of the independent and dependent variables and correlations among the variables are shown in Table 5.

Table 5: Mean Scores, Standard Deviations, and Correlations among Study Variables (N = 790)

Variable	M	SD	1	2	3	4	5	6	7	8	9	10
1. Volunteer tenure	2.51	.65	-									
2. Senior pastor tenure	2.51	.71	.15**	-								
3. Congregational size	3.13	1.34	.06	.53**	-							
4. Servant leadership	3.57	.44	-.04	-.04	.04	-						
5. Transformational leadership	3.28	.47	-.07	-.08	.05	.65**	-					
6. Transactional leadership	1.70	.58	.00	.08*	-.03	-.02	.13**	-				
7. Trust	3.07	.36	-.04	-.07	-.05	.52**	.63**	.08*	-			
8. Value congruence	3.10	.34	-.06	-.07	-.01	.48**	.60**	08*	.66**	-		
9. Extrinsic motivation	1.27	.78	-.03	.01	-.04	-.05	.02	.25**	-.01	-.03	-	
10. Intrinsic motivation	3.24	.57	.03	.03	.13*	.26**	.35**	.09*	.29**	.26**	.18**	-

* $p < .05$. ** $p < .01$.

Leadership Style

Volunteers perceived senior pastors to more typically exercise servant and transformational behaviors than transactional behaviors. This is evident in the high mean scores for servant leadership (M=3.57) and transformational leadership (M=3.28), compared with the low mean score for transactional leadership (M=1.70). It is also evident in the large (r > .50; Pallant, 2011) positive correlation between servant and transformational leadership (r = .65) which represents 42.25% of the variance in each variable. By contrast, transformational leadership had only had a small (r < .25; Pallant, 2011) positive correlation with transactional leadership (r = .13) representing 1.69% of variance. Servant leadership had no significant correlation with transactional leadership.

Volunteer Motivation

Volunteers typically believed that they were intrinsically rather than extrinsically motivated. This is evident in the high mean score for intrinsic motivation ($M=3.24$) and the low mean score for extrinsic motivation ($M=1.27$). There was a small positive correlation between intrinsic and extrinsic motivation ($r=.18$) representing 3.24% of variance.

Leadership Style and Volunteer Motivation

Servant leadership had a medium ($r=.25 - .50$; Pallant, 2011) positive correlation with intrinsic motivation ($r=.26$) representing 6.76% of variance. Transformational leadership also had a medium positive correlation with intrinsic motivation ($r=.35$) representing 12.25% of variance. Transactional leadership had a very small positive correlation with intrinsic motivation ($r=.09$) representing .81% of variance. Both transformational and servant leadership behaviors inspire intrinsic motivation in volunteers. The larger effect of transformational leadership is likely linked to the intentional focus of transformational leaders on inspiring followers to performance beyond expectation by engaging in exemplary and visionary leadership behaviors.

Transactional leadership had a medium positive correlation with extrinsic motivation ($r=.25$) representing 6.25% of variance. Neither servant nor transformational leadership had a signficant correlation with extrinsic motivation. Transactional leadership behaviors produce extrinsic motivation, but servant and transformational leadership behaviors do not.

Hypothesis 1 was supported, with the servant leadership behaviors of senior pastors being positively related to volunteer intrinsic motivation.

Leadership Style and Volunteer Trust and Value Congruence

The mean scores for trust ($M=3.07$) and value congruence ($M=3.10$) were high, indicating that volunteers typically trusted senior pastors and believed that their values aligned. Servant leadership had a large positive correlation with trust (r=.52) representing 27% of variance, and also with value congruence (r =.48) representing 23% of variance. Transformational leadership also had large positive correlations with trust (r=.63) representing 39.7% of variance, and with value congruence (r = .60) representing 36% of variance. Transactional leadership had a small positive correlation with trust (r=.08) representing 0.6% of variance, and with value congruence (r=.08) representing 0.6% of variance. Servant and transformational leadership behaviors inspire trust and value congruence in volunteers. The larger effect of transformational leadership is likely linked to the intentional focus of transformational leaders on inspiring followers to performance beyond expectation by engaging in exemplary and visionary leadership behaviors.

Hypothesis 2 was supported, with the servant leadership behaviors of senior pastors being positively related to volunteer trust in and value congruence with the leader.

Discussion

The goal of this study was to examine the relationships between the servant leadership behaviors of senior pastors and the levels of motivation, trust, and value congruence experienced by volunteers. The study found that servant leadership is significantly positively related to volunteer intrinsic motivation, trust, and value congruence. These results are similar to those found by Fogarty (2013) in relation to the impact of transformational leadership on volunteer motivation, trust, and value congruence. Study findings are summarised in Table 6.

Table 6: Summary of Correlation Analysis Results

Variable	Trust	Value Congruence	Intrinsic Motivation	Extrinsic Motivation
Servant	++	++	++	-
Transformational	++	++	++	-
Transactional	+	+	+	++

Note. ++ large or medium positive relationship; + small positive relationship; – no relationship.

The significant positive correlations between servant and transformational leadership and intrinsic motivation are consistent with servant and transformational leadership theories. Such theories posit that such leadership styles establish moral and inspirational relationships with followers and motivate them to work for transcendental goals and for aroused higher-level needs for self-actualisation (Winston & Fields, 2015; Bass, 1985). They are also consistent with self-determination theory which connects intrinsic motivation to internal motivators to fulfil the needs for autonomy, competence, and relatedness (Deci and Ryan, 2000, 2008). The practice of servant and transformational behaviors by non-profit leaders is likely to reinforce intrinsic motivation among volunteers.

The significant positive correlation between transactional leadership and extrinsic motivation is consistent with transactional leadership theory which posits that such leadership establishes an exchange relationship with followers offering rewards for services rendered (Bass, 1985; Burns, 1978). It is also consistent with self-determination theory which connects extrinsic motivation to external and instrumental motivators (Deci and Ryan, 2000, 2008). The practice of transactional behaviors by non-profit leaders is likely to reinforce extrinsic motivation among volunteers.

The significant positive correlations between servant and transformational leadership and trust and value congruence are also consistent with previous findings (Winston & Fields, 2015; Bass, 1985; Bennis and Nanus, 1985; Podsakoff et al. 1990). The practice of servant and transformational behaviors by non-profit leaders is likely to reinforce trust and value congruence among volunteers.

Theoretical Implications

This study contributed to the leadership and motivation literature by: (a) connecting servant leadership theory with self-determination theory in order to examine the relationship between leadership behavior and volunteer motivation in non-profit organisations, and thereby demonstrating (b) positive relationships between servant leadership and intrinsic motivation, trust, and value congruence in volunteers. Fogarty (2013) had identified similar relationships between transformational leadership and intrinsic motivation, trust, and value congruence. The findings of this study indicate that servant leadership has similar impacts on transformational leadership, and is therefore an effective leadership style for leading volunteers.

Practical Implications

Non-profit organisations that depend on volunteer workers require leaders who can inspire intrinsic motivation in volunteers (Larsson and Ronnmark, 1996; Riggio et al., 2004). The organisational problems of shorter tenure and poorer task performance are less likely to occur among volunteers in non-profit organisations where leaders exercise servant leadership behaviors directed towards the enhancement of volunteer intrinsic motivation, trust, and value congruence. Therefore, this study provides the following practical implications for non-profit organisations: (a) leader selection criteria should incorporate evidence of effective demonstration of servant leadership behaviors; (b) leader training should incorporate instruction and guidance in servant leadership behaviors; and (c) leadership strategies should incorporate the goal of building volunteer intrinsic motivation.

References

Andersen J.A. (2009). "When a Servant-Leader Comes Knocking." *Leadership & Organization Development Journal* 30, 1: 4-15.

Australian Christian Churches (2010). ACC 2010 Church Census Report. Sydney, Australia: ACC National Office.

Avolio B.J & B.M. Bass. (1988). "Transformational Leadership, Charisma and Beyond." In Emerging Leadership Vistas, edited by J.G. Hunt, B.R. Baliga, H.P. Dachler, and C.A. Schrieisheim, 29-50. Emsford, NY: Pergamon Press.

_____. (1995). "Individual Consideration Viewed at Multiple Levels of Analysis: A Multi-level Framework for Examining the Diffusion of Transformational Leadership." *Leadership Quarterly* 6: 199-218.

_____. (2004). Multifactor Leadership Questionnaire: Manual and Sampler Set (3rd ed.). Palo Alto, CA: Mind Garden.

Avolio B.J., B.M. Bass and D.I. Jung D.I. (1999). "Re-examining the Components of Transformational and Transactional Leadership Using the Multifactor Leadership Questionnaire." *Journal of Occupational and Organizational Psychology* 72: 441-462.

Bae K.. (2001). Transformational Leadership and Its Application in Church Organization (Ph.D. dissertation). Retrieved from ProQuest Dissertations and Theses database. (UMI No. 3005838).

Balswick J. and W. Wright. (1988). "A Complementary-Empowering Model of Ministerial Leadership. *Pastoral Psychology* 37, 1: 1-14.

Barbuto J.E. and D.W.Wheeler. (2006). Scale Development and Construct Clarification of Servant Leadership. Group & Organization Management 31, 3: 300-326.

Barrett C.K. (1971). The First Epistle to the Corinthians (2nd ed.). London, UK: A & C Black.

Barth K. (1962). The Epistle to the Philippians. Richmond, VA: John Knox.

Bass B.M. (1985). Leadership and Performance Beyond Expectations. New York, NY: Free Press.

_____. (1998). Transformational Leadership: Industry, Military, and Educational Impact. Mahwah, NJ: Erlbaum.

Bass B.M. and B.J. Avolio. (1990). "The Implications of Transformational and Transactional Leadership for Individual, Team, and Organizational Development." In Research in Organizational Change and Development edited by R. Woodman and W. Passmore, 231-272. Greenwich, CT: JAI Press.

_____. (2000). Effects on Platoon Readiness of Transformational/Transactional Platoon Leadership. Ft Belvoir, VA: US Army Research Institute for the Behavioral and Social Sciences.

Bennis W. and B. Nanus. (1985). Leaders. New York, NY: Harper & Row.

Burns J.M. (1978). Leadership. New York, NY: Harper & Row.

Butler D.M. and R.D. Herman. (1999). "Effective Ministerial Leadership." *Nonprofit Management & Leadership*, 9,3: 229-239.

Callahan S.H. (1996). A Delphi Study of the Competencies Needed by Leaders of Roman Catholic Faith Communities in Western Washington Through the Year 2000 (Ph.D. dissertation). Retrieved from ProQuest Dissertations and Theses database. (UMI No. 9716963).

Catano V.M., M. Pond and E.K. Kelloway (2001). "Exploring Commitment and Leadership in Voluntary Organizations." *Leadership and Organization Development Journal* 22, 5/6: 256-263.

Choi K. (2006). The Impact of Motivational Language and Transformational Leadership of the Pastor on Volunteers' Job Satisfaction in Korean Southern Baptist Churches in the

United States (Ph.D. dissertation). Retrieved from ProQuest Dissertations and Theses database. (UMI No. 3243509).

Crain-Gully D.I. (2003). Exploring Transformational Leadership Characteristics Among African American Church Leaders in the San Francisco Bay Area (Ph.D. dissertation). Retrieved from ProQuest Dissertations and Theses database. (UMI No. 3082000).

Deci E.L., H. Eghrari, B.C. Patrick, and D.R. Leone. (1994). "Facilitating Internalization: The Self Determination Theory Perspective." *Journal of Personality* 61, 1: 119-142.

Deci E.L. and R.M. Ryan. (2000). "The "What" and "Why" of Goal Pursuits: Human Needs and the Self-determination of Behavior." *Psychological Inquiry* 11, 4: 227-268.

_____. (2008). "Self-Determination Theory: A Macrotheory of Human Motivation, Development, and Health." *Canadian Psychology* 49, 3: 182-185.

Druskat V.U. (1994). "Gender and Leadership Style: Transformational and Transactional Leadership in the Roman Catholic Church." *Leadership Quarterly* 5: 99-119.

Epitropaki O. and R. Martin. (2004)." Implicit Leadership Theories in Applied Settings: Factor Structure, Generalizability and Stability Over Time." *Journal of Applied Psychology* 89, 2: 293-310.

Farling M., A. Stone, and B. Winston. (1999). "Servant Leadership: Setting the Stage for Empirical Research." *Journal of Leadership Studies* 61, 2: 49-72.

Fee G.D. (1987). The First Epistle to the Corinthians. Grand Rapids, MI: Eerdmans.

_____. (1995). Paul's Letter to the Philippians. Grand Rapids, MI: Eerdmans.

Fogarty S.G. (2013). The Impact of Senior Pastor Leadership Behaviors on Volunteer Motivation (Ph.D. dissertation).

Graham J.W. (1991). "Servant Leadership in Organizations: Inspirational and Moral." *The Leadership Quarterly* 2: 105-119.

Greenleaf R K. (1977). Servant Leadership: A Journey into the Nature of Legitimate Power and Greatness. New York: Paulist Press.

Hair J.F., W.C. Black, B.J. Babin, and R.E. Anderson. (2010). Multivariate Data Analysis (7th ed.). Upper Saddle River, NJ: Prentice Hall.

Johnson B. (2007). The Perceived Leadership Crisis Within the Baptist Church: An Exploratory Empirical Investigation of Selected Churches in Memphis, Tennessee (Ph.D. dissertation). Retrieved from ProQuest Dissertations and Theses database. (UMI No. 3251346).

Judge T.A. and J.E. Bono. (2000). "Five-Factor Model of Personality and Transformational Leadership." *Journal of Applied Psychology* 85, 5: 751-765.

Judge T.A. and R.F. Piccolo. (2004). "Transformational and Transactional Leadership: A Meta-Analytic Test of Their Relative Validity." *Journal of Applied Psychology* 89, 755-768.

Jung D.I. and B.J. Avolio. (2000). "Opening the Black Box: An Experimental Investigation of the Mediating Effects of Trust and Value Congruence on Transformational and Transactional Leadership." *Journal of Organizational Behavior* 21, 8: 949-964.

Knudsen D.N. (2006). The Effect of Transformational Leadership on Growth in Specialized Non-profit Organizations: Churches (Ph.D. dissertation). Retrieved from ProQuest Dissertations and Theses database. (UMI No. 3231161).

Larsson S. and L. Ronnmark. (1996). "The Concept of Charismatic Leadership: Its Application to an Analysis of Social Movements and a Voluntary Organization in Sweden." *The International Journal of Public Sector Management* 9, 7: 32-41.

Laub J.A. (1999). Assessing the Servant Organization: Development of the Servant Organizational Leadership Assessment (SOLA) Instrument. Unpublished Ph.D. dissertation. Florida Atlantic University, Boca Raton, FL.

Lichtman S.L. and H.N. Malony. (1990). "Effective Ministerial Style as Perceived by Denominational Leadership." *Pastoral Psychology* 38, 3: 161-171.

Liden R.C., S.J. Wayne, H. Zhao, and D. Henderson. (2008). "Servant Leadership: Development of a Multidimensional Measure and Multi-level Assessment." *The Leadership Quarterly* 19, 2: 161-177.

Millette V. and M. Gagné. (2008). "Designing Volunteers' Tasks to Maximize Motivation, Satisfaction and Performance: The Impact of Job Characteristics on Volunteer Engagement." *Motiv Emot* 32: 11-22.

Morris L. (1980). The First Epistle of Paul to the Corinthians. Grand Rapids, MI: Eerdmans.

Offermann L.R., J.K. Kennedy, and & P.W. Wirtz. (1994). "Implicit Leadership Theories: Content, Structure, and Generalizability." *Leadership Quarterly* 5, 1, 43-58.

Onnen M.K. (1987). The Relationship of Clergy Leadership Characteristics to Growing or Declining Churches (Unpublished Ph.D. dissertation). University of Louisville, Louisville, KY.

Pallant J. (2011). SPSS Survival Manual (4th ed.). Crows Nest, Australia: Allen & Unwin.

Paternoster R., R. Brame, P. Mazerolle, and A. Piquero. (1998). "Using the Correct Statistical Test for the Equality of Regression Coefficients." *Criminology* 36, 4: 859-866.

Patterson K. (2003). Servant Leadership: A Theoretical Model (Ph.D. dissertation). Retrieved from ProQuest-UMI AAT 3082719.

Phillips L.C. and M.H. Phillips. (2010). "Volunteer Motivation and Reward Preference: An Empirical Study of Volunteerism in a Large, Not-For-Profit Organization." *SAM Advanced Management Journal* 75, 4: 12-19.

_____. (2011, Winter). "Altruism, Egoism, or Something Else: Rewarding Volunteers Effectively and Affordably." *Southern Business Review*: 23-35.

Podsakoff P. S. Mackenzie, R. Moorman, and R. Fetter. (1990). "Transformational Leader Behaviors and Their Effects on Followers' Trust in Leaders, Satisfaction, and Organizational Citizenship Behaviors." *Leadership Quarterly* 1: 107-142.

Posner B. (1992). "Person–Organization Values Congruence: No Support for Individual Differences as a Moderating Influence." *Human Relations* 45, 4: 351-362.

_____. (2010). "Another Look at the Impact of Personal and Organizational Values Congruency." *Journal of Business Ethics* 97: 535-541.

Posner B.Z., J.M. Kouzes, and W.H. Schmidt. (1985). "Shared Values Make a Difference: An Empirical Test of Corporate Culture." *Human Resource Management* 24, 3: 293-310.

Riggio R.E., B.M. Bass, and S.S. Orr. (2004). "Transformational Leadership in Nonprofit Organizations. In Improving Leadership in Nonprofit Organizations, edited by R.E. Riggio and S.S. Orr, 49-62. San Francisco, CA: Jossey-Bass.

Rowold J. (2008). "Effects of Transactional and Transformational Leadership in Pastors." *Pastoral Psychology* 56: 403-411.

Rowold J. & Rohmann A. (2009). "Relationships Between Leadership Styles and Followers' Emotional Experience and Effectiveness in the Voluntary Sector." *Nonprofit and Voluntary Sector Quarterly* 38, 2: 270-286.

Sendjaya, S., Sarros, J.C. & Santora, J.C. (2008). "Defining and Measuring Servant Leadership Behaviour in Organizations." *Journal of Management Studies* 45, 2.

Shamir B., House R., & Arthur M. (1993). "The Motivational Effects of Charismatic Leadership: A Self-Concept Based Theory." *Organization Science* 4, 2: 1-17.

Snyder M. & Omoto A.M. (2004). "Volunteers and Volunteer Organizations: Theoretical Perspectives and Practical Concerns. In Improving Leadership in Nonprofit Organizations edited by R.E. Riggio and S.S. Orr, 163-179. San Francisco, CA: Jossey-Bass.

Son J. (2003). An Analysis of Leadership Styles and Practices among Korean Senior Pastors (Ph.D. dissertation). Retrieved from ProQuest Dissertations and Theses database. (UMI No. 3080173).

Stone A.G., Russell R.F., and K. Patterson. (2004). "Transformational versus servant leadership: A difference in leader focus." *Leadership & Organization Development Journal* 25: 349–61.

Thurston, B. B. and J.M. Ryan. (2005). Philippians and Philemon. Collegeville, MN: Liturgical Press.

Van Dierendonck D. (2011) "Servant Leadership: A Review and Synthesis." *Journal of Management* 37, 4:1228-1261.

Wilson J. and T. Janoski. (1995). "The Contribution of Religion to Volunteer Work." *Sociology of Religion* 56, 2:137-152.

Wilson J. and M. Musick. (1997). "Who Cares? Toward an Integrated Theory of Volunteer Work." *American Sociological Review* 62, 5:694-713.

Winton B.E and D. Fields. (2015). "Seeking and Measuring the Essential Behaviors of Servant Leadership." *Leadership & Organization Development Journal* 36, 4.

Witherington B. III (1994). Friendship and Finances in Philippi: The Letter of Paul to the Philippians. Valley Forge, PA: Trinity Press International.

Yammarino F.J. and B.M Bass. (1990). "Transformational Leadership and Multiple Levels of Analysis." *Human Relations* 43, 10:975-995.

Yammarino F.J., W.D. Spangler and B.M. Bass. (1993). "Transformational Leadership and Performance: A Longitudinal Investigation." *Leadership Quarterly* 4:81-102.

Yukl G. (2006). Leadership in Organizations (6th ed.). Upper Saddle River, NJ: Pearson Prentice Hall.

PROFILES OF CONTRIBUTORS

George Flattery, EdD
Chancellor, Global University and Founder, Network211

Stephen Fogarty, PhD
President, Alphacrusis College, Sydney, Australia.

Kay Fountain, PhD
*Academic Dean, Asia Pacific Theological Seminary
Baguio, Philippines*

Carl Gibbs, PhD
*Team Leader Publication, Africa's Hope and Vice-provost
of Pan-Africa Theological Seminary (PAThs)*

Robert Houlihan, DMin
*Former dean of the College of Christian Ministries and
Religion and presently the professor of World Mission and
Leadership at Southeastern University
Lakeland, Florida, USA*

Dave Johnson, DMiss
*Faculty, Asia Pacific Theological Seminary
Baguio, Philippines*

Paul Lewis, PhD
*Faculty, Assemblies of God Theological Seminary
Springfield, Missouri, USA*

Robert Love, PhD
Provost Emeritus, Global University

Robert Menzies, PhD
Director of Synergy, Kunming, China

Joel Tejedo, DMin
*Faculty, Asia Pacific Theological Seminary
Baguio, Philippines*

www.ingramcontent.com/pod-product-compliance
Lightning Source LLC
Chambersburg PA
CBHW062015220426
43662CB00010B/1340